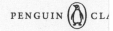

PENGUIN CL

D0497410

LANDSCAPE WITH FIGU
PROSE WRITI

RICHARD JEFFERIES (1848–87) was probably the most imaginative and certainly the least conventional of country writers. He
never worked the land and did not always live in the countryside, but in his articles and essays he single-handedly created the
modern idea of English 'nature writing'.

He wrote an astonishing amount in his short life, including
novels (most famously *Bevis* and the hugely influential post-
apocalypse novel *After London*), an autobiography, *The Story of
My Heart*, and numerous essays on the English countryside, both
about the people who lived and worked there and about its
animals and plants.

After an education at Oxford, RICHARD MABEY worked as a lec-
turer in social studies, then as a senior editor at Penguin Books.
He became a full-time writer in 1974 and is the author of some
thirty books, including *Weeds: How Vagabond Plants Gate-
crashed Civilisation and Changed the Way We Think About
Nature* (2010); *Whistling in the Dark: In Pursuit of the Nightingale* (1993), winner of the East Anglia Book Award, 2010, in a
revised version entitled *The Barley Bird: Notes on a Suffolk
Nightingale; Beechcombings: The Narratives of Trees* (2007); the
ground-breaking and best-selling *Flora Britannica* (1996), winner
of a National Book Award; and *Glibert White,* which won the
Whitbread Biography Award in 1986. His recent memoir, *Nature
Cure* (2005), which describes how reconnecting with the wild
helped him break free from debilitating depression, was short-
listed for three major literary awards: the Whitbread, the
Ondaatje, and the J. R. Ackerley prizes. He writes for the *Guardian, New Statesman* and *Granta,* and contributes frequently to
BBC radio. He has written a personal column in *BBC Wildlife*
magazine since 1986, and was made a Fellow of the Royal Society
of Literature in 2011.

30130 5060 6402 0

RICHARD JEFFERIES

Landscape with Figures: Selected Prose Writings

Edited and with an Introduction and Preface by
RICHARD MABEY

PENGUIN BOOKS

PENGUIN CLASSICS

Published by the Penguin Group
Penguin Books Ltd, 80 Strand, London WC2R ORL, England
Penguin Group (USA) Inc., 375 Hudson Street, New York, New York 10014, USA
Penguin Group (Canada), 90 Eglinton Avenue East, Suite 700, Toronto, Ontario, Canada M4P 2Y3
(a division of Pearson Penguin Canada Inc.)
Penguin Ireland, 25 St Stephen's Green, Dublin 2, Ireland (a division of Penguin Books Ltd)
Penguin Group (Australia), 707 Collins Street, Melbourne, Victoria 3008, Australia
(a division of Pearson Australia Group Pty Ltd)
Penguin Books India Pvt Ltd, 11 Community Centre, Panchsheel Park, New Delhi – 110 017, India
Penguin Group (NZ), 67 Apollo Drive, Rosedale, Auckland 0632, New Zealand
(a division of Pearson New Zealand Ltd)
Penguin Books (South Africa) (Pty) Ltd, Block D, Rosebank Office Park,
181 Jan Smuts Avenue, Parktown North, Gauteng 2193, South Africa

Penguin Books Ltd, Registered Offices: 80 Strand, London WC2R ORL, England

www.penguin.com

This selection, originally entitled *Landscape with Figures: An Anthology of Richard Jefferies's Prose*,
first published in Penguin English Library 1983
First published, with a new preface, in Penguin Classics 2013
002

Introduction copyright © Richard Mabey, 1983
New preface copyright © Richard Mabey, 2013
All rights reserved

Set in 10.25/12.25pt PostScript Adobe Sabon
Typeset by Jouve (UK), Milton Keynes
Printed in Great Britain by Clays Ltd, St Ives plc

ISBN: 978-0-141-39289-9

www.greenpenguin.co.uk

Contents

LANDSCAPE WITH FIGURES: SELECTED PROSE WRITINGS

Part One:
Writings on Agricultural and Social Affairs
(1872–80)

Part Two:
Natural History Writings (1878–86)

Part Three:
Late Essays (1882–7)

Preface to New Edition

Richard Jefferies died of tuberculosis in 1887, aged thirty-eight. In a writing life of little more than twenty years, he showed signs of becoming a literary polymath, publishing nine works of fiction and more than 450 essays and pieces of journalism. They range from a tone poem on 'The Lions in Trafalgar Square', through slight 'nature notes' and political brickbats on the misdemeanours of agricultural labourers, to metaphysical meditations on human perception. What links them is a nagging, inquisitive and, just occasionally, toxic curiosity about what, in the great scheme of things, was the relationship between human beings, nature and the land.

It's not surprising that in Jefferies' own breakneck career this passion moved through distinct phases. It began in his teens, with strictly journalistic and often deeply conservative surveys of the worlds of farming and gamekeeping, shifted to sharper enquiries into natural history, and concluded with a kind of inclusive synthesis, in which human nature, the 'more-than-human world', and the deep mysteries of consciousness all become part of a single 'field-play'. Jefferies was trying urgently to work out who he was, as a displaced, rootless, professional peerer, being rapidly invaded by one of the more destructive manifestations of nature.

Jefferies first perched on my shoulder when I was about twelve years old, and has lurked (not always enjoyably) in the shadows ever since. What fascinates me is how Jefferies' phases – 'movements', if you like – have been echoed both in my own life, and in the shifting focus of public interest. When I first came across him, I was an adolescent nature-romantic,

inclined to solitariness. His numinous landscape writing touched
something quite deep and undefined in me, and I aped his style
shamelessly in school essays. When I was sixteen I won a prize
for one of these pastiches, and chose Jefferies' 'spiritual autobiography', *The Story of My Heart,* as my reward. It is a
measure of how tastes change that the staff in charge of prizes
had never heard of either it or its author, and suspected from
the title that it was some cheap novelette. So it had to be vetted.
They might just as well not have bothered. I found it incompre-
hensible once I'd been presented with the thin volume, and it
still seems to me a faintly distasteful piece of pre-New Age
self-indulgence.

Half a century on, the reading public is more aware of Jefferies, especially his special contribution to what is now known
as 'nature writing', as distinct from 'natural history writing'. I
find I'm constantly discovering new aspects of him here as well.
His instinctive grasp of ecology was always obvious. Even in
his most despairing moments, he understood the individual
human's inseparability from the rest of creation, however indifferent creation was to him. But a sharpening of our contemporary
interest in what, precisely, these links are has helped highlight
what a precocious observer Jefferies was. He was a kind of
hedge-scientist, reasoning through analogy, forging explana-
tions by the application of reason and intuition to acute
observation. It's not a respectable scientific mode these days,
but it creates a space where human imagination can meet the
constantly evolving, experimenting pool of life. Jefferies was
surprisingly modern in his ideas about perception, too. He was
aware of the dangerous subjectivity – but also creativity – of
the senses, of how cultural context, psychological preconcep-
tion, even pure optical illusion, shape the way nature appears
to us. The mutability of the perceived world – and of evolving
life itself – were, in the end, a single phenomenon to him.

I chose the selection in *Selected Prose* (which was originally
published as *Landscape with Figures: An Anthology of Richard
Jefferies's Prose*) in the early nineteen-eighties, when interest in
Jefferies reflected current political and social worries, and
focused on his writings about the uneasy relations between

country and city, the future of democracy, the idea of the 'organic' community. I suspect that this aspect of his work is likely to come to the fore again, and I hope that its inclusion here, alongside his more immediately popular nature writing, will help give a more balanced view of an unusual, troubled, but always relevant, writer.

Richard Mabey
Norfolk, 2012

Introduction

Nearly a century after his death it is still hard to say exactly what kind of writer Richard Jefferies was. On the strength of the few of his books that are still widely read – *The Game-keeper at Home, Nature Near London, Wildlife in a Southern County* – he is recognized as probably the most imaginative observer of the natural world of his century. More generally he is regarded as a 'country' writer, and that will certainly do as a rough description of his working territory. But in any less literal sense it is a definition which immediately begs the most important question about his work, for there is nothing conventionally rural about Jefferies. He was never a land-worker and for a good deal of his career did not even live in the countryside. His writing rarely has the qualities of peace, quiet and timelessness that are supposed to characterize 'rustic' literature. He can appear, sometimes inside a single piece of writing, as a small-town journalist, a romantic radical, a social historian and an apologist for the landowning class. The closer he is read the more the major concern of his work appears to be an implicit questioning of what a 'country writer' is, an exploration of the relationships that are possible between a reflective outsider, marginal in all senses to the real business of the land, and the hard imperatives of life in the fields. To what extent is the 'countryside' not just a fact of geography and a place of work but an emblem of a whole range of social and spiritual values? And if there are intangible estates, who are the rightful inheritors?

The more urban our society becomes, the more relevant these questions seem, and it is no wonder that in some quarters

Jefferies' life has been mythological. In the most telling version –
out of the Golden Age by the Romantics – chance brings
together this visionary spirit, born of ancient English farming
stock, and the last remnants of an unblemished and untroubled
countryside. The reality was rather different. Jefferies was
raised on an unsuccessful smallholding in a county where, just
twenty years before, labourers had fought pitched battles with
the yeoman farmers. He began writing during the great agricultural depression of the 1870s, and died, after years of suffering,
when he was only thirty-eight, from tuberculosis.

We have to remember this history when reading Jefferies.
But equally, I believe, we have to remember the myths. A feature of his writing is the way it taps and exposes our
preconceptions about country life. In his huge output of essays
and articles almost all our current beliefs and worries are
prefigured.

In this anthology I have tried to sketch the development of Jefferies' thinking on social, political and ecological matters as it
is expressed in these essays and articles. (His fiction is outside
the scope of this collection, and is in any case less interesting.)
The sheer range of his output was formidable. In a working life
of not much more than twenty years he published nine novels
and ten volumes of non-fiction. Another ten collections
appeared posthumously. His non-fiction works were mostly
quarried from more than 450 essays and articles he contributed
to some thirty different publications, from the *Live Stock Journal* to the *Pall Mall Gazette*. He would write with equal
willingness (though not always equal facility) technical pieces
for the farming press, improving articles for home encyclope-
dias and propaganda for Tory journals. In the high-circulation
tabloids he pioneered the 'country diary', and the distinctive
discursive style he developed is still echoed in a score of local
newspapers. In almost the same breath, it seems, he was able to
retreat into mystical reveries of the kind typified by *The Story
of My Heart*, and then burst into radical sermonizing. Partly he
wrote as any freelance will, what he was paid to write by his
editors; yet the shifts also happened unprompted, as Jefferies

revised yet again his opinion of where he belonged in the rural scheme of things.

Although Jefferies' willingness to change his mind has sometimes been used as a reason for dismissing his work as trivial or untrustworthy, it is refreshing to find this kind of flexibility in 'country' writing. For a *motif* that is so important in English literature, the countryside has been portrayed from a notoriously narrow set of views, and only exceptionally by those who worked on it themselves. Permanence and peace, consequently, have been sighted more often than change and conflict, and natural harmony (though this is often illusory too) taken to include social harmony. At worst, the indigenous human has been absorbed completely into the natural landscape as another kind of sturdy and contented ruminant. This is a damaging process, and as Raymond Williams has pointed out, 'A fault can then occur in the whole ordering of the mind. Defence of a "vanishing countryside" . . . can become deeply confused with that defence of the old rural order which is in any case being expressed by the landlords, the rentiers, and their literary sympathizers.'*

Although an excess of pastoral naïvety has produced, understandably, a suspicion of onlookers' and outsiders' versions of the rural experience, this can lead to another kind of bias, in which all such views are dismissed as aesthetic indulgences. Yet the cycles of birth, death, harvest and renewal which characterize the agricultural and natural worlds have been a powerful source of symbols at every level in our culture, even for those who do not live close to them. And there is a sense in which a settled rural landscape, whose pattern of fields, farms and churches embodies the history of a hundred generations, *is* a vision of Eden, no matter what temptation and toil lie hidden behind it.

There has been no shortage of writers willing to ignore this problem of perspective and depict the countryside in simple black or white terms. Jefferies' accomplishment was to portray it in all shades with an equal vehemence and within the compass

* *The Country and the City*, Chatto & Windus, 1973.

of a single working life. Although in the short term his versatility can look like shallowness or opportunism, in the context of his whole work it seems more like a rare kind of honesty.

The central character in what Jefferies once called 'The Field-Play' is the land-worker himself. The shift in the way he is depicted – from laggard to victim to hero – is the most striking expression of the movement of Jefferies' thinking. Even his physical characteristics are viewed in different ways. In the early 1870s he is described as a rather badly designed machine. Ten years later he is being explicitly compared to the form of a classical sculpture.

Typically, it was with a shrewd, unflattering sketch of the Wiltshire labourer (to-day it would rank as an exposé) that Jefferies pushed his writing before a national audience in 1872. The Agricultural Labourers' Union had been formed just two years earlier and there was mounting concern amongst land-owners about its likely impact on the farm. Jefferies was working on the *North Wilts Herald* at the time, and realized that he was well placed to make an entry into the debate. He had a lifetime's experience of observing agricultural affairs, an adaptable and persuasive style, and enough ambition not to be averse to saying what his readers wanted to hear. So he composed the first of his now celebrated letters to *The Times* on the life and habits of the Wiltshire labourer, and in particular his uncouthness, laziness and more than adequate wages. It was by any standards a callous piece, written with apparent objectivity but in fact with a calculated disdain that at times reduces the worker to little more than a beast of burden:

> As a man, he is usually strongly built, broad-shouldered, and massive in frame, but his appearance is spoilt by the clumsiness of his walk and the want of grace in his movements ... The labourer's muscle is that of a cart-horse, his motions lumbering and slow. His style of walk is caused by following the plough in early childhood, when the weak limbs find it a hard labour to pull the heavy nailed boots from the thick clay soil. Ever afterwards he walks as if it were an exertion to lift his legs.

Jefferies was wearing his contempt on his sleeve, of course; but when he returned to the subject in the *Manchester Guardian* thirteen years later, it is hard to credit that it is the same man writing. Even the title of the piece (like those of many of his later essays) has a new subtlety, being less a description of what was to come than a frame of reference within which to read it; 'One of the New Voters' had little to do with voting or party loyalties but a great deal, implicitly, with the human right to the franchise. It recounted with meticulous detail and controlled anger a day in the life of Roger the reaper. Although he is still an abstraction, not a person, Roger is an altogether more real and sympathetic character than his predecessors. No longer an intemperate idler, but a man tied to long hours of dispiriting work without the capital or political power to find a way out, he none the less keeps his own private culture intact. Jefferies describes a scene in a pub after the day's work is over.

> You can smell the tobacco and see the ale; you cannot see the indefinite power which holds men there – the magnetism of company and conversation. *Their* conversation, not *your* conversation; not the last book, the last play; not saloon conversation; but theirs – talk in which neither you nor any one of your condition could really join. To us there would seem nothing at all in that conversation, vapid and subjectless; to them it means much. We have not been through the same circumstances: our day has been differently spent, and the same words have therefore a varying value. Certain it is, that it is conversation that takes men to the public-house. Had Roger been a horse he would have hastened to borrow some food, and, having eaten that, would have cast himself at once upon his rude bed. Not being an animal, though his life and work were animal, he went with his friends to talk.

This was a remarkable recognition from a man who just a few years earlier had seen nothing but vacant faces amongst the labouring class. But what really lifts this essay above the level of ephemeral social comment is that Jefferies sets it in the context of the great drama of the harvest, in which toil, sunshine,

beer and butterflies, cornfield weeds and the staff of life, were
mixed together in perplexing contradiction.

> The golden harvest is the first scene; the golden wheat, glorious
> under the summer sun. Bright poppies flower in its depths, and
> convolvulus climbs the stalks. Butterflies float slowly over the
> yellow surface as they might over a lake of colour. To linger by it,
> to visit it day by day, and even to watch the sunset by it, and see
> it pale under the changing light, is a delight to the thoughtful
> mind. There is so much in the wheat, there are books of medita-
> tion in it, it is dear to the heart. Behind these beautiful aspects
> comes the reality of human labour – hours upon hours of heat
> and strain; there comes the reality of a rude life, and in the end
> little enough of gain. The wheat is beautiful, but human life is
> labour.

The central paradox of rural life has never been more plainly
put. In another intense late essay, 'Walks in the Wheat-fields'
(1887), Jefferies likens the blinding, desperate gathering-in of
the harvest to 'gold fever . . . The whole village lived in the
field . . . yet they seemed but a handful buried in the tunnels of
the golden mine . . .' The double meaning of 'living in' here is
very forceful; at the beginning of the piece he compares the
shape of a grain of wheat to an embryo or 'a tiny man or
woman . . . settled to slumber'. In the wheat-field, he suggests,
'Transubstantiation is a fact . . .'

In his last years Jefferies was increasingly preoccupied with
the paradoxes that emerged when men lived close to nature.
They seemed trapped in one way by their physical and bio-
logical needs, and in another by their sensibilities. If the ritual
of harvest was paradoxical, so was all labour, which, depending on where you stood, could seem an act of nature or necessity,
dignity or slavery. So, for that matter, was nature itself, which
could be simultaneously cruel and beautiful. Jefferies' concern
with these ambiguities was in part a reflection of his own uncertain social position, as a man who had devoted his life to the
expression of rural life, but who had no real role in it himself.
He found no solutions to this enigma; but as he explores some

of its more practical ramifications – could villages be centres of social change as well as social stability, for instance? what were the respective rights of owners, workers and tourists over the land? – his mixed feelings of exclusion and concern come increasingly close to our modern attitudes towards the countryside.

Richard Jefferies seemed destined to be a displaced person from childhood. He was born into a declining smallholding at Coate near Swindon in 1848. Although he was later to idealize both Coate and his father (who appears as the splendid, doomed figure of farmer Iden in the novel *Amaryllis at the Fair*, 1887) it does not seem to have been an especially happy household. A description of Coate in a letter from Jefferies' father has a bitterness whose roots, one suspects, reach back to a time before Richard began upgrading his literary address to 'Coate Farm':

> How he could think of describing Coate as such a pleasant place and deceive so I could not imagine, in fact nothing scarcely he mentions is in Coate proper only the proper one was not a pleasant one Snodshill was the name on my Waggon and cart, he styled in Coate Farm it was not worthy of the name of Farm it was not Forty Acres of Land.*

When he was four years old, Richard was sent away from Snodshill to live with his aunt in Sydenham. He stayed there for five years, visiting his parents for just one month's holiday a year. When he was nine he returned home, but was quickly despatched to a succession of private schools in Swindon. Shunted about as if he were already a misfit, it is no wonder that he developed into a moody and solitary adolescent. He began reading Rabelais and the Greek Classics and spent long days roaming about Marlborough Forest. He had no taste for farm-work, and his father used to point with disgust to 'our Dick poking about in them hedges'. When he was sixteen Richard

---

* Quoted in *Richard Jefferies: Man of the Fields*, ed. S. J. Looker and C. Porteous, 1965.

ran away from home with his cousin, first to France and then to Liverpool, where he was found by the police and sent back to Swindon.

This habit of escape into fantasy or romantic adventure (it was later to become a characteristic of his fiction) must have been aggravated by the real-life decline of Coate. In 1865 the smallholding was badly hit by the cattle plague that was sweeping across southern England, and a short while later fourteen acres had to be sold off. Richard had left school for good by this time, and in 1866 started work in Swindon on a new Conservative paper, the *North Wilts Herald*. He was employed as a jack-of-all-trades reporter and proof-reader, but seemed to spend a good deal of his time composing short stories for the paper. They were a collection of orthodox Victorian vignettes of thwarted love, murder and historical romance, mannered in tone and coloured by antiquarian and classical references.* Although they are of no real literary value, they may have been useful to Jefferies as a way of testing and exercising his imaginative powers.

The next few years brought further frustrations and more elaborate retreats. In 1868 he began to be vaguely ill and had to leave his job on the *Herald*. In 1870 he took a long recuperative holiday in Brussels. He was extravagantly delighted by the women, the fashions, the manners, the sophistication of it all, and from letters to his aunt it is clear what he was beginning to think of the philistinism of Wiltshire society.

But circumstances forced him to return there in 1871, and to a situation that must have seemed even less congenial than when he had left. With the farm collapsing around them his parents resented his idleness and irresponsibility. He had no job and no money. He was able to sell a few articles to his old newspaper, but they were not enough, and he had to pawn his gun. His life began to slip into an anxious, hand-to-mouth existence that has more in common with the stereotype of the urban freelance than with a supposed 'son of the soil'. He started novels, but was repeatedly diverted by a procession of

---

* Collected by Grace Toplis as *The Early Fiction of Richard Jefferies*, 1890.

psychosomatic illnesses. He wrote a play, and a dull and deriva-
tive memoir on the family of his prospective member of
Parliament, Ambrose Goddard. The most unusual projects in
this period were two pamphlets: the self-explanatory *Reporting, Editing and Authorship: Practical Hints for Beginners*, and
Jack Brass, Emperor of England. This was a right-wing broad-
sheet that ridiculed what Jefferies saw as the dangers of
populism.

> ... Educate! educate! educate! Teach every one to rely on their
> own judgement, so as to destroy the faith in authority, and lead
> to a confidence in their own reason, the surest method of
> seduction ...

It was a heavy-handed satire, and though it may not have been
intended very seriously, Jefferies was to remember it with
embarrassment in later years.

But by this stage he had already made a more substantial
political and literary debut with his letters to *The Times* on the
subject of the Wiltshire labourer. It is important to remember
the context in which these appeared. Agricultural problems of
one kind or another had been central issues in British politics
for much of the nineteenth century. But the land-workers themselves had been given sparse attention. And though they had been
impoverished by the cumulative effects of farm mechanization,
wage and rent levels, and the appropriation of the common-
lands, their own protests had been sporadic and ineffectual.
Then in 1870 Joseph Arch and some of his fellow-workers
gathered together illicitly in their Warwickshire village and
formed the Agricultural Labourers' Union.

This was a new development in the countryside, and raised
new anxieties amongst landowners. The rioting and rick-burning
of the 1820s had fitted into a familiar stereotype of peasant
behaviour, and had been comparatively easily contained. But
organization was a different matter, and seemed to introduce
an ominously urban challenge to the rural order and, by implication, to the social fabric of the nation which rested on it.

Jefferies' hybrid background may have helped him understand

these worries better than most, and it was the sense of moral affront sounded in his letters that won him sympathy from the landowners. The correspondence became the subject of an editorial in *The Times*, and Jefferies was soon offered more journalistic work in the same vein. Over the next few years he wrote copiously on rural and agricultural affairs for journals such as *Fraser's Magazine* and the *Live Stock Journal*. Collectively these pieces are more informed and compassionate than the *Times* letters. Jefferies sympathizes with the sufferings of the labourers and their families, but believed that many of their habitual responses to trouble – particularly their reluctance to accept responsibility for their own fate – simply made matters worse. Wage demands alienated the farmers, who were their natural patrons and allies. Drink led to the kind of family break-ups described in 'John Smith's Shanty' (1874). The only certain remedies were hard work and self-discipline.

This has been a perennial theme in Conservative philosophy, and there are times when Jefferies' recommendations have a decidedly modern ring, as, for instance, in 'The Labourer's Daily Life' (1874): 'The sense of [home] ownership engenders a pride in the place, and all his better feelings are called into play.' Yet even at this early stage, Jefferies' conservatism has a liberal edge, and anticipates the libertarian, self-help politics of his later years. He speaks out in favour of allotments, libraries, cottage hospitals, women's institutes and other mutual associations as means towards parish independence. And he begins to suggest that the farm and the village – the basic units of rural life – owed their survival and strength not so much to some immemorial order but precisely to their capacity to incorporate change and new ideas into a well-tried framework.

The increasing amount of work Jefferies was doing for London-based journals encouraged him to move to Surbiton in 1877, when he was twenty-eight years of age. Rather to his surprise he enjoyed London, discovering in it not only many unexpectedly green corners, but an exciting quality of movement and vivacity. As Claude Monet was to do in his paintings of Leicester Square and Westminster Bridge, Jefferies saw the rush of traffic and the play of streetlights almost as if they were

natural events. In 'The Lions in Trafalgar Square' even the
people are absorbed:

> At summer noontide, when the day surrounds us and it is bright
> light even in the shadow, I like to stand by one of the lions and
> yield to the old feeling. The sunshine glows on the dusky crea-
> ture, as it seems, not on the surface but under the skin, as if it
> came up from out of the limb. The roar of the rolling wheels sinks
> and becomes distant as the sound of a waterfall when dreams are
> coming. All abundant life is smoothed and levelled, the abrupt-
> ness of the individuals lost in the flowing current like separate
> flowers drawn along in a border, like music heard so far off that
> the notes are molten and the theme only remains.

'Lions', like most of the London essays, was written during a
later phase of Jefferies' life. Perhaps because of his uncertainty
about his own social role, he rarely wrote about his current
circumstances, but about what he had just left behind. In Swindon, much of his work was concerned with the fantasy world
of his adolescence. In Surbiton he is remembering his life at
Coate, albeit in a rather idealized form.

The pieces that were to make up his first fully-fledged
non-fiction work, *The Gamekeeper at Home*, were amongst
these reminiscences, and were initially published in serial form
in the *Pall Mall Gazette* between December 1877 and Spring
1878. It is of some significance that Jefferies chose as his sub-
jects 'the master's man' and the practical business of policing
a sporting estate. The game laws were a crucial instrument
for expressing and maintaining the class structure of the
nineteenth-century countryside. Although poaching was an
economic necessity for many families, it was also an act of defi-
ance against the presumptions of landowners. They, for their
part, often viewed the taking of wild animals from their land as
a more fundamental breach of their 'natural' rights than out-
right stealing.

Jefferies doesn't challenge this assumption in *The Gamekeeper at Home*. In a chapter on the keeper's enemies, for
instance, he moves smoothly from weasels, stoats and magpies

to 'semi-bohemian trespassers', boys picking sloes and old women gathering firewood. '... how is the keeper to be certain,' he argues, 'that if the opportunity offered these gentry would not pounce upon a rabbit or anything else?'

This strand in Jefferies' writing reaches a kind of culmination in *Hodge and His Masters*. This collection of portraits of the rural middle class – speculators, solicitors, landowners, parsons – was serialized in the London *Standard* between 1878 and 1880. Its hero is the self-made, diligent yeoman farmer. If he should fail it is because he has become lazy or drunk, or has forgotten his place in society:

> There used to be a certain tacit agreement among all men that those who possessed capital, rank or reputation should be treated with courtesy. That courtesy did not imply that the landowner, the capitalist, or the minister of religion, was necessarily himself superior. But it did imply that those who administered property really represented the general order in which all were interested ... These two characteristics, moral apathy and contempt of property – i.e. of social order – are probably exercising considerable influence in shaping the labourer's future.

Jefferies grows shriller as he outlines the agents of these malign forces – the unemployed, the poachers, the publicans, the dispossessed and the dependant. Hodge himself, the ordinary labourer, remains invisible, except when Jefferies is rebuking him, in now familiar style, for his greed, bad cooking, lack of culture and laziness. How lucky he is, Jefferies remarks, only to work in the hours of daylight. After this, it is hard to take seriously the book's closing note of regret about the insulting charity of the workhouse.

Yet alongside (and sometimes inside) these sour social commentaries he had begun writing short studies in natural history. They are lightly and sharply observed, and one senses Jefferies' relief at having an escape route from the troubled world of human affairs. *Wildlife in a Southern County* was serialized in the *Pall Mall Gazette* during 1878, and its contents give some indication of what a versatile writer he was. There are pieces on orchards, woods, rabbits, ants, stiles, the ague, and 'noises in the air'. The descriptions of the weather are especially convincing – perhaps because he saw this as one area which was beyond the corrupting influence of human society.

During this stage in his life his writing developed a characteristic discursiveness that was no doubt partly a result of his working as a jobbing journalist and having regularly to fill columns of a fixed length. Yet it was also a way of thinking. Many of the pieces are ramblings in an almost literal sense; anecdotes, observations, musings flit by as if they had been encountered and remarked upon during a walk.

In *Round About a Great Estate* (1880) this conversational style is employed to great effect and helps to make this the most unaffectedly charming of all Jefferies' books. It is an ingenuous, buoyant collection of parish gossip, of characters and events that seem to have been chanced upon by accident. Yet it is celebratory rather than nostalgic. Jefferies remarks in his preface to the original edition:

> In this book some notes have been made of the former state of things before it passes away entirely. But I would not have it therefore thought that I wish it to continue or return. My sympathies and hopes are with the light of the future, only I should like it to come from nature. The clock should be read by the sunshine, not the sun timed by the clock.

The worst thing that can be said about these natural history and documentary essays is not that they are inconsequential, but that they are impersonal and generalized. Even at his most perceptive, Jefferies viewed natural life with the same kind of detachment as he regarded the labourer. They aroused his curiosity but rarely his sympathy. But at the beginning of the 1880s a new intimacy starts to appear in his writing. He allows us to share specific experiences and deeply personal feelings. He seems, at last, to be *engaged*. A set of pieces on the fortunes of a trout trapped in a London brook, for instance, show us

Jefferies in a very unfamiliar light – concerned, sentimental and increasingly aware of his own vulnerability.

There can be little doubt that one of the major influences on Jefferies during these years was his deteriorating health. The illness that was eventually to kill him began in earnest in 1881, and was diagnosed as a generalized tuberculosis. During 1882 he went to Brighton to recuperate, but he found only temporary relief, and signs of his pain and disenchantment are visible in almost all the remainder of his work.

Much of this period, perhaps predictably, was taken up with escapist novels. *Greene Ferne Farm* (1880) is an old-fashioned pastoral with a dialect-speaking Chorus. *Bevis* (1882), a book for children, is set in Jefferies' boyhood Wiltshire, which the young heroes transform into a fabulous playground for their fantasies. *After London* (1885) is a bitter vision of the collapse of urban civilization and of the city reclaimed by forest and swamp. Yet even with, so to speak, a clean slate, Jefferies still chooses to create a woodland feudal society, complete with reconstituted poachers as savages. There is some fine descriptive writing in his fiction (particularly in *Amaryllis at the Fair*, which is based on an idealized version of his own family), yet as novels they have to be regarded as failures. They have no real movement, either in the development of the plot or of the individual characters. David Garnett described *Amaryllis* as 'a succession of stills, never a picture in motion',* and Jefferies himself declared he would have been happy to have seen it published as 'scenes of country life' rather than as a novel.

During the early 1880s he was also working on his 'soul-life', a kind of spiritual autobiography that was published as *The Story of My Heart* in 1883. Like all mystical works this is comprehensible to the degree to which one shares the writer's faith – which here is an intense pantheism. Yet the book is an account of a meditation rather than a complete religion. (Some of the short, rhythmical passages even read like mantras.) Typically Jefferies goes to a 'thinking place' – a tree, a stream, or

* Introduction to *Amaryllis at the Fair*, Dent, 1939.

more often the sea – lies under the sun and prays that he may have a revelation. He wishes to transcend the flesh, to transcend nature itself, though he cannot express what he wants, nor what, if anything, he has found. 'The only idea I can give,' he writes, 'is that there is another idea.' Yet if the mystical sections of *The Story* are typified by this kind of word-play – sincerely meant, no doubt, but meaningless – there is another strand of more earthly idealism in the book concerned with a belief in the perfectibility of man and the degradation of labour, themes that were to become increasingly prominent in his work.

Although it is mostly impenetrable, the soul-searching of *The Story of My Heart* seemed to liberate Jefferies from many of his social and literary uncertainties. After 1883 his writing has a new commitment and assurance of style. His viewpoint had changed radically. He had become, on almost every topic from economics to ecology, a progressive. He worries about trends in agricultural modernization and their likely implications for wildlife. He attacks the grubbing-out of hedgerows and the ploughing of old grassland. He defends the otter, and argues in favour of the townsman's right of access to the countryside (see particularly 'The Modern Thames', 1884).

These were specific expressions of a deeper change in Jefferies' whole ideology. By the mid-1880s he had begun to argue for the extension of the franchise, and at times to go beyond the humane concern of 'One of the New Voters' to an out-and-out socialist position. In a remarkable late essay, 'Primrose Gold in Our Village' (1887), he describes how the new Conservative alliances in the countryside, which had once opposed the labourers' vote, were now moving in to appropriate it. 'Primrose Gold' is unlike anything he had written previously. It is sophisticated, witty, elliptical and bitterly ironic. It also deals in allusion and metaphor, which are in short supply in his earlier, more literal writings. As Raymond Williams has remarked:

'Primrose Gold': the phrase is so exact. The simple flower as a badge of political manoeuvre; the yellow of the flower and of the money that is the real source of power; the natural innocence, the political dominance: it is all there.

In his late essays Jefferies begins to write of the politics, history and landscape of the countryside as if they were aspects of a single experience. This was especially true of his nature writing. Although he would still turn in slight pieces on seaside beaches and song birds when it was required of him, he was beginning to suggest that nature was not something apart from us, but a world that we were part of and in which we might see reflected some of our own qualities as living creatures. In 'Out of Doors in February' (1882) for instance, he explains the optimism he saw in the images of winter, and in the living world's annual triumph over dark and cold:

> The lark, the bird of the light, is there in the bitter short days. Put the lark then for winter, a sign of hope, a certainty of summer. Put, too, the sheathed bud, for if you search the hedge you will find the buds there, on tree and bush, carefully wrapped around with the case which protects them as a cloak. Put, too, the sharp needles of the green corn ... One memory of the green corn, fresh beneath the sun and wind, will lift up the heart from the clods.

That was one kind of answer to the enigma of the toiler in the field: nature, as a redemptive force that could smooth away the distortions of civilization. In 'Golden Brown' (1884) Jefferies writes enviously of the health and habits of the Kent fruit-pickers, and of 'the life above this life to be obtained from the constant presence with the sunlight and the stars'.

Yet at no time had he believed that complete human fulfilment could be achieved by a simple surrender to natural (or artificially rustic) rhythms. In an odd and not always rational way he also believed in that specifically human concept, progress. As early as 1880 he had declared that his sympathies and hopes were with 'the light of the future'. He wanted, in Edward Thomas's wonderfully exact phrase, 'the light railway to call at the farmyard gate'.*

But for Jefferies himself neither nature nor progress could any longer provide a release. He spent 1887, the last year of his

---

* *Richard Jefferies*, 1909; Faber edition 1978.

life, as an invalid in Goring, in pain and poverty. His view of the world was confined to what he could glimpse through a window, and his thoughts by that paradox that had haunted him, in one form or another, for most of his life. He had dreamed of men living with the easy grace of birds in flight, yet realized that the self-awareness that made that ambition possible would prevent it ever being fulfilled. In 'Hours of Spring' he writes mournfully of 'the old, old error: I love the earth and therefore the earth loves me.' Man was in the unique and probably unenviable position of being both part of nature and a conscious interpreter of it. Hence the crises of perspective that affected young political commentator and nostalgic old man-of-the-fields alike.

These last essays, particularly 'Walks in the Wheat-fields' and 'My Old Village', are poignant and embittered, but written with great power and clarity. In the end – inevitably perhaps – he returns to mysticism and, in 'Nature and Books' for example, rejects both naturalistic and scientific analyses of the colour of flowers: 'I want the inner meaning and the understanding of wild flowers in the meadow ... Why are they? What end? What purpose?'

There is a passage in the novel *Amaryllis at the Fair*, written at the start of this final illness, that catches exactly the conflict between consciousness and animality that runs right through Jefferies' work. The hero, Iden, has just eaten a dinner which has been described in minute and sensuous detail. As he settles down in a chair to sleep, a mouse runs up his trouser leg to eat the crumbs in his lap:

> One great brown hand was in his pocket, close to them – a mighty hand, beside which they were pygmies indeed in the land of the giants. What would have been the value of their lives between a finger and thumb that could crack a ripe and strong-shelled walnut? ...
>
> Yet the little things fed in perfect confidence. He was so still, so *very* still – quiescent – they feared him no more they did the wall; they could not hear his breathing. Had they been giften with human intelligence that very fact would have excited their

suspicions. Why so very, *very* still? Strong men, wearied by work, do not sleep quietly; they breathe heavily. Even in firm sleep we move a little now and then, a limb trembles, a muscle quivers, or stretches itself.

But Iden was so still it was evident he was really wide awake and restraining his breath, and exercising conscious command over his muscles, that this scene might proceed undisturbed.

Now the strangeness of the thing was in this way: Iden set traps for mice in the cellar and the larder, and slew them there without mercy. He picked up the trap, swung it round, opening the door at the same instant, and the wretched captive was dashed to death upon the stone flags of the floor. So he hated them and persecuted them in one place, and fed them in another.

A long psychological discussion might be held upon this apparent inconsistency, but I shall leave analysis to those who like it, and go on recording facts. I will make only one remark. That nothing is consistent that is human. If it was not inconsistent it would have no association with a living person.

From the merest thin slit, as it were, between his eyelids, Iden watched the mice feed and run about his knees till, having eaten every crumb, they descended his leg to the floor.

Richard Mabey, 1983

Note on the Text

Rather than follow a strictly chronological order, I have arranged the pieces that follow in a way that may help illustrate the development of Jefferies' thinking. I have also put them into three rough groups (agricultural and social affairs; natural history; general, philosophical essays) that correspond to the three main phases of his career, though there are of course overlaps both in time and subject matter.

Landscape with Figures:
Selected Prose Writings

PART ONE

WRITINGS ON AGRICULTURAL AND SOCIAL AFFAIRS

(1872–80)

Wiltshire Labourers

First published in *The Times*, 12 November 1872
First collected in *The Toilers of the Field*, 1892

Sir, – The Wiltshire agricultural labourer is not so highly paid as those of Northumberland, nor so low as those of Dorset; but in the amount of his wages, as in intelligence and general position, he may fairly be taken as an average specimen of his class throughout a large portion of the kingdom.

As a man, he is usually strongly built, broad-shouldered, and massive in frame, but his appearance is spoilt by the clumsiness of his walk and the want of grace in his movements. Though quite as large in muscle, it is very doubtful if he possesses the strength of the seamen who may be seen lounging about the ports. There is a want of firmness, a certain disjointed style, about his limbs, and the muscles themselves have not the hardness and tension of the sailor's. The labourer's muscle is that of a cart-horse, his motions lumbering and slow. His style of walk is caused by following the plough in early childhood, when the weak limbs find it a hard labour to pull the heavy nailed boots from the thick clay soil. Ever afterwards he walks as if it were an exertion to lift his legs. His food may, perhaps, have something to do with the deadened slowness which seems to pervade everything he does – there seems a lack of vitality about him. It consists chiefly of bread and cheese, with bacon twice or thrice a week, varied with onions, and if he be a milker (on some farms) with a good 'tuck-out' at his employer's expense on Sundays. On ordinary days he dines at the fashionable hour of six or seven in the evening – that is, about that time his cottage scents the road with a powerful odour of boiled cabbage, of which he eats an immense quantity. Vegetables are his luxuries, and a large garden, therefore, is the greatest blessing he can have. He eats huge onions raw; he has no idea of flavouring his food with them, nor of making those savoury and inviting messes or vegetable soups at which the French peasantry are so clever. In Picardy I have often dined in a peasant's cottage, and thoroughly enjoyed the excellent soup he puts upon the table for his ordinary meal. To dine in an English labourer's cottage would be impossible. His bread is generally good, certainly; but his bacon is the cheapest he can buy at small second-class shops – oily, soft, wretched stuff; his vegetables are cooked in detestable style, and eaten saturated with the pot liquor. Pot liquor is a favourite soup. I have known cottagers actually apply at farmers' kitchens not only for the pot liquor in which meat has been soddened, but for the water in which potatoes have been boiled – potato liquor – and sup it up with avidity. And this not in times of dearth or scarcity, but rather as a relish. They never buy anything but bacon; never butchers' meat. Philanthropic ladies, to my knowledge, have demonstrated over and over again even to their limited capacities that certain parts of butchers' meat can be bought just as cheap, and will make more savoury and nutritive food; and even now, with the present high price of meat, a certain proportion would be advantageous. In vain; the labourers obstinately adhere to the pig, and the pig only. When, however, an opportunity does occur the amount of food they will eat is something astonishing. Once a year, at the village club dinner, they gormandize to repletion. In one instance I knew of a man eating a plate of roast beef (and the slices are cut enormously thick at these dinners), a plate of boiled beef, then another of boiled mutton, and then a fourth of roast mutton, and a fifth of ham. He said he could not do much to the bread and cheese; but didn't he go into the pudding! I have even heard of men stuffing to the fullest extent of their powers, and then retiring from the table to take an emetic of mustard and return to a second gorging. There is scarcely any limit to their power of absorbing beer. I have known reapers and mowers make it their boast that they could lie on their backs and never take the wooden bottle (in the shape of a small barrel) from their lips till they had drunk a gallon, and from the feats I have seen I verily believe it a fact.

The beer they get is usually poor and thin, though sometimes in harvest the farmers bring out a taste of strong liquor, but not till the work is nearly over; for from this very practice of drinking enormous quantities of small beer the labourer cannot drink more than a very limited amount of good liquor without getting tipsy. This is why he so speedily gets inebriated at the alehouse. While mowing and reaping many of them lay in a small cask.

They are much better clothed now than formerly. Corduroy trousers and slops are the usual style. Smock-frocks are going out of use, except for milkers and faggers. Almost every labourer has his Sunday suit, very often really good clothes, sometimes glossy black, with the regulation 'chimney-pot'. His unfortunate walk betrays him, dress how he will. Since labour has become so expensive it has become a common remark among the farmers that the labourer will go to church in broadcloth and the masters in smock-frocks. The labourer never wears gloves – that has to come with the march of the times; but he is particularly choice over his necktie. The women must dress in the fashion. A very respectable draper in an agricultural district was complaining to me the other day that the poorest class of women would have everything in the fashionable style, let it change as often as it would. In former times, if he laid in a stock of goods suited to tradesmen, and farmers' wives and daughters, if the fashion changed, or they got out of date, he could dispose of them easily to the servants. Now no such thing. The quality did not matter so much, but the style must be the style of the day – no sale for remnants. The poorest girl, who had not got two yards of flannel on her back, must have the same style of dress as the squire's daughter – Dolly Vardens, chignons, and parasols for ladies who can work all day reaping in the broiling sun of August! Gloves, kid, for hands that milk the cows!

The cottages now are infinitely better than they were. There is scarcely room for further improvement in the cottages now erected upon estates. They have three bedrooms, and every appliance and comfort compatible with their necessarily small size. It is only the cottages erected by the labourers themselves on waste plots of ground which are open to objection. Those he builds himself are, indeed, as a rule, miserable huts, disgraceful to a Christian country. I have an instance before me at this moment where a man built a cottage with two rooms and no staircase or upper apartments, and in those two rooms eight persons lived and slept – himself and wife, grown-up daughters, and children. There was not a scrap of garden attached, not enough to grow half-a-dozen onions. The refuse and sewage was flung into the road, or filtered down a ditch into the brook which supplied that part of the village with water. In another case at one time there was a cottage in which twelve persons lived. This had upper apartments, but so low was the ceiling that a tall man could stand on the floor, with his head right through the opening for the staircase, and see along the upper floor under the beds! These squatters are the curse of the community. It is among them that fever and kindred infectious diseases break out; it is among them that wretched couples are seen bent double with rheumatism and affections of the joints caused by damp. They have often been known to remain so long, generation after generation, in these wretched hovels, that at last the lord of the manor, having neglected to claim quit-rent, they can defy him, and claim them as their own property, and there they stick, eyesores and blots, the fungi of the land. The cottages erected by farmers or by landlords are now, one and all, fit and proper habitations for human beings; and I verily believe it would be impossible throughout the length and breadth of Wiltshire to find a single bad cottage on any large estate, so well and so thoroughly have the landed proprietors done their work. On all farms gardens are attached to the cottages, in many instances very large, and always sufficient to produce enough vegetables for the resident. In villages the allotment system has been greatly extended of late years, and has been found most beneficial, both to owners and tenants. As a rule the allotments are let at a rate which may be taken as £4 per annum – a sum which pays the landlord very well, and enables the labourer to remunerate himself. In one village which came under my observation the clergyman of the parish has turned a portion of his glebe land into allotments – a most

excellent and noble example, which cannot be too widely followed or too much extolled. He is thus enabled to benefit almost
every one of his poor parishioners, and yet without destroying
that sense of independence which is the great characteristic of
a true Englishman. He has issued a book of rules and conditions under which these allotments are held, and he thus places
a strong check upon drunkenness and dissolute habits, indul-
gence in which is a sure way to lose the portions of ground.
There is scarcely an end to the benefits of the allotment system.
In villages there cannot be extensive gardens, and the allotments supply their place. The extra produce above that which
supplies the table and pays the rent is easily disposed of in
the next town, and places many additional comforts in the
labourer's reach. The refuse goes to help support and fatten the
labourer's pig, which brings him in profit enough to pay the rent
of his cottage, and the pig, in turn, manures the allotment.
Some towns have large common lands, held under certain conditions; such are Malmesbury, with 500 acres, and Tetbury (the
common land of which extends two miles), both these being
arable, &c. These are not exactly in the use of labourers, but
they are in the hands of a class to which the labourer often
rises. Many labourers have fruit-trees in their gardens, which,
in some seasons, prove very profitable. In the present year, to
my knowledge, a labourer sold £4 worth of apples; and another
made £3, 10s. off the produce of one pear tree, pears being
scarce.

To come at last to the difficult question of wages. In Wiltshire there has been no extended strike, and very few meetings
upon the subject, for the simple reason that the agitators can
gain no hold upon a county where, as a mass, the labourers are
well paid. The common day-labourer receives 10s., 11s., and
12s. a week, according to the state of supply and demand for
labour in various districts; and, if he milks, 1s. more, making
13s. a week, now common wages. These figures are rather
below the mark; I could give instances of much higher pay. To
give a good idea of the wages paid I will take the case of a hill
farmer (arable, Marlborough Downs), who paid this last summer during harvest 18s. per week per man. His reapers often

earned 10s. a day – enough to pay their year's rent in a week. These men lived in cottages on the farm, with three bedrooms each, and some larger, with every modern appliance, each having a garden of a quarter of an acre attached and close at hand, for which cottage and garden they paid 1s. per week rent. The whole of these cottages were insured by the farmer himself, their furniture, &c., in one lump, and the insurance policy cost him, as nearly as possible, 1s. 3d. per cottage per year. For this he deducted 1s. per year each from their wages. None of the men would have insured unless he had insisted upon doing it for them. These men had from six to eight quarts of beer per man (over and above their 18s. a week) during harvest every day. In spring and autumn their wages are much increased by piece-work, hoeing, &c. In winter the farmer draws their coal for them in his waggons, a distance of eight miles from the nearest wharf, enabling them to get it at cost price. This is no slight advantage, for, at the present high price of coal, it is sold, delivered in the villages, at 2s. per cwt. Many who cannot afford it in the week buy a quarter of a cwt. on Saturday night, to cook their Sunday's dinner with, for 6d. This is at the rate of £2 per ton. Another gentleman, a large steam cultivator in the Vale, whose name is often before the public, informs me that his books show that he paid £100 in one year in cash to one cottage for labour, showing the advantage the labourer possesses over the mechanic, since his wife and child can add to his income. Many farmers pay £50 and £60 a year for beer drunk by their labourers – a serious addition to their wages. The railway companies and others who employ mechanics do not allow them any beer. The allowance of a good cottage and a quarter of an acre of garden for 1s. per week is not singular. Many who were at the Autumn Manoeuvres of the present year may remember having a handsome row of houses, rather than cottages, pointed out to them as inhabited by labourers at 1s. per week. In the immediate neighbourhood of large manufacturing towns 1s. 6d. a week is sometimes paid; but then these cottages would in such positions readily let to mechanics for 3s., 4s., and even 5s. per week. There was a great outcry when the Duke of Marlborough issued an order that the cottages on his estate should in future only be let to such men as worked upon the farms where those cottages were situated. In reality this was the very greatest blessing the Duke could have conferred upon the agricultural labourer; for it ensured him a good cottage at a nearly nominal rent and close to his work; whereas in many instances previously the cottages on the farms had been let at a high rate to the mechanics, and the labourer had to walk miles before he got to his labour. Cottages are not erected by landowners or by farmers as paying speculations. It is well known that the condition of things prevents the agricultural labourer from being able to pay a sufficient rent to be a fair percentage upon the sum expended. In one instance a landlord has built some cottages for his tenant, the tenant paying a certain amount of interest on the sum invested by the landlord. Now, although this is a matter of arrangement, and not of speculation – that is, although the interest paid by the tenant is a low percentage upon the money laid out, yet the rent paid by the labourers inhabiting these cottages to the tenant does not reimburse him what he pays his landlord as interest – not by a considerable margin. But then he has the advantage of his labourers close to his work, always ready at hand.

Over and above the actual cash wages of the labourer, which are now very good, must be reckoned his cottage and garden, and often a small orchard, at a nominal rent, his beer at his master's expense, piece-work, gleaning after harvest, &c., which alter his real position very materially. In Gloucestershire, on the Cotswolds, the best-paid labourers are the shepherds, for in that great sheep-country much trust is reposed in them. At the annual auctions of shearlings which are held upon the large farms a purse is made for the shepherd of the flock, into which every one who attends is expected to drop a shilling, often producing £5. The shepherds on the Wiltshire Downs are also well paid, especially in lambing-time, when the greatest watchfulness and care are required. It has been stated that the labourer has no chance of rising from his position. This is sheer cant. He has very good opportunities of rising, and often does rise, to my knowledge. At this present moment I could mention a person who has risen from a position scarcely equal to that of a labourer, not only to have a farm himself, but to place his sons in farms. Another has just entered on a farm; and several more are on the high-road to that desirable consummation. If a labourer possesses any amount of intelligence he becomes head-carter or head-fagger, as the case may be; and from that to be assistant or under-bailiff, and finally bailiff. As a bailiff he has every opportunity to learn the working of a farm, and is often placed in entire charge of a farm at a distance from his employer's residence. In time he establishes a reputation as a practical man, and being in receipt of good wages, with very little expenditure, saves some money. He has now little difficulty in obtaining the promise of a farm, and with this can readily take up money. With average care he is a made man. Others rise from petty trading, petty dealing in pigs and calves, till they save sufficient to rent a small farm, and make that the basis of larger dealing operations. I question very much whether a clerk in a firm would not find it much more difficult, as requiring larger capital, to raise himself to a level with his employer than an agricultural labourer does to the level of a farmer.

Many labourers now wander far and wide as navvies, &c., and perhaps when these return home, as most of them do, to agricultural labour, they are the most useful and intelligent of their class, from a readiness they possess to turn their hand to anything. I know one at this moment who makes a large addition to his ordinary wages by brewing for the small inns, and very good liquor he brews, too. They pick up a large amount of practical knowledge.

The agricultural women are certainly not handsome; I know no peasantry so entirely uninviting. Occasionally there is a girl whose nut-brown complexion and sloe-black eyes are pretty, but their features are very rarely good, and they get plain quickly, so soon as the first flush of youth is past. Many have really good hair in abundance, glossy and rich, perhaps from its exposure to the fresh air. But on Sundays they plaster it with strong-smelling pomade and hair-oil, which scents the air for yards most unpleasantly. As a rule, it may safely be laid down that the agricultural women are moral, far more so than those of the town. Rough and rude jokes and language are, indeed, too common; but that is all. No evil comes of it. The fairs are the chief cause of immorality. Many an honest, hard-working servant-girl owes her ruin to these fatal mops and fairs, when liquor to which she is unaccustomed overcomes her. Yet it seems cruel to take from them the one day or two of the year on which they can enjoy themselves fairly in their own fashion. The spread of friendly societies, patronized by the gentry and clergy, with their annual festivities, is a remedy which is gradually supplying them with safer, and yet congenial, amusement. In what may be termed lesser morals I cannot accord either them or the men the same praise. They are too ungrateful for the many great benefits which are bountifully supplied them – the brandy, the soup, and fresh meat readily extended without stint from the farmer's home in sickness to the cottage are too quickly forgotten. They who were most benefited are often the first to most loudly complain and to backbite. Never once in all my observation have I heard a labouring man or woman make a grateful remark; and yet I can confidently say that there is no class of persons in England who receive so many attentions and benefits from their superiors as the agricultural labourers. Stories are rife of their even refusing to work at disastrous fires because beer was not immediately forth-coming. I trust this is not true; but it is too much in character. No term is too strong in condemnation for those persons who endeavour to arouse an agitation among a class of people so short-sighted and so ready to turn against their own benefactors and their own interest. I am credibly informed that one of these agitators, immediately after the Bishop of Gloucester's unfortunate but harmlessly intended speech at the Gloucester Agricultural Society's dinner – one of these agitators mounted a platform at a village meeting and in plain language incited and advised the labourers to duck the farmers! The agricultural women either go out to field-work or become indoor servants. In harvest they hay-make – chiefly light work, as raking – and reap, which is much harder labour; but then, while reaping they work their own time, as it is done by the piece. Significantly enough, they make longer hours while reaping. They are notoriously late to arrive, and eager to return home, on the hay-field. The children help both in haymaking and reaping. In spring and autumn they hoe and do other piece-work. On pasture farms they beat clots or pick up stones out of the way of the mowers' scythes. Occasionally, but rarely now, they milk. In winter they wear gaiters, which give the ankles a most ungainly appearance. Those who go out to service get very low wages at first from their extreme awkwardness, but generally quickly rise. As dairy-maids they get very good wages indeed. Dairymaids are scarce and valuable. A dairymaid who can be trusted to take charge of a dairy will sometimes get £20 besides her board (liberal) and sundry perquisites. These often save money, marry bailiffs, and help their husbands to start a farm.

In the education provided for children Wiltshire compares favourably with other counties. Long before the passing of the recent Act in reference to education the clergy had established schools in almost every parish, and their exertions have enabled the greater number of places to come up to the standard required by the Act, without the assistance of a School Board. The great difficulty is the distance children have to walk to school, from the sparseness of population and the number of outlying hamlets. This difficulty is felt equally by the farmers, who, in the majority of cases, find themselves situated far from a good school. In only one place has anything like a cry for education arisen, and that is on the extreme northern edge of the county. The Vice-Chairman of the Swindon Chamber of Agriculture recently stated that only one-half of the entire population of Inglesham could read and write. It subsequently appeared that the parish of Inglesham was very sparsely populated, and that a variety of circumstances had prevented vigorous efforts being made. The children, however, could attend schools in adjoining parishes, not farther than two miles, a distance which they frequently walk in other parts of the country.

Those who are so ready to cast every blame upon the farmer, and to represent him as eating up the earnings of his men and enriching himself with their ill-paid labour, should remember that farming, as a rule, is carried on with a large amount of borrowed capital. In these days, when £6 an acre has been expended in growing roots for sheep, when the slightest derangement of calculation in the price of wool, meat, or corn, or the loss of a crop, seriously interferes with a fair return for capital invested, the farmer has to sail extremely close to the wind, and only a little more would find his canvas shaking. It was only recently that the cashier of the principal bank of an agricultural county, after an unprosperous year, declared that such another season would make almost every farmer insolvent. Under these circumstances it is really to be wondered at that they have done as much as they have for the labourer in the last few years, finding him with better cottages, better wages, better education, and affording him better opportunities of rising in the social scale. – I am, Sir, faithfully yours,

RICHARD JEFFERIES
COATE FARM, SWINDON, *Nov.* 12, 1872

The Labourer's Daily Life

First published in *Fraser's Magazine*, November 1874
First collected in *The Toilers of the Field*, 1892

Many labourers can trace their descent from farmers or well-to-do people, and it is not uncommon to find here and there a man who believes that he is entitled to a large property in Chancery, or elsewhere, as the heir. They are very fond of talking of these things, and naturally take a pride in feeling themselves a little superior in point of ancestry to the mass of labourers.

How this descent from a farmer to a labourer is managed there are at this moment living examples going about the country. I knew a man who for years made it the business of his life to go round from farm to farm soliciting charity, and telling a pitiful tale of how he had once been a farmer himself. This tale was quite true, and as no class likes to see their order degraded, he got a great deal of relief from the agriculturists where he was known. He was said to have been wild in his youth, and now in his old age was become a living representative of the farmer reduced to a labourer.

This reduction is, however, usually a slow process, and takes two generations to effect – not two generations of thirty years each, but at least two successors in a farm.

Perhaps the decline of a farming family began in an accession of unwonted prosperity. The wheat or the wool went up to a high price, and the farmer happened to be fortunate and possessed a large quantity of those materials. Or he had a legacy left him, or in some way or other made money by good fortune rather than hard work. This elated his heart, and thinking to rise still higher in life, he took another, or perhaps two more large farms. But to stock these required more money than he could produce, and he had to borrow a thousand or so. Then the difficulty of attending to so large an acreage, much of it distant from his home, made it impossible to farm in the best and most profitable manner. By degrees the interest on the loan ate up all the profit on the new farms. Then he attempted to restore the balance by violent high farming. He bought manures to an unprecedented extent, invested in costly machinery – anything to produce a double crop. All this would have been very well if he had had time to wait till the grass grew; but meantime the steed starved. He had to relinquish the additional farms, and confine himself to the original one with a considerable loss both of money and prestige. He had no energy to rise again; he relapsed into slow, dawdling ways, perpetually regretting and dwelling on the past, yet making no effort to retrieve it.

This is a singular and strongly marked characteristic of the agricultural class, taken generally. They work and live and have their being in grooves. So long as they can continue in that groove, and go steadily forward, without much thought or trouble beyond that of patience and perseverance, all goes well; but if any sudden jolt should throw them out of this rut, they seem incapable of regaining it. They say, 'I have lost my way; I shall never get it again.' They sit down and regret the past, granting all their errors with the greatest candour; but the efforts they make to regain their position are feeble in the extreme.

So our typical unfortunate farmer folds his hands, and in point of fact slumbers away the rest of his existence, content with the fireside and a roof over his head, and a jug of beer to drink. He does not know French, he has never heard of Metternich, but he puts the famous maxim in practice, and, satisfied with to-day, says in his heart, *Après nous le Déluge*. No one disturbs him; his landlord has a certain respect and pity for him – respect, perhaps, for an old family that has tilled his land for a century, but which he now sees is slowly but irretrievably passing away. So the decayed farmer dozes out his existence.

Meantime his sons are coming on, and it too often happens that the brief period of sunshine and prosperity has done its evil work with them too. They have imbibed ideas of gentility and desire for excitement utterly foreign to the quiet, peaceful life of an agriculturist. They have gambled on the turf and become involved. Notwithstanding the fall of their father from his good position, they still retain the belief that in the end they shall find enough money to put all to rights; but when the end comes there is a deficiency. Among them there is perhaps one more plodding than the rest. He takes the farm, and keeps a house for the younger children. In ten years he becomes a bankrupt, and the family are scattered abroad upon the face of the earth. The plodding one becomes a bailiff, and lives respectably all his life; but his sons are never educated, and he saves no money; there is nothing for them but to go out to work as farm labourers.

Such is something like the usual way in which the decline and fall of a farming family takes place, though it may of course arise from unforeseen circumstances, quite out of the control of the agriculturist. In any case the children graduate downwards till they become labourers. Nowadays many of them emigrate, but in the long time that has gone before, when emigration was not so easy, many hundreds of families have thus become reduced to the level of the labourers they once employed. So it is that many of the labourers of to-day bear names which less than two generations ago were well known and highly respected over a wide tract of country. It is natural for them to look back with a certain degree of pleasure upon that past, and some may even have been incited to attempt to return to the old position.

But the great majority, the mass, of the agricultural labourers have been labourers time out of mind. Their fathers were labourers, their grandfathers and their great-grandfathers have all worked upon the farms, and very often almost continuously during that long period of time upon the farms in one parish. All their relations have been, and still are, labourers, varied by one here who has become a tinker, or one there who keeps a small roadside beerhouse. When this is the case, when a man and all his ancestors for generations have been hewers of wood and drawers of water, it naturally follows that the present representative of the family holds strongly to the traditions, the instincts, acquired during the slow process of time. What those instincts are will be better gathered from a faithful picture of his daily life.

Most of the agricultural labourers are born in a thatched cottage by the roadside, or in some narrow lane. This cottage is usually an encroachment. In the olden time, when land was cheap, and the competition for it dull, there were many strips and scraps which were never taken any notice of, and of which at this hour no record exists either in the parochial papers or the Imperial archives. Probably this arose from the character of the country in the past, when the greater part was open, or, as it was called, champaign land, without hedge, or ditch, or landmark. Near towns a certain portion was enclosed generally by the great landowners, or for the use of the tradesmen. There was also a large enclosure called the common land, on which all burgesses or citizens had a right to feed so many cattle, sheep, or horses. As a rule the common land was not enclosed by hedges in fields, though instances do occur in which it was. There were very few towns in the reign of Charles II that had not got their commons attached to them; but outside and beyond these patches of cultivation round the towns the country was open, unenclosed, and the boundaries ill-defined. The king's highway ran from one point to another, but its course was very wide. Roads were not then macadamized and strictly confined to one line. The want of metalling, and the consequent fearful ruts and sloughs, drove vehicles and travellers further and further from what was the original line, till they formed a track perhaps a score or two of yards wide. When fields became more generally enclosed it was still only in patches, and these strips and spaces of green sward were left utterly uncared for and unnoticed. These were encamped upon by the gipsies and travelling folk, and their unmolested occupation no doubt suggested to the agricultural labourer that he might raise a cottage upon such places, or cultivate it for his garden.

I know of one spot at this present moment which was enclosed by an agricultural labourer fully sixty years ago. It is an oval piece of ground of considerable size, situated almost exactly in the centre of a very valuable estate. He and his descendants continued to crop this garden of theirs entirely unmolested for the whole of that time, paying no rent whatever. It soon, however, became necessary to enlarge the size of the fields, which were small, in order to meet the requirements of the modern style of agriculture. This oval piece was surrounded by hedges of enormous growth, and the cultivator was requested to remove to another piece more out of the way. He refused to do so, and when the proprietors of the surrounding estate came to inquire into the circumstances they found that they could do nothing. He had enjoyed undisturbed possession for sixty years; he had paid no rent – no quit-rent or manor dues of any kind. But still further, when they came to examine the maps and old documents, no mention whatever appeared of this particular patch of ground. It was utterly unnoticed; it was not recorded as any man's property. The labourer therefore retained possession. This was an extraordinary case, because the encroachment took place in the middle of a cultivated estate, where one would have thought the tenants would have seen to it.

Commonly the squatters pitched on a piece of land – a long unused strip – running parallel to the highway or lane. This was no one's property; it was the property of the nation, which had no immediate representative to look after its interests. The surrounding farmers did not care to interfere; it was no business of theirs. The highway board, unless the instance was very glaring, and some actual obstruction of the road was caused, winked at the trespass. Most of them were farmers, and did not wish to interfere with a poor man, who they knew had no other way of getting a house of his own. By-and-by, when the cottage was built, the labourer was summoned to the court-leet of the manor, and was assessed in quit-rent, a mere nominal sum, perhaps fourpence or a shilling a year. He had no objection to this, because it gave him a title. As long as the quit-rent was duly paid, and he could produce the receipt, he was safe in the occupation of his cottage, and no one could turn him out. To be assessed by the court-leet in fact established his title. Some of these court-leets or manor courts are only held at intervals of three years, or even more, and are generally composed of farmers, presided over by the legal agent of the lord of the manor. The tenants of the manor attend to pay their quit-rent for the preceding years, and it often happens that if the cottager has been ill, or is weak and infirm, the farmers composing the court subscribe and pay the quit-rent for him.

The first step when a labourer intends to become a squatter is to enclose the strip of land which he has chosen. This he does by raising a low bank of earth round it, on which he plants elder bushes, as that shrub grows quickest, and in the course of two seasons will form a respectable fence. Then he makes a small sparred gate which he can fasten with a padlock, and the garden is complete. To build the cottage is quite another matter. That is an affair of the greatest importance, requiring some months of thought and preparation. The first thing is to get the materials. If it is a clay country, of course bricks must be chosen; but in stone countries there are often quarries on the farm on which he works. His employer will let him have a considerable quantity of stone for nothing, and the rest at a nominal charge, and will lend him a horse and cart at a leisure season; so that in a very short time he can transport enough stone for his purpose. If he has no such friend, there is almost sure to be in every parish a labouring man who keeps a wretched horse or two, fed on the grass by the road-side, and gains his living by hauling. Our architect engages this man at a low price to haul his materials for him. The lime to make mortar he must buy. In the parish there is nearly sure to be at least one native mason, who works for the farmers, putting up pig-styes, mending walls, and doing small jobs of that kind. This is the builder who engages to come on Saturday afternoons or in the evenings, while the would-be householder himself is the hod-bearer and mixes the mortar. Nine times out of ten the site for the cottage is chosen so as to have a ditch at the back. This ditch acts at once as the cesspool and the sewer, and, unless it happens to have a good fall, speedily becomes a nuisance to the neighbourhood. A certain quantity of wood is of course required in building even this humble edifice. This is either given by the farmers or is purchased at a nominal rate.

The ground plan is extremely simple. It consists of two rooms, oblong, and generally of the same size – one to live in, the other to sleep in – for the great majority of the squatters' hovels have no upstair rooms. At one end there is a small shed for odds and ends. This shed used to be built with an oven, but now scarcely any labourers bake their own bread, but buy of the baker. The walls of the cottage having been carried up some six feet, or six feet six – just a little higher than a man's head – the next process is to construct the roof, which is a very simple process. The roof is then thatched, sometimes with flags cut from the brooks, but more usually with straw, and practically the cottage is now built, for there are no indoor fittings to speak of. The chimney is placed at the end of the room set apart for day use. There is no ceiling, nothing between the floor and the thatch and rafters, except perhaps at one end, where there is a kind of loft. The floor consists simply of the earth itself rammed down hard, or sometimes of rough pitching-stones, with large interstices between them. The furniture of this room is of the simplest description. A few chairs, a deal table, three or four shelves, and a cupboard, with a box or two in the corners, constitute the whole. The domestic utensils are equally few, and strictly utilitarian. A great pot, a kettle, a saucepan, a few plates, dishes and knives, half-a-dozen spoons, and that is about all. But on the mantelpiece there is nearly sure to be a few ornaments in crockery, bought from some itinerant trader. The walls are whitewashed. The bedroom is plainly and rudely furnished. Some cottages do not even attain to this degree of comfort. They consist of four posts set in the ground which support the cross-beam and the roof, and the walls are made of wattle and daub, i.e., of small split willow sticks, put upright and daubed over with coarse plaster. The roofs of these cottages are often half hidden with rank grass, moss, and sillgreen, a vegetation perhaps encouraged by the drippings from a tree overhanging the roof; and the situation of the cottage is itself in many cases low and damp.

But there is a class of squatters, who possess habitations more fit for human beings. These were originally built by men who had saved a little money, had showed, perhaps, a certain talent for hedge carpentering or thatching, become tinkers, or even blacksmiths. In such capacities a man may save a little money – not much, perhaps £30 or £40 at furthest. With the aid of this he manages to build a very tidy cottage, in the face of the statement made by architects and builders that a good cottage cannot be erected under £120. Their dwellings do not, indeed, compete with the neat, prim, and business-like work of the professional builder; but still they are roomy and substantial cottages. The secret of cheapness lies in the fact that they work themselves at the erection, and do not entrust some one else with a contract. Moreover, they make shifts and put up with drawbacks as no business-man could possibly do. The materials they purchase are cheap and of second-class condition, but good enough to hold together and to last some time. Their rude beams and rafters would not satisfy the eye of a landed proprietor, but they hold up the roof-tree equally well. Every pound they spend goes its full length, and not a penny is wasted. After a while a substantial-looking cottage rises up, whitewashed and thatched. It has an upper storey with two rooms, and two, at least, downstairs, with the inevitable lean-to or shed, without which no labourer's cottage is complete. This is more like a house, the residence of a man, than that of the poorer squatter. The floor is composed of flag-stones, in this case always carefully washed and holystoned. There are the same chairs and deal table as in the poorer cottage, but there are many more domestic utensils, and the chimney-piece is ornamented with more crockery figures. A few coarse prints hang against the walls. Some of these old prints are great curiosities in their way – hardly valuable enough for a collection, but very amusing. A favourite set of prints is the ride of Dick Turpin of York on Black Bess, representing every scene in that famous gallop. The upstair rooms are better furnished, and the beds often really good.

Some of these cottages in summer-time really approach something of that Arcadian beauty which is supposed to prevail in the country. Everything, of course, depends upon the character of the inmates. The dull tint of the thatch is relieved here and there by great patches of sillgreen, which is religiously preserved as a good herb, though the exact ailments for which it is 'good' are often forgotten. One end of the cottage is often completely hidden with ivy, and woodbine grows in thickest profusion over the porch. Near the door there are almost always a few cabbage-rose trees, and under the windows grow wall-flowers and hollyhocks, sweet peas, columbine, and sometimes the graceful lilies of the valley. The garden stretches in a long strip from the door, one mass of green. It is enclosed by thick hedges, over which the dog-rose grows, and the wild convolvulus will blossom in the autumn. Trees fill up every available space and corner – apple trees, pear trees, damsons, plums, bullaces – all varieties. The cottagers seem to like to have at least one tree of every sort. These trees look very nice in the spring when the apple blossom is out, and again in the autumn when the fruit is ripe. Under the trees are gooseberry bushes, raspberries, and numbers of currants. The patches are divided into strips producing potatoes, cabbage, lettuce, onions, radishes, parsnips; in this kitchen produce, as with the fruit, they like to possess a few of all kinds. There is generally a great bunch of rhubarb. In odd corners there are sure to be a few specimens of southernwood, mugwort, and other herbs; not for use, but from adherence to the old customs. The 'old people' thought much of these 'yherbs', so they must have some too, as well as a little mint and similar potherbs. In the windows you may see two or three geraniums, and over the porch a wicker cage, in which the 'ousel cock, with orange-tawny bill', pours out his rich, melodious notes. There is hardly a cottage without its captive bird, or tame rabbit, or mongrel cur, which seems as much attached to his master as more high-bred dogs to their owners.

These better cottages are extremely pleasing to look upon. There is an old English, homely look about them. I know a man now whose cottage is ornamented much in the way I have described, a man of sixty, who can neither read nor write, and is rude and uncouth in speech, yet everything about him seems pleasant and happy. To my eye the thatch and gables, and picturesque irregularity of this class of cottages, are more pleasing than the modern glaring red brick and prim slate of dwellings built to order, where everything is cut with a precise uniformity.

If a man can be encouraged to build his own house, depend upon it it is better for him and his neighbours than that he should live in one which is not his own. The sense of ownership engenders a pride in the place, and all his better feelings are called into play. Some of these cottagers, living in such houses as these, are the very best labourers to be had. They stay on one farm a lifetime, and never leave it – an invaluable aid to a farmer. They frequently possess some little special knowledge of carpentering or blacksmith's work, which renders them extremely useful, and at the same time increases their earnings. These men are the real true peasantry, quiet and peaceful, yet strong and courageous. These are the class that should be encouraged by every possible means: a man who keeps his little habitation in the state I have described, who ornaments it within, and fills his garden with fruit and flowers, though he may be totally unable to read or to speak correctly, is nevertheless a good and useful citizen, and an addition to the stability of the State.

Though these cottages are worth the smallest sums comparatively, it is interesting to note with what pride and satisfaction the possessors contemplate leaving them to their children. Of course this very feeling, where there are quarrelsome relations, often leads to bickerings and strife. It is astonishing with what tenacity a man who thinks he has a claim to a part of such a small estate will cling to his cause, and will not hesitate to spend to maintain his claim all his little earnings on the third-class lawyers whom the agricultural poor mostly patronize. Even after every shadow of legal chance is gone, he still loudly declares his right; and there is more squabbling about the inheritance of these places than over the succession to great domains.

Another class of labourers' cottages is found chiefly in the villages. These were not originally erected for the purpose to which they are now applied; they were farmhouses in the days when small farms were the rule, or they were built for tradesmen who have long since departed. These buildings are divided into two, three, or more habitations, each with its family; and many makeshifts have to be resorted to to render them decent and comfortable. This class of cottage is to be avoided if possible, because the close and forced intercourse which must take place between the families generally leads to quarrels. Perhaps there is one pump for the entire building, and one wants to use it just at the moment that another requires water; or there is only one gateway to the court, and the passage is obstructed by the wheelbarrow of the other party. It is from these places that the greater part of the malcontents go up to the magistrates in petty sessions. It is rare, indeed, that the cottager living more or less isolated by the side of the road appears in a court of law. Of course, in these villages there are cottages which have been built expressly for the use of labouring men, and these, like those in the open country, may be divided into three classes – the hovel, the cottage proper, and the model modern cottage.

In the villages there is almost sure to be one or more cottages which carries one's idea of Lilliputian dwellings to the extreme. These are generally sheds or outhouses which have been converted into cottages. I entered one not long since which consisted of two rooms, one above and one below, and each of these rooms could not have measured, at a guess, more than six feet six across. I had heard of this place, and expected to find it a perfect den of misery and wretchedness. No such thing. To my surprise the woman who opened the door was neatly clad, clean, and bright. The floor of the cottage was of ordinary flag-stones, but there was a ceiling whitewashed and clean. A good fire was burning in the grate – it was the middle of winter – and the room felt warm and comfortable. The walls were completely covered with engravings from the *Illustrated London News*. The furniture was equal to the furniture of the best cottages, and everything was extremely clean. The woman said they were quite comfortable; and although they could have had a larger cottage many times since, they never wished to change, as they had no children. That of course made a great difference. I never should have thought it possible for two human beings to have existed, much less been comfortable, in such a diminutive place. Another cottage I know contains but one room altogether, which is about eight feet square; it is inhabited by a solitary old woman, and looks like a toy-house. One or two such places as these may be found in most villages, but it does not by any means follow that because they are small the inhabitants are badly off. The condition they are found in depends entirely upon the disposition of the inmates. If they are slatternly and dirty, the largest cottages would not improve them.

In some rural villages a great many cottages may be observed sadly out of repair – the thatch coming off and in holes, the windows broken, and other signs of dilapidation. This is usually set down to the landlord's fault, but if the circumstances are inquired into, it will often be found that the fault lies with the inmates themselves. These cottages are let to labourers at a merely nominal rent, and with them a large piece of allotment ground. But although they thus get a house and garden almost free, they refuse to do the slightest or simplest repairs. If the window gets broken – 'Oh, let it stop; the landlord can do that.' If a piece of thatch comes off – 'Oh, 'tisn't my house; let the landlord do it up.' So it goes on till the cottage is ready to tumble to pieces. What is the landlord to do? In his heart he would like to raze the whole village to the ground and rebuild it afresh. But there are not many who afford such an expense. Then, if it were done, the old women and old men, and infirm persons who find a home in these places, would be driven forth. If the landlord puts up two hundred new cottages, he finds it absolutely necessary to get some kind of return for the capital invested. He does not want more than two and a half per cent; but to ask that means a rise of perhaps a shilling a week. That is enough; the labourer seeks another tumbledown place where he can live for tenpence a week, and the poor and infirm have to go to the workhouse. So, rather than be annoyed with the endless complaints and troubles, to say nothing of the inevitable loss of money, the landlord allows things to go on as they are.

Among our English cottages in out-of-the-way places may be found curious materials for the study of character in humble life. In one cottage you may find an upright, stern-featured man, a great student of the Bible, and fond of using its language whenever opportunity offers, who is the representative of the old Puritan, though the denomination to which he may belong is technically known as the Methodist. He is stern, hard, uncompromising – one who sets duty above affection. His children are not spoiled because the rod is spared. He stands aloof from his fellows, and is never seen at the cottage alehouse, or lingering in groups at the cross-roads. He is certain to be at the 'anniversary', i.e., the commemoration of the foundation of the Methodist chapel of the parish. The very next cottage may contain the antithesis of this man. This is a genius in his way. He has some idea of art, as you may gather from the fanciful patches into which his garden is divided. He has a considerable talent for construction, and though he has never been an apprentice he can do something towards mending a cart or a door. He makes stands with wires to put flowers in for the farmers' parlours, and strings the dry oak-apples on wire, which he twists into baskets, to hold knicknackeries. He is witty, and has his jest for everybody. He can do something of everything – turn his hand any way – a perfect treasure on the farm. In the old days there was another character in most villages; this was the rhymer. He was commonly the fiddler too, and sang his own verses to tunes played by himself. Since the printing-press has come in, and flooded the country with cheap literature, this character has disappeared, though many of the verses these men made still linger in the countryside.

The ordinary adult farm labourer commonly rises at from four to five o'clock; if he is a milker, and has to walk some little distance to his work, even as early as half-past three. Four was the general rule, but of late years the hour has grown later. He milks till five or half-past, carries the yokes to the dairy, and draws water for the dairymaid, or perhaps chops up some wood for her fire to scald the milk. At six he goes to breakfast, which consists of a hunch of bread and cheese as the rule, with now and then a piece of bacon, and as a milker he receives his quart of beer. At breakfast there is no hurry for half-an-hour or so; but some time before seven he is on at the ordinary work of the day. If a milker and very early riser, he is not usually put at the heavy jobs, but allowances are made for the work he has already done. The other men on the farm arrive at six. At eleven, or half-past, comes luncheon, which lasts a full hour, often an hour and a quarter. About three o'clock the task of milking again commences; the buckets are got out with a good deal of rattling and noise, the yokes fitted to the shoulders, and away he goes for an hour or hour and a half of milking. That done, he has to clean up the court and help the dairymaid put the heavier articles in place; then another quart of beer, and away home. The time of leaving off work varies from half-past five to half-past six. At ordinary seasons the other men leave at six, but in haymaking or harvest time they are expected to remain till the job in hand that day is finished, often till eight or half-past. This is compensated for by a hearty supper and almost unlimited beer. The women employed in field labour generally leave at four, and hasten home to prepare the evening meal. The evening meal is the great event of the day. Like the independent gentleman in this one thing, the labourer dines late in the day. His midday meal, which is the farmer's dinner, is his luncheon. The labourer's dinner is taken at half-past six to seven in the evening, after he has got home, unlaced his heavy and cumbrous boots, combed his hair, and washed himself. His table is always well supplied with vegetables, potatoes, and particularly greens, of which he is peculiarly fond. The staple dish is, of course, a piece of bacon, and large quantities of bread are eaten. It is a common thing now, once or twice in the week, for a labourer to have a small joint of mutton, not a prime joint, of course, but still good and wholesome meat. Many of them live in a style, so far as eating and drinking is concerned, quite equal to the small farmers, and far superior to what these small farmers were used to. Instead of beer, the agricultural labourer frequently drinks tea with his dinner – weak tea in large quantities. After the more solid parts comes a salad of onions or lettuce. These men eat quantities which would half kill many townspeople. After dinner, if it is the season of the year, they go out to the allotment and do a little work for themselves, and then, unless the alehouse offers irresistible attractions, to bed. The genuine agricultural labourer goes early to bed. It is necessary for him, after the long toil of the day, on account of the hour at which he has to rise in the morning.

Men employed on arable farms, as carters, for instance, have to rise even earlier than dairymen. They often begin to bait their horses at half-past three, or rather they used to. This operation of baiting is a most serious and important one to the carter. On it depends the appearance of his team – with him a matter of honest and laudable ambition. If he wishes his horses to look fat and well, with smooth shiny coats, he must take the greatest care with their food, not to give them too much or too little, and to vary it properly. He must begin feeding a long time before his horses start to plough. It is, therefore, an object with him to get to rest early. In the winter time especially the labouring poor go to bed very soon, to save the expense of candles.

By the bye, the cottagers have a curious habit, which deserves to be recorded even for its singularity. When the good woman of the cottage goes out for half-an-hour to fetch a pail of water, or to gossip with a neighbour, she always leaves the door-key in the keyhole *outside*. The house is, in fact, at the mercy of any one who chooses to turn the key and enter. This practice of locking the door and leaving the key in it is very prevalent. The presence of the key is to intimate that the inmate has gone out, but will shortly return; and it is so understood by the neighbours. If a cottager goes out for the day, he or she locks the door, and takes the key with them; but if the key is left in the door, it is a sign that the cottager will be back in ten minutes or so.

The alehouse is the terrible bane of the labourer. If he can keep clear of that, he is clean, tidy, and respectable; but if he once falls into drinking habits, good-bye to all hopes of his rising in his occupation. Where he is born there will he remain, and his children after him.

Some of the cottagers who show a little talent for music combine under the leadership of the parish clerk and the patronage of the clergyman, and form a small brass band which parades the village at the head of the Oddfellows or other benefit club once a year. In the early summer, before the earnest work of harvest begins, and while the evenings begin to grow long, it is not unusual to see a number of the younger men at play at cricket in the meadow with the more active of the farmers. Most populous villages have their cricket club, which even the richest farmers do not disdain to join, and their sons stand at the wicket.

The summer is the labourer's good season. Then he can make money and enjoy himself. In the summer three or four men will often join together and leave their native parish for a ramble. They walk off perhaps some forty or fifty miles, take a job of mowing or harvesting, and after a change of scenery and associates, return in the later part of the autumn, full of the things they have seen, and eager to relate them to the groups at the cross-roads or the alehouse. The winter is under the best circumstances a hard time for the labourer. It is not altogether that coals are dear and firewood growing scarcer year by year, but every condition of his daily life has a harshness about it. In the summer the warm sunshine cast a glamour over the rude walls, the decaying thatch, and the ivy-covered window. The blue smoke rose up curling beside the tall elm-tree. The hedge parting his garden from the road was green and thick, the garden itself full of trees, and flowers of more or less beauty. Mud floors are not so bad in the summer; holes in the thatch do not matter so much; an ill-fitting window-sash gives no concern. But with the cold blasts and ceaseless rain of winter all this is changed. The hedge next the road is usually only elder, and this, once the leaves are off, is the thinnest, most miserable of shelters. The rain comes through the hole in the thatch (we are speaking of the large class of poor cottages), the mud floor is damp, and perhaps sticky. If the floor is of uneven stones, these grow damp and slimy. The cold wind comes through the ill-fitting sash, and drives with terrible force under the door. Very often the floor is one step lower than the ground outside, and consequently there is a constant tendency in rainy weather for the water to run or soak in. The elm-tree overhead, that appeared so picturesque in summer, is now a curse, for the great drops fall perpetually from it upon the thatch and on the pathway in front of the door. In great storms of wind it sways to and fro, causing no little alarm, and boughs are sometimes blown off it, and fall upon the roof-tree. The thatch of the cottage is saturated; the plants and grasses that almost always grow on it, and the moss, are vividly, rankly green; till all dripping, soaked, overgrown with weeds, the wretched place looks not unlike a dunghill. Inside, the draught is only one degree better than the smoke. These low chimneys, overshadowed with trees, smoke incessantly, and fill the room with smother. To avoid the draught, many of the cottages are fitted with wooden screens, which divide the room, small enough before, into two parts, the outer of which, towards the door, is a howling wilderness of draught and wet from under the door; and the inner part close, stuffy, and dim with smoke driven down the chimney by the shifting wind. Here the family are all huddled up together close over the embers. Here the cooking is done, such as it is. Here they sit in the dark, or in such light as is supplied by the carefully hoarded stock of fuel, till it is time to go to bed, and that is generally early enough. So rigid is the economy practised in many of these cottages that a candle is rarely if ever used. The light of the fire suffices, and they find their beds in the dark. Even when a labourer has risen in the scale, and has some small property, the enforced habits of early life cling to him; and I have frequently found men who were really worth some little money sitting at eight o'clock on a dark winter's night without a candle or lamp, their feet close to a few dying embers. The older people especially go to bed early. Going to some cottages once for a parish paper that had been circulated for signature, I rapped at the closed door. This was at half-past seven one evening in November. Again and again I hammered at the door; at last an old woman put her head out of the window, and the following colloquy ensued: –

'What do 'ee want?'

'The paper; have you signed it?'

'Lor, I doan't know. He's on the table – a bin ther ever since a come. Thee's can lift th' latch an' take 'un. *We bin gone to bed this two hours.*'

They must have gone upstairs at half-past five. To rise at five of a summer's morning, and see the azure of the sky and the glorious sun, may be, perhaps, no great hardship, although there are few persons who could long remain poetical on bread and cheese. But to rise at five on a dark winter's morning is a very different affair. To put on coarse nailed boots, weighing fully seven pounds, gaiters up above the knee, a short greatcoat of some heavy material, and to step out into the driving rain and trudge wearily over field after field of wet grass, with the furrows full of water; then to sit on a three-legged stool, with mud and manure half-way up the ankles, and milk cows with one's head leaning against their damp, smoking hides for two hours, with the rain coming steadily drip, drip, drip – this is a very different affair.

The 'fogger' on a snowy morning in the winter has to encounter about the most unpleasant circumstances imaginable. Icicles hang from the eaves of the rick, and its thatch is covered with snow. Up the slippery ladder in the dark morning, one knee out upon the snow-covered thatch, he plunges the broad hay-knife in and cuts away an enormous truss – then a great prong is stuck into this, a prong made on purpose, with extra thick and powerful handle, and the truss, well bound round with a horse-hair rope, is hoisted on the head and shoulders. This heavy weight the fogger has to carry perhaps half-a-mile through the snow; the furrows in the field are frozen over, but his weight crashes through the ice, slush into the chilly water. Rain, snow, or bitter frost, or still more bitter east winds – 'harsh winds', as he most truly calls them – the fogger must take no heed of either, for the cows must be fed.

A quart of threepenny ale for breakfast, with a hunch of bread and cheese, then out to work again in the weather, let it be what it may. The cowyards have to be cleaned out – if not done before breakfast – the manure thrown up into heaps, and the heaps wheeled outside. Or, perhaps, the master has given him a job of piece-work to fill up the middle of the day with – a hedge to cut and ditch. This means more slush, wet, cold, and discomfort. About six or half-past he reaches home, thoroughly saturated, worn-out, cross, and 'dummel'. I don't know how to spell that word, nor what its etymology may be, but it well expresses the dumb, sullen churlishness which such a life as this engenders. For all the conditions and circumstances of such a life tend to one end only – the blunting of all the finer feelings, the total erasure of sensitiveness. The coarse, half-cooked cabbage, the small bit of fat and rafty bacon, the dry bread and

pint of weak tea, makes no very hearty supper after such a day
as this. The man grows insensible to the weather, so cold and
damp; his bodily frame becomes crusted over, case-hardened;
and with this indifference there rises up at the same time a corresponding dulness as regards all moral and social matters.

Generally the best conditions of cottage life are to be found
wherever there are, say, three or four great, tall, strong, unmar-
ried sons lodging in the house with their aged parents. Each of
these pays a small sum weekly for his lodging, and often an
additional sum for the bare necessaries of life. In the aggregate
this mounts up to a considerable sum, and whatever is bought
is equally shared by the parents. They live exceedingly well.
Such young men as these earn good wages, and now and then
make extra time, and come home with a pocketful of money.
Even after the inevitable alehouse has claimed its share, there
still remains enough to purchase fresh meat for supper; and it
is not at all unusual in such cottages to find the whole family
supping at seven (it is, in fact, dining) on a fairly good joint of
mutton, with every species of common vegetables. In one case
that was brought under my notice three brothers lived with
their aged mother. They were all strong, hard-working men,
and tolerably steady. In that cottage there were no less than
four separate barrels of beer, and all on tap. Four barrels in one
cottage seems an extraordinary thing, yet it resolved itself very
simply. The cottage was the mother's; they gave her so much
for lodging, and she had her own barrel of beer, so that there
should be no dispute. The three brothers were mowers – mowers
drink enormous quantities of liquor – and with the same view to
prevent dispute each had his own especial barrel. Families like
this live fairly well, and have many little comforts. Still, at the
best, in winter it is a rough and uncomfortable existence.

In the life of the English agricultural labourers there is absolutely no poetry, no colour. Even their marriages – times when
if ever in life poetry will manifest itself – are sober, dull, tame,
clumsy, and colourless. I say sober in the sense of tint, for to get
drunk appears to be the one social pleasure of the marriage-day.
They, of course, walk to church; but then that walk usually
leads across fields full of all the beauties of the spring or the

summer. There is nothing in the walk itself to flatten down the occasion. But the procession is so dull – so utterly ungenial – a stranger might pass it without guessing that a wedding was toward. Except a few rude jests; except that there is an attempt to walk arm-in-arm (it is only an attempt, for they forget to allow for each other's motions); except the Sunday dresses, utterly devoid of taste, what is there to distinguish this day from the rest? There is the drunken carousal, it is true, all the afternoon and evening. There are no fête days in the foreign sense in the English labourer's life. There are the fairs and feasts, and a fair is the most melancholy of sights. Showmen's vans, with pictures outside of unknown monsters; merry-go-rounds, nut stalls, gingerbread stalls, cheap Jacks, and latterly photographic 'studios'; behind all these the alehouse; the beating of drums and the squalling of pigs, the blowing of horns, and the neighing of horses trotted out for show, the roar of a rude crowd – these constitute a country fair. There is no colour – nothing flowery or poetical about this festival of the labourer.

The village feasts are still less interesting. Here and there the clergyman of the parish has succeeded in turning what was a rude saturnalia into a decorous 'fête', with tea in a tent. But generally the feasts are falling into rapid disuse, and would perhaps have died away altogether had not the benefit societies often chosen that day for their annual club-dinner. A village feast consists of two or three gipsies located on the greensward by the side of the road, and displaying ginger-beer, nuts, and toys for sale; an Aunt Sally; and, if the village is a large one, the day may be honoured by the presence of what is called a rifle-gallery; the 'feast' really and truly does not exist. Some two or three of the old-fashioned farmers have the traditional roast beef and plum-pudding on that day, and invite a few friends; but this custom is passing away. In what the agricultural labourer's feast nowadays consists no one can tell. It is an excuse for an extra quart or two of beer, that is all.

This dulness is not, perhaps, the fault of the labourer. It may be that it is the fault of the national character, shown more broadly in the lower class of the population. Speaking nationally, we have no fête days – there is no colour in our mode of life. These English agricultural labourers have no passion plays, no peasant plays, no rustic stage and drama, few songs, very little music. The club-dinner is the real fête of the labourer; he gets plenty to eat and drink for that day. It is this lack of poetical feeling that makes the English peasantry so uninteresting a study. They have no appreciation of beauty. Many of them, it is true, grow quantities of flowers; but barely one in a thousand could arrange those flowers in a bouquet.

The alehouse forms no inconsiderable part of the labourer's life. It is at once his stock exchange, his reading-room, his club, and his assembly rooms. It is here that his benefit society holds its annual dinner. The club meetings take place weekly or monthly in the great room upstairs. Here he learns the news of the day; the local papers are always to be found at the public-house, and if he cannot read himself he hears the news from those who can. In the winter he finds heat and light, too often lacking at home; at all times he finds amusement; and who can blame him for seizing what little pleasure lies in his way? As a rule the beerhouse is the only place of amusement to which he can resort: it is his theatre, his music-hall, picture-gallery, and Crystal Palace. The recent enactments bearing upon the licensed victuallers have been rather hard upon the agricultural labourer. No doubt they are very excellent enactments, especially those relating to early closing; but in the villages and outlying rural districts, where life is reduced to its most rude and simple form, many of the restrictions are unjust, and deprive the labourer of what he feels to be his legitimate right. Playing at nine-pins, for instance, is practically forbidden, so also dominoes. Now, it was a great thing to put down skittle-sharping and cheating at gambling generally – a good thing to discourage gambling in every form – but in these thinly-populated outlying agricultural parishes, where money is scarce and wages low, there never existed any temptation to allure skittle-sharpers and similar cheaters to the spot. The game at skittles was a legitimate game – a fair and honest struggle of skill and strength. Nine times out of ten it was played only for a quart of ale, to be drunk by the loser as well as the winner in good fellowship. Why deprive the man who labours all day in wet and storm of so simple a pleasure in the evening? The conditions are very different to those existing in large manufacturing towns, and some modification of the law ought to be made. The agricultural labourer has no cheap theatre at which he can spend an hour, no music-hall, no reading-room; his only resource is the public-house. Now that he is practically deprived of his skittles and such games, he has no amusement left except to drink, or play at pitch and toss on the quiet, a far worse pastime than skittles. Skittles, of course, are allowed provided the players play for love only; but what public-house keeper cares to put up the necessary arrangements on such terms? The labourer will have his quart in the evening, and, despite of all 'cry' to the contrary, I believe it to be his right to have that quart; and it is better, if he must have it, that his whole thoughts should not be concentrated on the liquor – that he should earn it by skill and strength. There is an opprobrium about the public-house, and let us grant that it is at least partially deserved – but where else is the labourer to go? He cannot for ever work all day and sit in his narrow cabin in the evening. He cannot always read, and those of his class who do read do so imperfectly. A reading-room has been tried, but as a rule it fails to attract the *purely agricultural labourer*. The shoemaker, the tailor, the village post-master, grocer, and such people may use it; also a few of the better-educated of the young labourers, the rising generation; but not the full-grown labourer with a wife and family and cottage. It does good undoubtedly; in the future, as education extends, it will become a place of resort. But at present it fails to reach the adult genuine agricultural labourer. For a short period in the dead of the winter the farmers and gentry get up penny readings in many places, but these are confined to at most one evening a week. What, then, is the labourer to do? Let any one put himself in his place, try to realize his feelings and circumstances. At present, till education extends, he must go to the public-house. Is he to be punished and deprived of his game of skill because in large towns it bears evil fruit? Surely the law could be somewhat modified, and playing permitted under some restrictions.

The early closing has been an unalloyed good in these rural districts. The labourer is a steady drinker. He does not toss down glasses of stiff brandy and whisky. His beer requires time to produce an effect. The last hour does the mischief. Since the earlier closing the village streets have been comparatively free from drunken men. In any case, the agricultural labourer is the most lamb-like of drunkards. He interferes with no one. He unhinges no gates, smashes no windows, does no injury. He either staggers home or quietly lies on the grass till the liquor passes off. He is not a quarrelsome man. He does not fight with knuckle-dusters or kick with his heavy boots. His fights, when he does fight, are very harmless affairs. No doubt his drunkenness is an offence; but it is comparatively innocuous to the general public.

Religious feeling does not run high among the labourers. A large proportion of them are Nonconformists – principally Methodists. But this is not out of any very decided notion as to the difference of ceremony or theological dogma; it arises out of a class feeling. They say, or rather they feel, that this is *their* church. The parish church is the church of the farmers and the gentry. There is no hostility to the clergyman of the parish, no bitter warfare of sect against sect, or of Methodist against Churchman. But you see very few of the farmers go to chapel. The labourer goes there, and finds his own friends – his cousins and uncles – his wife's relations. He is among his own class. There is no feeling of inferiority. The religion taught, the service, the hymns, the preacher, all are his. He has a sense of proprietorship in them. He helps to pay for them. The French peasant replied to the English tourist, who expressed surprise at the fanatic love of the populace for the first Napoleon – 'he was as much a tyrant as King Louis was.' 'Ah, but Napoleon was *our* king.' So the labourers feel that this is their religion. Therefore it is that so many of them gather together (where there are no chapels) in the cottage of some man who takes the lead, and sit, with doors and windows shut, crammed together to pray and listen to others pray. Any of them who wishes can, as it were, ascend the pulpit here. This is why in so many parishes the pews of the parish church are comparatively empty so far as agricultural labourers are concerned. The best of clergymen must fail to fill them under such disadvantages.

It is very difficult not only for the clergyman, but for others who wish to improve the condition of the labourer, to reach him. Better cottages are, of course, a most effectual way, but it is not in the power of every one to confer so substantial a benefit. Perhaps one of the best means devised has been that of cottage flower-shows. These are, of course, not confined to flowers; in fact, the principal part of such shows consists of table vegetables and fruit. By rigidly excluding all gardeners, and all persons not strictly cottage people, the very best results have often been arrived at in this way. For if there is one thing in which the labourer takes an interest it is his garden and his allotment. To offer him prizes for the finest productions of his garden touches the most sensitive part of his moral organization. It is wonderful what an amount of emulation these prizes excite – emulation not so much for the value of the prize as for the distinction. These competitions tend besides to provide him with a better class of food, for he depends largely upon vegetables.

There is nothing connected with the condition of the agricultural poor that is better worth the attention of improvers than the style of cookery pursued in these cottages. A more wretched cookery probably does not exist on the face of the earth. The soddened cabbage is typical of the whole thing. Since higher wages have come in it has become possible for the labourer in many cases to provide himself with better food, such as mutton – the cheap parts – more bacon, pork, and so on; but the women do not know how to make the most of it. It is very difficult to lay down a way in which this defect may be remedied; for there is nothing a man, let him be never so poor, so deeply resents as an inspection of the contents of his pot. He would sooner eat half-raw bacon than have the teaching forced on him – how to make savoury meals of the simple provisions within his reach; nor can he be blamed for this sturdy independent feeling. Possibly the establishment of schools of cookery in villages might do much good. They might be attached to the new schools now building throughout the country. The labourer, from so long living upon coarse, ill-cooked food, acquires an artificial taste. Some men eat their bacon raw; others will drink large quantities of vinegar, and well they may need it to correct by its acidity the effects of strong unwholesome cabbage. The cottage cook has no idea of those nutritious and pleasant soups which can be made to form so important a feature in the economy of daily life.

The labourer is in a lower degree of the same class as the third-rate working farmer of the past. He is the old small dairy farmer in a coarser shape. With a little less education, ruder manners, with the instincts of eating, drinking, and avarice more prominently displayed, he presents in his actual condition at this day a striking analogy to the agriculturist of a bygone time. In fact, those farmers of twenty or thirty acres, living in cottage-like homesteads, were barely distinguishable as far as *personnel* went from the labourers among whom they lived. This being the case, it is not surprising to find that the labourer of this day presents in general characteristics a marked affinity in ideas and sentiments to those entertained by the old farmer. He has the same paternal creed in a more primeval form. He considers his children as his absolute property. He rules them with a rod of iron, or rather of ground-ash. In fact, the ground-ash stick is his social religion. The agricultural labouring poor are very rough and even brutal towards their children. Not that they are without affection towards them, but they are used to thrash them into obedience instead of leading them into it by the gentle means of moral persuasion.

Bystanders would call the agricultural labourer cruel. Carters, for instance, had till lately a habit of knocking the boys under their control about in a brutal manner. But I do not think that in the mass of cases it arose from deliberate cruelty, but from a species of stolid indifference or insensibility to suffering. Somehow they do not seem to understand that others suffer, whether this arises from the rough life they lead, the endless battle with the weather, the hard fare – whether it has grown up out of the circumstances surrounding them. The same unfeeling brutality often extends to the cattle under their care. In this there has been a decided improvement of late years; but it is not yet extinct.

These are some of the lights and shades of the labourer's daily life impartially presented.

The Gamekeeper at Home:
The Man Himself – His House, and Tools

First published as a serial in the
Pall Mall Gazette, 1877–8
First collected in *The Gamekeeper at Home*, 1878

The keeper's cottage stands in a sheltered 'coombe', or narrow hollow of the woodlands, overshadowed by a mighty Spanish chestnut, bare now of leaves, but in summer a noble tree. The ash wood covers the slope at the rear; on one side is a garden, and on the other a long strip of meadow with elms. In front, and somewhat lower, a streamlet winds, fringing the sward, and across it the fir plantations begin, their dark sombre foliage hanging over the water. A dead willow trunk thrown from bank to bank forms a rude bridge; the tree, not even squared, gives little surface for the foot, and in frosty weather a slip is easy. From this primitive contrivance a path, out of which others fork, leads into the intricacies of the covers, and from the garden a wicket-gate opens on the ash wood. The elms in the meadow are full of rooks' nests, and in the spring the coombe will resound with their cawing; these black bandits, who do not touch it at other times, will then ravage the garden to feed their hungry young, despite ingenious scarecrows. A row of kennels, tenanted by a dozen dogs, extends behind the cottage: lean retrievers yet unbroken, yelping spaniels, pointers, and perhaps a few greyhounds or fancy breeds, if 'young master' has a taste that way.

Beside the kennels is a shed ornamented with rows upon rows of dead and dried vermin, furred and feathered, impaled for their misdeeds; and over the door a couple of horseshoes nailed for luck – a superstition yet lingering in the by-ways of the woods and hills. Within are the ferret hutches, warm and dry; for the ferret is a shivery creature, and likes nothing so well as to nozzle down in a coat-pocket with a little hay. Here are spades and billhooks, twine and rabbit nets, traps, and other odds and ends scattered about with the wires and poacher's implements impounded from time to time.

In a dark corner there lies a singular-looking piece of mechanism, a relic of the olden times, which when dragged into the light turns out to be a man-trap. These terrible engines have long since been disused – being illegal, like spring-guns – and the rust has gathered thickly on the metal. But, old though it be, it still acts perfectly, and can be 'set' as well now as when in bygone days poachers and thieves used to prod the ground and the long grass, before they stepped among it, with a stick, for fear of mutilation.

The trap is almost precisely similar to the common rat-trap or gin still employed to destroy vermin, but greatly exaggerated in size, so that if stood on end it reaches to the waist, or above. The jaws of this iron wolf are horrible to contemplate – rows of serrated projections, which fit into each other when closed, alternating with spikes a couple of inches long, like tusks. To set the trap you have to stand on the spring – the weight of a man is about sufficient to press it down; and, to avoid danger to the person preparing this little surprise, a band of iron can be pushed forward to hold the spring while the catch is put into position, and the machine itself is hidden among the bushes or covered with dead leaves. Now touch the pan with a stout walking-stick – the jaws cut it in two in the twinkling of an eye. They seem to snap together with a vicious energy, powerful enough to break the bone of the leg; and assuredly no man ever got free whose foot was once caught by these terrible teeth.

The keeper will tell you that it used to be set up in the corner of the gardens and orchard belonging to the great house, and which in the pre-policemen days were almost nightly robbed. He thinks there were quite as many such traps set in the gardens just outside the towns as ever there were in the woods and preserves of the country proper. He recollects but one old man (a mole-catcher) who actually had experienced in his youth the sensation of being caught; he went lame on one foot, the sinews having been cut or divided. The trap could be chained to its place if desired; but, as a matter of fact, a chain was unnecessary, for no man could possibly drag this torturing clog along.

Another outhouse attached to the cottage contains a copper for preparing the food for both quadrupeds and birds. Some poultry run about the mead, and perhaps with them are feeding the fancy foreign ducks which in summer swim in the lake before the hall.

The cottage is thatched and oddly gabled – built before 'improvements' came into fashion – yet cosy; with walls three feet thick, which keep out the cold of winter and the heat of summer. This is not solid masonry; there are two shells, as it were, filled up between with rubble and mortar rammed down hard.

Inside the door the floor of brick is a step below the level of the ground. Sometimes a peculiar but not altogether unpleasant odour fills the low-pitched sitting room – it is emitted by the roots burning upon the fire, hissing as the sap exudes and boils in the fierce heat. When the annual fall of timber takes place the butts of the trees are often left in the earth, to be afterwards grubbed and split for firewood, which goes to the great house or is sold. There still remain the roots, which are cut into useful lengths and divided among the upper employés. From elm and oak and ash, and the crude turpentine of the fir, this aromatic odour, the scent of the earth in which they grew, is exhaled as they burn.

The ceiling is low and crossed by one huge square beam of oak, darkened by smoke and age. The keeper's double-barrelled gun is suspended from this beam: there are several other guns in the house, but this, the favourite, alone hangs where it did before he had children – so strong is habit; the rest are yet more out of danger. It has been a noble weapon, though now showing signs of age – the interior of the breech worn larger than the rest of the barrel from constant use; so much so that, before it was converted to a breech-loader, the wad when the ramrod pushed it down would slip the last six inches, so loosely fitting as to barely answer its purpose of retaining the shot; so that when cleaned out, before the smoke fouled it again, he had to load with paper. This in a measure anticipated the 'choke-bore', and his gun was always famous for its killing power. The varnish is worn from the stock by incessant friction against his coat, showing the real grain of the walnut-wood, and the trigger-guard with the polish of the sleeve shines like silver. It has been his companion for so many years that it is not strange he should feel an affection for it; no other ever fitted the shoulder so well, or came with such delicate precision to the 'present' position. So accustomed is he to its balance and 'hang' in the hand that he never thinks of aiming; he simply looks at the object, still or moving, throws the gun up from the hollow of his arm, and instantly pulls the trigger, staying not a second to glance along the barrel. It has become almost a portion of his body, answering like a limb to the volition of will without the intervention of reflection. The hammers are chased and ele-gantly shaped – perfectly matching: when once the screw came loose, and the jar of a shot jerked one off among the dead leaves apparently beyond hope of recovery, he never rested night or day till by continuous search and sifting the artistic piece of metal was found. Nothing destroys the symmetry of a gun so much as hammers which are not pairs; and well he knew that he should never get a smith to replace that delicate piece of workmanship, for this gun came originally from the hands of a famous maker, who got fifty, or perhaps even seventy guineas for it years ago. It did not shoot to please the purchaser – guns of the very best character sometimes take use to get into thor-ough order – and was thrown aside, and so the gun became the keeper's.

These fine old guns often have a romance clinging to them, and sometimes the history is a sad one. Upstairs he still keeps the old copper powder-flask curiously chased and engraved, yet strong enough to bear the weight of the bearer, if by chance he sat down upon it while in his pocket, together with the shot-belt and punch for cutting out the wads from cardboard or an old felt hat. These the modern system of loading at the breech has cast aside. Here, also, is the apparatus for filling empty cartridge-cases – a work which in the season occupies him many hours.

Being an artist in his way, he takes a pride in the shine and polish of his master's guns, which are not always here, but come down at intervals to be cleaned and attended to. And woe be to the first kid gloves that touch them afterwards; for a gun, like a sardine, should be kept in fine oil, not thickly encrusting it, but, as it were, rubbed into and oozing from the pores of the metal and wood. Paraffin is an abomination in his eyes (for preserving from rust), and no modern patent oil, he thinks, can compare with a drop of gin for the locks – the spirit never congeals in cold weather, and the hammer comes up with a clear, sharp snick. He has two or three small screwdrivers and gunsmith's implements to take the locks to pieces; for gentlemen are sometimes careless and throw their guns down on the wet grass, and if a single drop of water should by chance penetrate under the plate it will play mischief with the works, if the first speck of rust be not forthwith removed.

His dog-whistle hangs at his buttonhole. His pocket-knife is a basket of tools in itself, most probably a present from some youthful sportsman who was placed under his care to learn how to handle a gun. The corkscrew it contains has seen much service at luncheon-time, when under a sturdy oak, or in a sheltered nook of the lane, where the hawthorn hedge and the fern broke the force of the wind, a merry shooting party sat down to a well-packed hamper and wanted some one to draw the corks. Not but what the back of the larger blade has not artistically tapped off the neck of many a bottle, hitting it gently upwards against the rim. Nor must his keys be forgotten. The paths through the preserves, where they debouch on a public lane or road, are closed with high-sparred wicket gates, well pitched to stand the weather, and carefully locked, and of course he has a key. His watch, made on purpose for those who walk by night, tells him the time in the densest darkness of the woods. On pressing a spring and holding it near the ear, it strikes the hour last past, then the quarters which have since elapsed; so that even when he cannot see an inch before his face he knows the time within fifteen minutes at the outside, which is near enough for practical purposes.

In personal appearance he would be a tall man were it not that he has contracted a slight stoop in the passage of the years, not from weakness or decay of nature, but because men who walk much lean forward somewhat, which has a tendency to round the shoulders. The weight of the gun, and often of a heavy game-bag dragging downwards, has increased this defect of his figure, and, as is usual after a certain age, even with those who lead a temperate life, he begins to show signs of corpulency. But these shortcomings only slightly detract from the manliness of his appearance, and in youth it is easy to see that he must have been an athlete. There is still plenty of power in the long sinewy arms, brown hands, and bull-neck, and intense vital energy in the bright blue eye. He is an ash-tree man, as a certain famous writer would say; hard, tough, unconquerable by wind or weather, fearless of his fellows, yielding but by slow and imperceptible degrees to the work of time. His neck has become the colour of mahogany, sun and tempest have left their indelible marks upon his face; and he speaks from the depths of his broad chest, as men do who talk much in the open air, shouting across the fields and through copses. There is a solidity in his very footstep, and he stands like an oak. He meets your eye full and unshirkingly, yet without insolence; not as the labourers do, who either stare with sullen ill-will or look on the earth. In brief, freedom and constant contact with nature have made him every inch a man; and here in this nineteenth century of civilized effeminacy may be seen some relic of what men were in the old feudal days when they dwelt practically in the woods. The shoulder of his coat is worn a little where the gun rubs, and so is his sleeve; otherwise he is fairly well dressed.

Perfectly civil to every one, and with a willing manner towards his master and his master's guests, he has a wonderful knack of getting his own way. Whatever the great house may propose in the shooting line, the keeper is pretty certain to dispose of in the end as he pleases; for he has a voluble 'silver' tongue, and is full of objections, reasons, excuses, suggestions, all delivered with a deprecatory air of superior knowledge which he hardly likes to intrude upon his betters, much as he would regret to see them go wrong. So he really takes the lead, and in nine cases in ten the result proves he is right, as minute local knowledge naturally must be when intelligently applied.

Not only in such matters as the best course for the shooting party to follow, or in advice bearing upon the preserves, but in concerns of a wider scope, his influence is felt. A keen, shrewd judge of horseflesh – (how is it that if a man understands one animal he seems to instinctively see through all?) – his master in a careless way often asks his opinion before concluding a bargain. Of course the question is not put direct, but 'By-the-by, when the hounds were here you saw so-and-so's mare; what do you think of her?' The keeper blurts out his answer, not always flattering or very delicately expressed; and his view is not forgotten. For when a trusted servant like this accompanies his master often in solitary rambles for hours together, dignity must unbend now and then, however great the social difference between them; and thus a man of strong individuality and a really valuable gift of observation insensibly guides his master.

Passing across the turnips, the landlord, who perhaps never sees his farms save when thus crossing them with a gun, remarks that they look clean and free from weeds; whereupon the keeper, walking respectfully a little in the rear, replies that so-and-so, the tenant, is a capital farmer, a preserver of foxes and game, but has suffered from the floods – a reply that leads to inquiries, and perhaps a welcome reduction of rent. On the other hand, the owner's attention is thus often called to abuses. In this way an evilly-disposed keeper may, it is true, do great wrongs, having access to the owner and, in familiar phrase, 'his ear'. I am at present delineating the upright keeper, such as are in existence still, notwithstanding the abuse lavished upon them as a class – often, it is to be feared, too well deserved. It is not difficult to see how in this way a man whose position is lowly may in an indirect way exercise a powerful influence upon a large estate.

He is very 'great' on dogs (and, indeed, on all other animals); his opinion is listened to and taken by everybody round about who has a dog, and sometimes he has three or four under treatment for divers ills. By this knowledge many 'tips' are gained, and occasionally he makes a good thing by selling a pup at a high price. He may even be seen, with his velveteen jacket carefully brushed, his ground-ash stick under his arm, and hat in hand, treading daintily for fear of soiling the carpet with his shoe, in the anteroom, gravely prescribing for the ailing pug in which the ladies are interested.

At the farmhouses he is invited to sit down and take a glass, being welcome for his gossip of the great house, and because, having in the course of years been thrown into the society of all classes, he has gradually acquired a certain tact and power of accommodating himself to his listener. For the keeper, when he fulfils his duty in a quiet way as a man of experience does, is by no means an unpopular character. It is the too officious man who creates a feeling among the tenants against himself and the whole question of game. But the quiet experienced hand, with a shrewd knowledge of men as well as the technicalities of his profession, grows to be liked by the tenantry, and becomes a local authority on animal life.

Proud, and not without reason, of his vigour and strength, he will tell you that though between fifty and sixty he can still step briskly through a heavy field-day, despite the weight of reserve ammunition he carries. He can keep on his feet without fatigue from morn till eve, and goes his rounds without abating one inch of the distance. In one thing alone he feels his years – i.e. in pace; and when 'young master', who is a disciple of the modern athletic school, comes out, it is about as much as ever he can do to keep up with him over the stubble. Never once for the last thirty years has he tossed on a bed of sickness; never once has he failed to rise from his slumber refreshed and ready for his labour. His secret is – but let him tell it in his own words:

'It's indoors, sir, as kills half the people; being indoors three parts of the day, and next to that taking too much drink and vittals. Eating's as bad as drinking; and there ain't nothing like fresh air and the smell of the woods. You should come out here in the spring, when the oak timber is throwed (because, you see, the sap be rising, and the bark strips then), and just sit down on a stick fresh peeled – I means a trunk, you know – and sniff up the scent of that there oak bark. It goes right down your throat, and preserves your lungs as the tan do leather. And I've heard say as folk who work in the tan-yards never have no illness. There's always a smell from trees, dead or living – I could tell what wood a log was in the dark by my nose; and the air is better where the woods be. The ladies up in the great house sometimes goes out into the fir plantations – the turpentine scents strong, you see – and they say it's good for the chest; but, bless you, you must live in it. People go abroad, I'm told, to live in the pine forests to cure 'em: I say these here oaks have got every bit as much good in that way. I never eat but two meals a day – breakfast and supper: what you would call dinner – and maybe in the middle of the day a hunch of dry bread and an apple. I take a deal for breakfast, and I'm rather lear at supper; but you may lay your oath that's why I'm what I am in the way of health. People stuffs theirselves, and by consequence it breaks out, you see. It's the same with cattle; they're overfed, tied up in stalls and stuffed, and never no exercise, and mostly oily food too. It stands to reason they must get bad: and that's the real cause of these here rinderpests and pleuro-pneumonia and what-nots. At least that's my notion. I'm in the woods all day, and never comes home till supper – 'cept, of course, in breeding-time, to fetch the meal and stuff for the birds – so I gets the fresh air, you see; and the fresh air is the life, sir. There's the smell of the earth, too – 'specially just as the plough turns it up – which is a fine thing; and the hedges and the grass are as sweet as sugar after a shower. Anything with a green leaf is the thing, depend upon it, if you want to live healthy. I never signed no pledge; and if a man asks me to take a glass of ale, I never says him no. But I ain't got no barrel at home; and all the time I've been in this here place, I've never been to a public. Gentlemen give me tips – of course they does; and much obliged I be; but I takes it to my missus. Many's the time they've axed me to have a glass of champagne or brandy when we've had lunch under the hedge; but I says no, and would like a glass of beer best, which I gets, of course. No; when I drinks, I drinks ale: but most in general I drinks no strong liquor. Greatcoat! – cold weather! I never put no greatcoat on this thirty year. These here

woods be as good as a topcoat in cold weather. Come off the
open field with the east wind cutting into you, and get inside
they firs and you'll feel warm in a minute. If you goes into the
ash wood you must go in farther, because the wind comes more
between the poles.' Fresh air, exercise, frugal food and drink,
the odour of the earth and the trees – these have given him, as
he nears his sixtieth year, the strength and vitality of early
manhood.

He has his faults: notably, a hastiness of temper towards his
undermen, and towards labourers and wood-cutters who trans-
gress his rules. He is apt to use his ground-ash stick rather
freely without thought of consequences, and has got into
trouble more than once in that way. When he takes a dislike or
suspicion of a man, nothing will remove it; he is stubbornly
inimical and unforgiving, totally incapable of comprehending
the idea of loving an enemy. He hates cordially in the true
pagan fashion of old. He is full of prejudices, and has some
ideas which almost amount to superstitions; and, though he
fears nothing, has a vague feeling that sometimes there is 'summat' inexplicable in the dark and desolate places. Such is this
modern man of the woods.

The impressions of youth are always strongest with us, and
so it is that recollecting the scenes in which he passed his earlier
days he looks with some contempt upon the style of agriculture
followed in the locality; for he was born in the north, where the
farms are sometimes of a great area, though perhaps not so rich
in soil, and he cannot forgive the tenants here because they
have not got herds of three or four hundred horned cattle.
Before he settled down in the south he had many changes of
situation, and was thus brought in contact with a wonderful
number of gentlemen, titled or otherwise distinguished, whose
peculiarities of speech or appearance he loves to dwell upon. If
the valet sees the hero or the statesman too closely, so sometimes does the gamekeeper. A great man must have moments
when it is a relief to fling off the constant posturing necessary
before the world; and there is freshness in the gamekeeper's
unstudied conversation. The keeper thinks that nothing reveals
a gentleman's character so much as his 'tips'.

'Gentlemen is very curious in tips,' he says, 'and there ain't nothing so difficult as to know what's coming. Most in general them as be the biggest guns, and what you would think would come out handsome, chucks you a crown and no more; and them as you knows ain't much go in the way of money slips a sovereign into your fist. There's a deal in the way of giving it too, as perhaps you wouldn't think. Some gents does it as much as to say they're much obliged to you for kindly taking it. Some does it as if they were chucking a bone to a dog. One place where I was, the governor were the haughtiest man as ever you see. When the shooting was done – after a great party, you never knowed whether he were pleased or not – he never took no more notice of you than if you were a tree. But I found him out arter a time or two. You had to walk close behind him, as if you were a spaniel; and by-and-by he would slip his hand round behind his back – without a word, mind – and you had to take what was in it, and never touch your hat or so much as "Thank you, sir." It were always a five-pound note if the shooting had been good; but it never seemed to come so sweet as if he'd done it to your face.'

The keeper gets a goodly number of tips in the course of the year, from visitors at the great house, from naturalists who come now and then, from the sportsmen, and regularly from the masters of three packs of hounds; not to mention odd moneys at intervals in various ways, as when he goes round to deliver presents of game to the chief tenants on the estate or to the owner's private friends. Gentlemen who take an interest in such things come out every spring to see the young broods of pheasants – which, indeed, are a pretty sight – and they always leave something behind them. In the summer a few picnic parties come from the town or the country round about, having permission to enter the grounds. In the winter half a dozen young gentlemen have a turn at the ferreting; a great burrow is chosen, three or four ferrets put in at once without any nets, so that the rabbits may bolt freely, and then the shooting is like volleys of musketry fire. For sport like this the young gentlemen tip freely. After the rook-shooting party in the spring from the great house, with their rook-rifles and sometimes cross-

bows, have had the pick of the young birds, some few of the
tenants are admitted to shoot the remainder – a task that
spreads perhaps over two or even three days, and there is a
good deal of liquor and silver going about. Then gentlemen
come to fish in the mere, having got the necessary permission,
and they want bait and some attention, which the keeper's lad,
being an adept himself, can render better than any one else; and
so he too gets his share. Besides which, being swift of foot, and
with a shrewd idea which way the fox will run when the hunt
is up, he is to the fore when a lady or some timid gentleman
wants a gate opened – a service not performed in vain. For
breaking-in dogs also the keeper is often paid well; and, in
short he is one of those fortunate individuals whom all the
world tips.

Village Architecture:
The Cottage Preacher –
Cottage Society – The Shepherd –
Events of the Village Year

First published in the *Pall Mall Gazette*, 1878
First collected in *Wild Life in a Southern County*, 1879

Some few farmhouses, with cowyards and rickyards attached, are planted in the midst of the village, and these have cottages occupied by the shepherds and carters, or other labourers, who remain at work for the same employer all the year. These cottages are perhaps the best in the place, larger and more commodious, with plenty of space round them, and fair-sized gardens close to the door. The system of hiring for a twelve-month has been bitterly attacked; but as a matter of fact there can be no doubt that a man with a family is better off when settled in one spot with constant employment, and any number of odd jobs for his wife and children. The cottages not attached to any particular farm – belonging to various small owners – are generally much less convenient; they are huddled together, and the footpaths and rights of way frequently cross, and so lead to endless bickering.

Not the faintest trace of design can be found in the ground-plan of the village. All the odd nooks and corners seem to have been preferred for building sites; and even the steep side of the hill is dotted with cottages, with gardens at an angle of forty-five degrees or more, and therefore difficult to work. Here stands a group of elm trees; there half a dozen houses; next a cornfield thrusting a long narrow strip into the centre of the place; more cottages built with the back to the road, and the front door opening just the other way; a small meadow, a well, a deep lane, with banks built up of loose stone to prevent them slipping – only broad enough for one waggon to pass at once – and with cottages high above reached by steps; an open space where three more crooked lanes meet; a turnpike gate, and, of course, a beerhouse hard by it.

Each of these crooked lanes has its group of cottages and its own particular name; but all the lanes and roads passing through the village are known colloquially as 'the street'. There is an individuality, so to say, in these by-ways, and in the irregular architecture of the houses, which does not exist in the straight rows, each cottage exactly alike, of the modern blocks in the neighbourhood of cities. And the inhabitants correspond with their dwelling in this respect – most of them, especially the elder folk, being 'characters' in their way.

Such old-fashioned cottages are practically built around the chimney; the chimney is the firm nucleus of solid masonry or brickwork about which the low walls of rubble are clustered. When such a cottage is burned down the chimney is nearly always the only thing that remains, and against the chimney it is built up again. Next in importance is the roof, which, rising from very low walls, really encloses half of the inhabitable space.

The one great desire of the cottager's heart – after his garden – is plenty of sheds and outhouses in which to store wood, vegetables, and lumber of all kinds. This trait is quite forgotten as a rule by those who design 'improved' cottages for gentlemen anxious to see the labourers on their estates well lodged; and consequently the new buildings do not give so much satisfaction as might be expected. It is only natural that to a man whose possessions are limited, things like potatoes, logs of wood, chips, odds and ends should assume a value beyond the appreciation of the well-to-do. The point should be borne in mind by those who are endeavouring to give the labouring class better accommodation.

A cottage attached to a farmstead, which has been occupied by a steady man who has worked on the tenancy for the best part of his life, and possibly by his father before him, sometimes contains furniture of a superior kind. This has been purchased piece by piece in the course of years, some representing a little legacy – cottagers who have a trifle of property are very proud of making wills – and some perhaps the last remaining relics of former prosperity. It is not at all uncommon to find men like this, whose forefathers no great while since held farms, and even owned them, but fell by degrees in the social scale, till at last their grandchildren work in the fields for wages. An old chair or cabinet which once stood in the farmhouse generations ago is still preserved.

Upon the shelf may be found a few books – a Bible, of course; hardly a cottager who can read is without his Bible – and among the rest an ancient volume of polemical theology, bound in leather; it dates back to the days of the fierce religious controversies which raged in the period which produced Cromwell. There is a rude engraving of the author for frontispiece, title in red letter, a tedious preface, and the text is plentifully bestrewn with Latin and Greek quotations. These add greatly to its value in the cottager's eyes, for he still looks upon a knowledge of Latin as the essential of a 'scholard'. This book has evidently been handed down for many generations as a kind of heirloom, for on the blank leaves may be seen the names of the owners with the inevitable addition of 'his' or 'her book'. It is remarkable that literature of this sort should survive so long.

Even yet not a little of that spirit which led to the formation of so many contending sects in the seventeenth century lingers in the cottage. I have known men who seemed to reproduce in themselves the character of the close-cropped soldiers who prayed and fought by turns with such energy. They still read the Bible in its most literal sense, taking every word as addressed to them individually, and seriously trying to shape their lives in accordance with their convictions.

Such a man, who has been labouring in the hayfield all day, in the evening may be found exhorting a small but attentive congregation in a cottage hard by. Though he can but slowly wade through the book, letter by letter, word by word, he has caught the manner of the ancient writer, and expresses himself in an archaic style not without its effect. Narrow as the view must be which is unassisted by education and its broad sympathies, there is no mistaking the thorough earnestness of the cottage preacher. He believes what he says, and no persuasion, rhetoric, or force could move him one jot. His congregation approve his discourse with groans and various ejaculations. Men of this kind won Cromwell's victories; but to-day they are mainly conspicuous for upright steadiness and irreproachable moral character, mingled with some surly independence. They are not 'agitators' in the current sense of the term; the local agents of labour associations seem chosen from quite a different class.

Pausing once to listen to such a man, who was preaching in a roadside cottage in a loud and excited manner, I found he was describing, in graphic if rude language, the procession of a martyr of the Inquisition to the stake. His imagination naturally led him to picture the circumstances as corresponding to the landscape of fields with which he had been from youth familiar. The executioners were dragging the victim bound along a footpath across the meadows to the pile which had been prepared for burning him. When they arrived at the first stile they halted, and held an argument with the prisoner, promising him his life and safety if he would recant, but he held to the faith.

Then they set out again, beating and torturing the sufferer along the path, the crowd hissing and reviling. At the next stile a similar scene took place – promise of pardon, and scornful refusal to recant, followed by more torture. Again, at the third and last stile, the victim was finally interrogated, and, still firmly clinging to his belief, was committed to the flames in the centre of the field. Doubtless there was some historic basis for the story; but the preacher made it quite his own by the vigour and life of the local colouring in which he clothed it, speaking of the green grass, the flowers, the innocent sheep, the fagots, and so on, bringing it home to the minds of his audience to whom fagots and grass and sheep were so well known. They worked themselves into a state of intense excitement as the narrative approached its climax, till a continuous moaning formed a deep undertone to the speaker's voice. Such men are not paid, trained, or organized; they labour from goodwill in the cause.

Now and then a woman, too, may be found who lectures in the little cottage room where ten or fifteen, perhaps twenty, are packed almost to suffocation; or she prays aloud and the rest respond. Sometimes, no doubt, persons of little sincerity practise these things from pure vanity and the ambition of preaching – for there is ambition in cottage life as elsewhere; but the men and women I speak of are thoroughly in earnest.

Cottagers have their own social creed and customs. In their intercourse, one point which seems to be insisted upon particularly is a previous knowledge or acquaintance. The very people whose morals are known to be none of the strictest – and cottage morality is sometimes very far from severe – will refuse, and especially the women, to admit a strange girl, for instance, to sleep in their house for ample remuneration, even when introduced by really respectable persons. Servant-girls in the country where railways even now are few and far between often walk long distances to see mistresses in want of assistance, by appointment. They get tired; perhaps night approaches, and then comes the difficulty of lodging them if the house happens to be full. Cottagers make the greatest difficulty, unless by some chance it should be discovered that they met the girl's uncle or cousin years ago.

To their friends and neighbours, on the contrary, they are often very kind, and ready to lend a helping hand. If they seldom sit down to a social gathering among themselves, it is because they see each other so constantly during the day, working in the same fields, and perhaps eating their luncheon a dozen together in the same outhouse. A visitor whom they know from the next village is ever welcome to what fare there is. On Sundays the younger men often set out to call on friends at a distance of several miles, remaining with them all day; they carry with them a few lettuces, or apples from the tree in the garden (according to the season), wrapped up in a coloured handkerchief, as a present.

Some of the older shepherds still wear the ancient blue smock-frock, crossed with white 'facings' like coarse lace; but the rising generation use the greatcoat of modern make, at which their forefathers would have laughed as utterly useless in the rain-storms that blow across the open hills. Among the elder men, too, may be found a few of the huge umbrellas of a former age, which when spread give as much shelter as a small tent. It is curious that they rarely use an umbrella in the field, even when simply standing about; but if they go a short journey along the highway, they take it with them. The aged men sling these great umbrellas over the shoulder with a piece of tar cord, just as a soldier slings his musket, and so have both hands free – one to stump along with a stout stick and the other to carry a flag basket. The stick is always too lengthy to walk with as men use it in cities, carrying it by the knob or handle; it is a staff rather than a stick, the upper end projecting six or eight inches above the hand.

If any labourers deserve to be paid well, it is the shepherds: upon their knowledge and fidelity the principal profit of a whole season depends on so many farms. On the bleak hills in lambing time the greatest care is necessary; and the fold, situated in a hollow if possible, with the down rising on the east or north, is built as it were of straw walls, thick and warm, which the sheep soon make hollow inside, and thus have a cave in which to nestle.

The shepherd has a distinct individuality, and is generally a much more observant man in his own sphere than the ordinary labourer. He knows every single field in the whole parish, what kind of weather best suits its soil, and can tell you without going within sight of a given farm pretty much what condition it will be found in. Knowledge of this character may seem trivial to those whose days are passed indoors; yet it is something to recollect all the endless fields in several square miles of country. As a student remembers for years the type and paper, the breadth of the margin – can see, as it were, before his eyes the bevel of the binding and hear again the rustle of the stiff leaves of some tall volume which he found in a forgotten corner of a library, and bent over with such delight, heedless of dust and 'silver-fish' and the gathered odour of years – so the shepherd recalls *his* books, the fields; for he, in the nature of things, has to linger over them and study every letter: sheep are slow.

When the hedges are grubbed and the grass grows where the

hawthorn flowered, still the shepherd can point out to you where the trees stood – here an oak and here an ash. On the hills he has often little to do but ponder deeply sitting on the turf of the slope, while the sheep graze in the hollow, waiting for hours as they eat their way. Therefore by degrees a habit of observation grows upon him – always in reference to his charge; and if he walks across the parish off duty he still cannot choose but notice how the crops are coming on, and where there is most 'keep'. The shepherd has been the last of all to abandon the old custom of long service. While the labourers are restless, there may still be found not a few instances of shepherds whose whole lives have been spent upon one farm. Thus, from the habit of observation and the lapse of years, they often become local authorities; and when a dispute of boundaries or water rights or right of way arises, the question is frequently finally decided by the evidence of such a man.

Every now and then a difficulty happens in reference to the old green lanes and bridle-tracks which once crossed the country in every direction, but get fewer in number year by year. Sometimes it is desired to enclose a section of such a track to round off an estate: sometimes a path has grown into a valuable thoroughfare through increase of population; and then the question comes, Who is to repair it? There is little or no documentary evidence to be found – nothing can be traced except through the memories of men; and so they come to the old shepherd, who has been stationary all his life, and remembers the condition of the lane fifty years since. He always liked to drive his sheep along it – first, because it saved the turnpike tolls; secondly, because they could graze on the short herbage and rest under the shade of the thick bushes. Even in the helplessness of his old age he is not without his use at the very last, and his word settles the matter.

In the winter twilight, after a fall of snow, it is difficult to find one's way across the ploughed fields of the open plain, for it melts on the south of every furrow, leaving a white line where it has ledged on the northern side, till the furrows resemble an endless succession of waves of earth tipped with foam-flecks of snow. These are dazzling to the eyes, and there are few hedges or trees visible for guidance. Snow lingers sometimes for weeks on the northern slopes of the Downs – where shallow dry dykes, used as landmarks, are filled with it; the dark mass of the hill is streaked like the black hull of a ship with its line of white paint. Field work during what the men call 'the dark days afore Christmas' is necessarily much restricted and they are driven to find some amusement for the long evenings – such as blowing out candles at the alehouse with muzzle-loader guns for wagers of liquor, the wind of the cap alone being sufficient for the purpose at a short distance.

The children never forget St Thomas's Day, which ancient custom has consecrated to alms, and they wend their way from farmhouse to farmhouse throughout the parish; it is usual to keep to the parish, for some of the old local feeling still remains even in these cosmopolitan times. At Christmas sometimes the children sing carols, not with much success so far as melody goes, but otherwise successfully enough; for recollections of the past soften the hearts of the crustiest.

The young men for weeks previously have been practising for the mumming – a kind of rude drama requiring, it would seem, as much rehearsal beforehand as the plays at famous theatres. They dress in a fantastic manner, with masks and coloured ribbons; anything grotesque answers, for there is little attempt at dressing in character. They stroll round to each farmhouse in the parish, and enact the play in the kitchen or brewhouse; after which the whole company are refreshed with ale, and, receiving a few coins, go on to the next homestead. Mumming, however, has much deteriorated, even in the last fifteen or twenty years. On nights when the players were known to be coming, in addition to the farmer's household and visitors at that season, the cottagers residing near used to assemble, so that there was quite an audience. Now it is a chance whether they come round or not.

A more popular pastime with the young men, and perhaps more profitable, is the formation of a brass band. They practise vigorously before Christmas, and sometimes attain considerable proficiency. At the proper season they visit the farms in the evening, and as the houses are far apart, so that only a few can be called at in the hours available after work, it takes them some time to perambulate the parish. So that for two or three weeks about the end of the old and the beginning of the new year, if one chances to be out at night, every now and then comes the unwonted note of a distant trumpet sounding over the fields. The custom has grown frequent of recent years, and these bands collect a good deal of money.

The ringers from the church come too, with their hand bells, and ring pleasant tunes – which, however, on bells are always plaintive – standing on the crisp frozen grass of the green before the window. They are well rewarded, for bells are great favourites with all country people.

What is more pleasant than the jingling of the tiny bells on the harness of the cart-horses? You may hear the team coming with a load of straw on the waggon three furlongs distant; then step out to the road, and watch the massive yet shapely creatures pull the heavy weight up the hill, their glossy quarters scarcely straining, but heads held high showing the noble neck, the hoofs planted with sturdy pride of strength, the polished brass of the harness glittering, and the bells merrily jingling! The carter, the thong of his whip nodding over his shoulder, walks by the shaft, his boy ahead by the leader, as proud of his team as the sailor of his craft: even the whip is not to be lightly come by, but is chosen carefully, bound about with rows of brazen rings; neither could you or I knot the whipcord on to his satisfaction.

For there is a certain art even in so small a thing, not to be learned without time and practice; and his pride in whip, harness, and team is surely preferable to the indifference of a stranger, caring for nothing but his money at the end of the week. The modern system – men coming one day and gone the next – leaves no room for the growth of such feelings, and the art and mystery of the craft loses its charm. The harness bells, too, are disappearing; hardly one team in twenty carries them now.

Those who labour in the fields seem to have far fewer holidays than the workers in towns. The latter issue from factory and warehouse at Easter, and rush gladly into the country: at Whitsuntide, too, they enjoy another recess. But the farmer and the labourer work on much the same, the closing of banks and factories in no way interfering with the tilling of the earth or the tending of cattle. In May the ploughboys still remember King Charles, and on what they call 'shick-shack day' search for oak-apples and the young leaves of the oak to place with a spray of ash in their hats or buttonholes: the ash spray must have even leaves; an odd number is not correct. To wear these green emblems was thought imperative even within the last twenty years, and scarcely a labourer could be seen without them. The elder men would tell you – as if it had been a grave calamity – that they could recollect a year when the spring was so backward that not an oak leaf or oak-apple could be found by the most careful search for the purpose. The custom has fallen much into disuse lately: the carters, however, still attach the ash and oak leaves to the heads of their horses on this particular day.

Many village clubs or friendly societies meet in the spring, others in autumn. The day is sometimes fixed by the date of the ancient feast. The club and fête threaten, indeed, to supplant the feast altogether: the friendly society having been taken under the patronage of the higher ranks of residents. Here and there the feast-day, however (the day on which the church was dedicated), is still remembered, as in this village, where the elder farmers invite their friends and provide liberally for the occasion. Some of the gipsies still come with their stalls, and a little crowd assembles in the evening; but the glory of the true feast has departed.

The elder men, nevertheless, yet reckon by the feast-day; it is a fixed point in their calendar, which they construct every year, of local events. Such and such a fair is calculated to fall so many days after the first full moon in a particular month; and another fair falls so long after that. An old man will thus tell you the dates of every fair and feast in all the villages and little towns ten or fifteen miles round about. He quite ignores the modern system of reckoning time, going by the ancient ecclesiastical calendar and the moon. How deeply the ancient method must have impressed itself into the life of these people to still remain a kind of instinct at this late day!

The feasts are in some cases identified with certain well-recognized events in the calendar of nature; such as the ripening of cherries. It may be noticed that these, chancing thus to correspond pretty accurately on the average with the state of fruit, are kept up more vigorously than those which have no such aid to the memory. The Lady Day fair and Michaelmas fair at the adjacent market town are the two best recognized holidays of the year. The fair is sometimes called 'the mop', and stalwart girls will walk eight or nine miles rather than miss it. Maid-servants in farmhouses always bargain for a holiday on fair day. These two main fairs are the Bank Holidays of rural life. It is curious to observe that the developments of the age, railroads and manufactories, have not touched the traditional prestige of these gatherings.

For instance, you may find a town which, by the incidence of the railroad and the springing up of great industries, has shot far ahead of the other sleepy little places; its population may treble itself, its trade be ten times as large, its attractions one would imagine incalculably greater. Nothing of the kind: its annual fair is not nearly so important an event to the village mind as that of an old-world slumberous place removed from the current of civilization. This place, which is perhaps eight or nine miles by road, with no facilities of communication, has from time immemorial had a reputation for its fair. There, accordingly, the scattered rural population wends, making no account of distance and very little of weather: it is a country maxim that it always rains on fair day, and mostly thunders. There they assemble and enjoy themselves in the old-fashioned way, which consists in standing in the streets, buying 'fairings' for the girls, shooting for nuts, visiting all the shows, and so on.

To push one's way through such a crowd is no simple matter; the countryman does not mean to be rude, but he has not the faintest conception that politeness demands a little yielding. He has to be shoved, and makes no objection. A city crowd is to a certain extent mobile – each recognizes that he must give way. A country crowd stand stock still.

The thumping of drums, the blaring of trumpets, the toot-ling of pan-pipes in front of the shows, fill the air with a din which may be heard miles away, and seem to give the crowd intense pleasure – far more than the crack band of the Coldstream Guards could impart. Nor are they ever weary of gazing at the 'pelican of the wilderness' as the showman describes it – a mournful bird with draggled feathers standing by the entrance, a traditional part of his stock-in-trade. One attraction – perhaps the strongest – may be found in the fact that all the countryside is sure to be there. Each labourer or labouring woman will meet acquaintances from distant villages they have not seen or heard of for months. The rural gossip of half a county will be exchanged.

In the autumn after the harvest the gleaning is still an important time to the cottager, though nothing like it used to be. Reaping by machinery has made rapid inroads, and there is not nearly so much left behind as in former days. Yet half the women and children of the place go out and glean, but very few now bake at home; they have their bread from the baker, who comes round in the smallest hamlets. Possibly they had a more wholesome article in the olden time, when the wheat from their gleanings was ground at the village mill, and the flour made into bread at home. But the cunning of the mechanician has invaded the ancient customs; the very sheaves are now to be bound with wire by the same machine that reaps the corn. The next generation of country folk will hardly be able to understand the story of Ruth.

Hamlet Folk

First published in the *Pall Mall Gazette*, 1880
First collected in *Round About a Great Estate*, 1880

It happened one Sunday morning in June that a swarm of bees issued from a hive in a cottage garden near Okebourne church. The queen at first took up her position in an elm tree just outside the churchyard, where a large cluster of bees quickly depended from a bough. Being at a great height the cottager could not take them, and, anxious not to lose the swarm, he resorted to the ancient expedient of rattling fire-tongs and shovel together in order to attract them by the clatter. The discordant banging of the fire-irons resounded in the church, the doors being open to admit the summer air; and the noise became so uproarious that the clerk presently, at a sign from the rector, went out to stop it, for the congregation were in a grin. He did stop it, the cottager desisting with much reluctance; but, as if to revenge the bee-master's wrongs, in the course of the day the swarm, quitting the elm, entered the church and occupied a post in the roof.

After a while it was found that the swarm had finally settled there, and were proceeding to build combs and lay in a store of honey. The bees, indeed, became such a terror to nervous people, buzzing without ceremony over their heads as they stood up to sing, and caused such a commotion and buffeting with Prayer-books and fans and handkerchiefs, that ultimately the congregation were compelled to abandon their pews. All efforts to dislodge the bees proving for the time ineffectual, the rector had a temporary reading-desk erected in the porch, and there held the service, the congregation sitting on chairs and forms in the yard, and some on the stone tombs, and even on the sward under the shade of the yew tree.

In the warm dry hay-making weather this open-air worship was very pleasant, the flowers in the grass and the roses in the little plots about the tombs giving colour and sweet odours, while the swallows glided gracefully overhead and sometimes a blackbird whistled. The bees, moreover, interfered with the baptisms, and even caused several marriages to be postponed. Inside the porch was a recess where the women left their pattens in winter, instead of clattering iron-shod down the aisle.

Okebourne village was built in an irregular way on both sides of a steep coombe, just at the verge of the hills, and about a mile from the Chace; indeed, the outlying cottages bordered the park wall. The most melancholy object in the place was the ruins of a windmill; the sails and arms had long disappeared, but the wooden walls, black and rotting, remained. The windmill had its genius, its human representative – a mere wreck, like itself, of olden times. There never was a face so battered by wind and weather as that of old Peter, the owner of the ruin. His eyes were so light a grey as to appear all but colourless. He wore a smock-frock the hue of dirt itself, and his hands were ever in his pockets as he walked through rain and snow beside his cart, hauling flints from the pits upon the Downs.

If the history of the cottage-folk is inquired into it will often be found that they have descended from well-to-do positions in life – not from extravagance or crime, or any remarkable piece of folly, but simply from a long-continued process of muddling away money. When the windmill was new, Peter's forefathers had been, for village people, well off. The family had never done anything to bring themselves into disgrace; they had never speculated; but their money had been gradually muddled away, leaving the last little better than a labourer. To see him crawling along the road by his load of flints, stooping forward, hands in pocket, and then to glance at the distant windmill, likewise broken down, the roof open, and the rain and winds rushing through it, was a pitiful spectacle. For that old building represented the loss of hope and contentment in life as much as any once lordly castle whose battlements are now visited only by the jackdaw. The family had, as it were, foundered and gone down.

How they got the stray cattle into the pound it is difficult to imagine; for the gate was very narrow, and neither bullocks nor horses like being driven into a box. The copings of the wall on one side had been pushed over, and lay in a thick growth of nettles: this, almost the last of old village institutions, was, too, going by degrees to destruction.

Every hamlet used to have its representative fighting-man – often more than one – who visited the neighbouring villages on the feast-days, when there was a good deal of liquor flowing, to vaunt of their prowess before the local champions. These quickly gathered, and after due interchange of speeches not unlike the heroes of Homer, who harangue each other ere they hurl the spear, engaged in conflict dire. There was a regular feud for many years between the Okebourne men and the Clipstone 'chaps'; and never did the stalwart labourers of those two villages meet without falling to fisticuffs with right goodwill. Nor did they like each other at all the worse, and after the battle drank deeply from the same quart cups. Had these encounters found an historian to put them upon record, they would have read something like the wars (without the bloodshed) between the little Greek cities, whose population scarcely exceeded that of a village, and between which and our old villages there exists a certain similarity. A simplicity of sentiment, an unconsciousness as it were of themselves, strong local attachments and hatreds, these they had in common, and the Okebourne and Clipstone men thwacked and banged each other's broad chests in true antique style.

Hilary said that when he was a boy almost all the cottages in the place had a man or woman living in them who had attained to extreme old age. He reckoned up cottage after cottage to me in which he had known old folk up to and over eighty years of age. Of late the old people seemed to have somehow died out: there were not nearly so many now.

Okebourne Wick, a little hamlet of fifteen or twenty scattered houses, was not more than half a mile from Lucketts' Place; on the Overboro' road, which passed it, was a pleasant

roadside inn, where, under the sign of The Sun, very good ale
was sold. Most of the farmers dropped in there now and then,
not so much for a glass as a gossip, and no one from the neighbouring villages or from Overboro' town ever drove past
without stopping. In the 'tap' of an evening you might see the
labourers playing at 'chuck-board', which consists in casting a
small square piece of lead on to certain marked divisions of a
shallow tray-like box placed on the trestle-table. The lead,
being heavy, would stay where it fell; the rules I do not know,
but the scene reminded me of the tric-trac contests depicted by
the old Dutch painters.

Young Aaron was very clever at it. He pottered round the
inn of an evening and Saturday afternoons, doing odd jobs in
the cellar with the barrels; for your true toping spirit loves to
knock the hoops and to work about the cask, and carry the
jugs in answer to the cry for some more 'tangle-legs' – for thus
they called the strong beer. Sometimes a labourer would toast
his cheese on a fork in the flame of the candle. In the old days,
before folk got so choice of food and delicate of palate, there
really seemed no limit to the strange things they ate. Before the
railways were made, herds of cattle had of course to travel
the roads, and often came great distances. The drovers were at
the same time the hardiest and the roughest of men in that
rough and hardy time. As night came on, after seeing their herd
safe in a field, they naturally ate their supper at the adjacent
inn. Then sometimes, as a dainty treat with which to finish his
meal, a drover would call for a biscuit, large and hard, as broad
as his hand, and, taking the tallow candle, proceed to drip
the grease on it till it was well larded and soaked with the
melted fat.

At that date, before the Government stamp had been removed
from newspapers, the roadside inn was the centre and focus of
all intelligence. When the first railway was constructed up in
the North the Okebourne folk, like the rest of the world, were
with good reason extremely curious about this wonderful
invention, and questioned every passer-by eagerly for information. But no one could describe it, till at last a man, born in the

village, but who had been away for some years soldiering, returned to his native place. He had been serving in Canada and came through Liverpool, and thus saw the marvel of the age. At The Sun the folk in the evening crowded round him, and insisted upon knowing what a steam-engine was like. He did his best to describe it, but in vain; they wanted a familiar illustration, and could not be satisfied till the soldier, by a happy inspiration, said the only thing to which he could compare a locomotive was a great cannon on a timber-carriage. To us who are so accustomed to railways it seems a singular idea; but, upon reflection, it was not so inapt, considering that the audience had seen or heard something of cannons, and were well acquainted with timber-carriages. The soldier wished to convey the notion of a barrel or boiler mounted on wheels.

They kept up the institution of the parish constable, as separate and distinct from the policeman, till very recently at Okebourne, though it seems to have lapsed long since in many country places. One year Hilary, with much shrugging of shoulders, was forced into the office; and during his term there was a terrible set-to between two tribes of gipsies in the Overboro' road. They fought like tigers, making the lovely summer day hideous with their cries and shrieks – the women, the fiercer by far, tearing each other's hair. One fiendish creature drew her scissors, and, using them like a stiletto, drove the sharp point into a sister 'gip's' head.

'Where's the constable?' was the cry. Messengers rushed to Lucketts' Place; the barn, the sheds, the hayfield, all were searched in vain – Hilary had quite disappeared. At the very first sound he had slipped away to look at some cattle in Chequer's Piece, the very last and outlying field of the farms, full a mile away, and when the messengers got to Chequer's Piece of course he was up on the Down. So much for the parish constable's office – an office the farmers shirked whenever they could, and would not put in force when compelled to accept it.

How could a resident willingly go into a neighbour's cottage and arrest him without malice and scandal being engendered? If he did his duty he was abused; if he did not do it, it was hinted that he favoured the offender. As for the 'gip' who was stabbed, nothing more was heard of it; she 'traipsed' off with the rest.

Sometimes when the 'tangle-legs' got up into their heads the labourers felt an inclination to resume the ancient practices of their forefathers. Then you might see a couple facing each other in the doorway, each with his mug in one hand, and the other clenched, flourishing their knuckles. 'Thee hit I.' 'Thee come out in th' road and I'll let thee knaw.' The one knew very well that the other dared not strike him in the house, and the other felt certain that, however entreated, nothing would induce his opponent to accept the invitation and 'come out into th' road'.

The shadows of the elm have so far to fall that they become enlarged and lose the edge upon reaching the ground. I noticed this one moonlight night in early June while sitting on a stile where the footpath opened on the Overboro' road. Presently I heard voices, and immediately afterwards a group came round the curve of the highway. There were three cottage women, each with a basket and several packages; having doubtless been into Overboro' town shopping, for it was Saturday. They walked together in a row; and in front of them, about five yards ahead, came a burly labourer of the same party, carrying in his arms a large clock.

He had taken too much ale, and staggered as he walked, two steps aside to one forward, and indeed could hardly keep upright. His efforts to save himself and the clock from destruction led to some singular flexures of the body, and his feet traced a maze as he advanced, hugging the clock to his chest. The task was too much for his over-taxed patience: just opposite the stile he stood still, held his load high over his head, and shouting, 'Dang th' clock!' hurled it with all his force thirty feet against the mound, at the same time dropping a-sprawl. The women, without the least excitement or surprise, quietly endeavoured to assist him up; and, as he resisted, one of them remarked in the driest matter-of-fact tone, 'Ourn be just like un – as contrary as the wind.' She alluded to her own husband.

When I mentioned this incident afterwards to Mrs Luckett, she said the troubles the cottage women underwent on account of the 'beer' were past belief. One woman who did some work at the farmhouse kept her cottage entirely by her own exertions; her husband doing nothing but drink. He took her money from her by force, nor could she hide it anywhere but what he would hunt it out. At last in despair she dropped the silver in the jug on the wash-hand basin, and had the satisfaction of seeing him turn everything topsy-turvy in a vain attempt to find it. As he never washed, it never occurred to him to look in the water-jug.

The cottage women when they went into Overboro' shopping, she said, were the despair of the drapers. A woman, with two or three more to chorus her sentiments, would go into a shop and examine half-a-dozen dress fabrics, rubbing each between her work-hardened fingers and thumb till the shopkeeper winced, expecting to see it torn. After trying several and getting the counter covered she would push them aside, contemptuously remarking, 'I don't like this yer shallygallee (flimsy) stuff. Haven't 'ee got any gingham tackle?' Whereat the poor draper would cast down a fresh roll of stoutest material with the reply: 'Here, ma'am. Here's something that will wear like pin-wire.' This did better, but was declared to be 'gallus dear'.

Even within recent years, now and then a servant-girl upon entering service at the farmhouse would refuse to touch butcher's meat. She had never tasted anything but bacon at home, and could only be persuaded to eat fresh meat with difficulty, being afraid she should not like it. One girl who came from a lonely cottage in a distant 'coombe-bottom' of the Downs was observed never to write home or attempt to communicate with her parents. She said it was of no use; no postman came near, and the letters they wrote or the letters written to them never reached their destination. 'Coombe-bottom' is a curious duplication – either word being used to indicate a narrow valley or hollow. An unfortunate child who lived there had never been so well since the stone roller went over his head. She had a lover, but he was 'a gurt hummocksing noon-naw', so she was not sorry to leave him. The phrase might be translated, 'great loose-jointed idiot'.

They sometimes had lettuce-pudding for dinner, and thought nothing of eating raw bacon. In the snow the men wound hay-bands round their legs to serve as gaiters, and found it answered admirably. One poor girl had been subject to fits ever since a stupid fellow, during the hay-making, jokingly picked up a snake and threw it round her neck. Yet even in that far-away coombe-bottom they knew enough to put an oyster-shell in the kettle to prevent incrustation.

The rules of pronunciation understood about Okebourne seemed to consist in lengthening the syllables that are usually spoken quick, and shortening those that are usually long. Hilary said that years ago it really appeared as if there was something deficient in the organs of the throat among the labourers, for there were words they positively could not pronounce. The word 'reservoir', for instance, was always 'tezzievoy'; they could not speak the word correctly. He could not explain to me a very common expression among the men when they wished to describe anything unusual or strange for which they had no exact equivalent. It was always 'a sort of a meejick'. By degrees, however, we traced it back to 'menagerie'. The travelling shows of wild beasts at first so much astonished the villagers that everything odd and curious became a menagerie, afterwards corrupted to 'meejick'.

'Caddle no man's cattle' was a favourite proverb with a population who were never in a hurry. 'Like shot out of a show'l', to express extreme nimbleness, was another. A comfortless, bare apartment was 'gabern'; anything stirred with a pointed instrument was 'ucked' – whether a cow 'ucked' the fogger with her horn or the stable was cleaned out with the fork. The verb 'to uck' was capable indeed of infinite conjugation, and young Aaron, breaking off a bennet, once asked me to kindly 'uck' a grain of hay-dust out of his eye with it. When a heron rose out of the brook 'a moll ern flod away'.

With all their apparent simplicity some of the cottage folk were quite up to the value of appearances. Old Aaron had a little shop; he and his wife sold small packets of tea, tobacco, whipcord, and so forth. Sometimes while his wife was weighing out the sugar, old Aaron – wretched old deceiver – would come in rustling a crumpled piece of paper as if it were a bank-note, and handing it to her with much impressiveness of manner whisper loudly, 'Now you take un and put un away; and mind you don't mix um. You put he along with the fives and not with the tens.'

Hilary once showed me the heel of a boot which had just been mended by the hedge carpenter and cobbler who worked for him; and offered to bet that not all the scientific people in Europe, with microscope, spectrum analysis, all their appli-ances, could tell what leather the new heel-piece was made of. Unable to guess, I gave it up; it was of bacon. A pig that was never a 'good doer' was found in a ditch dead. There is always a competition among the labourers for a dead pig or sheep; it was the cobbler's turn, and he had it, cut it up, and salted it down. But when in course of time he came to partake of his side of bacon, behold it was so tough and dried up that even he could not gnaw it. The side hung in the cottage for months, for he did not like to throw it away, and could not think what to do with it, for the dogs could not eat it. At last the old fellow hit upon the notion of using it as leather to mend shoes; so half his customers walked about the world on bacon heels.

So far as I could discover, the cottage folk did not now use many herbs. They made tea sometimes of the tormentil, whose little yellow flowers appear along the furrows. The leaves of the square-stemmed figwort, which they called 'cresset' or 'cressil', were occasionally placed on a sore; and the yarrow – locally 'yarra' – was yet held in estimation as a salve or ointment.

It would be possible for any one to dwell a long time in the midst of a village, and yet never hear anything of this kind and obtain no idea whatever of the curious mixture of the gro-tesque, the ignorance and yet cleverness, which go to make up hamlet life. But so many labourers and labouring women were continually in and out of the kitchen at Lucketts' Place that I had an opportunity of gathering these items from Mrs Luckett and Cicely. Years since they had employed even more labour, before machinery came into use so much: then as many as twenty-four women might have been counted in one hayfield, all in regular rank like soldiers, turning the hay 'wallows' with their rakes. 'There's one thing now you have forgotten,' said Cicely. 'They pick the canker-roses off the briars and carry them in the pocket as a certain preventive of rheumatism.'

Minute Cultivation –
A Silver Mine

First published in the *Live Stock Journal*, 26 July 1878
First collected in *Chronicles of the Hedges*, 1948

Is it absolutely necessary that agriculture should be for ever confined to two methods of culture only; must a farm never produce anything but cereals or grass? No matter what the size of a field may be, whether it be five, ten, or fifty acres, there seems to be a fixed immutable law that the whole of it must be devoted to one purpose. There must be fifty acres grass, or there must be fifty acres corn. This remarkable uniformity, which is so characteristic of English agriculture, has of course its advantages, as in the case of arable land, where a large area can be better worked by machinery than a small one. But then for that to be an advantage, it presupposes the crop a profitable one, whereas the general experience is notoriously that wheat-farming is not profitable. Landlords are constantly finding their farms in the wheat counties returned upon their hands, because the tenants are no longer able to work them, or because they prefer to retire upon the capital they still have left. This is an old story, but it increases one's astonishment that landlords and tenants alike do not turn their attention to a fresh system of culture, instead of adhering to a plan proved unsuitable to the conditions of the age. Grass we know is profitable, on account of livestock, and the recent development of the dairy; yet even on grass farms some modification, if only on a small scale, might be found to give better returns. But the idea that anything else could be cultivated besides corn and grass – the idea of any other agriculture besides arable and pasture being possible – does not appear to occur to them.

Yet every condition of modern life points in the direction of minute cultivation. Look at the millions of people in great cities (and small cities, too, for the matter of that) who cannot grow a single vegetable or a single apple for their own use. They must either go without these most desirable and health-giving articles of diet, or buy them. If bought – not to say anything of the high price of fruit – the article is found too frequently to have lost half the relish, and three-fourths of its dietary value, because it is not fresh. It is not fresh because it has had to travel many hundreds or even thousands of miles, and in order to stand that ordeal it has had to be gathered long before ripe. There is nothing so delicious as a ripe English apple, nothing so wholesome; but where are you to get it? If you chance to have friends in the country perhaps you may; if not, you will find, upon inquiry, that your dessert apples have come all the way from America, and have cost you a pretty sum. At the same moment we are told that large areas of land are being returned upon the landlord's hands because wheat-farming is unprofitable. An obstinate traditionary rule requires that under any and every circumstance such and such farms shall grow nothing but corn (as the primary crop), let the result be what it may. Meantime thousands upon thousands of pounds are sent out of the country for such a simple thing as fruit. And the point lies in this, that in despite of the expenditure on foreign fruit supplies, there is never enough good fruit to be got – the demand is so much greater than the supply. Just in the flush of the season there may be an overplus, because everybody now endeavours to be first in the market, and this race causes a temporary block. But inquire later on; ask at Christmas, or in the spring, and the reply will be, no apples but Americans, and these not over good. Now it is just here that English growers ought to step in. Our climate is not a forcing one; stimulants are required to get home productions forward enough to compete with those of brighter skies. English fruit should, then, be of the keeping kind – apples, for instance, that would come in at Christmas, and later than that. Our grandmothers used to pride themselves on producing from their stores a fine apple eight months old; there are sorts, unless we mistake, that will keep much longer; the conditions of the times are such that what they only practised as a pleasure might be made to yield a large profit.

Not, of course, that wheat fields of fifty acres are to be turned bodily into orchards; but why not add to the one general yield of the farm some secondary produce of a high value in the market? Apples are only given as an example. All other kinds of fruit, without exception, pay well. Why should not a farmer take a corner of a large field, say one of fifty acres, and fencing off five out of the fifty, devote that five to vegetables or to fruit? He might find the five so profitable as to induce an enlargement of the venture. Transit now is so easy that no difficulties could arise on that score. Under his very eyes he sees the common, uneducated labourer eager to get a large allotment – competing for a cottage that happens to have a good strip of garden; and labourers' gardens, let it be observed, are always full as they can hold of fruit-trees. They know full well that a good crop on one single tree will pay their rent; a fair crop throughout their little orchard will not only pay their rent, but supply the family with clothes. The ignorant labourer sighs for a morsel of land, knowing from the experience of his friends and relations that his spade would literally dig up silver from it. The farmer with 400 acres looks at his yellow wheat, shakes his head with the market prices in his hand, and mournfully informs his landlord's agent that he must give it up, and go and eke out an existence upon the interest of the money he has not yet sunk. Could any contrast be more telling? The thing speaks for itself; but so strong is tradition and custom that loud as the voice may be it is unheeded. With his 400 acres the farmer, too, has this great advantage over the labourer's silver mine of one quarter acre. This one quarter acre is of course in one position only; it may be damp, it may be dry, the aspect may be north or east. He cannot move on. But on the 400 acres every variety of aspect may be found, and in all probability one or more varieties of soil. By cultivating a few acres on the garden system at one extremity of the farm, where the soil is naturally moist, it can be readily irrigated, and another few acres at the other extremity, where it is naturally dry and can stand a great deal of rain without injury, he may make himself in a measure independent of the season. Whether wet or dry one or other plot would pay. There is a mine of wealth yet on every farm in this country, if only men could be brought to step out of the old jog-trot round. In order to sow a seed of reflection in his mind that may grow and germinate, let any farmer ask himself the question, why should my great field yonder yield only one crop, and that of a doubtful value? Having reflected on that, let him next visit the nearest allotment-grounds; or, better still, the nearest cottage gardens (as trees, even fruit-trees, are excluded from allotments very often) and inquire why the ignorant labourer is so anxious for a slice, however small, of earth. It is because minute cultivation returns a hundred-fold, and every spadeful of earth glistens with specks of precious ore.

The Amateur Poacher:
Oby and His System –
The Moucher's Calendar

First published as a serial in the *Pall Mall Gazette*, 1879
First collected in *The Amateur Poacher*, 1879

One dark night, as I was walking on a lonely road, I kicked against something, and but just saved myself from a fall. It was an intoxicated man lying at full length. As a rule, it is best to let such people alone; but it occurred to me that the mail-cart was due: with two horses harnessed tandem-fashion, and travelling at full speed, the mail would probably go over him. So I seized the fellow by the collar and dragged him out of the way. Then he sat up, and asked in a very threatening tone who I was. I mentioned my name: he grunted, and fell back on the turf, where I left him.

The incident passed out of my mind, when one afternoon a labourer called, asking for me in a mysterious manner, and refusing to communicate his business to any one else. When admitted, he produced a couple of cock pheasants from under his coat, the tail feathers much crumpled, but otherwise in fine condition. These he placed on the table, remarking, 'I ain't forgot as you drawed I out of the raud thuck night.' I made him understand that such presents were too embarrassing; but he seemed anxious to do 'summat', so I asked him to find me a few ferns and rare plants.

This he did from time to time; and thus a species of acquaintanceship grew up and I learned all about him. He was always called 'Oby' (i.e. Obadiah), and was the most determined poacher of a neighbouring district – a notorious fighting man – hardened against shame, an Ishmaelite openly contemning authority and yet not insensible to kindness. I give his history in his own language – softening only the pronunciation, that would otherwise be unintelligible.

'I lives with my granny in Thorney-lane: it be outside the village. My mother be married agen, you see, to the smith: her have got a cottage as belongs to her. My brother have got a van and travels the country; and sometimes I and my wife goes with him. I larned to set up a wire when I went to plough when I were a boy, but never took to it regular till I went a-navigating [navvying] and seed what a spree it were.

'There ain't no such chaps for poaching as they navigators in all England: I means where there be a railway a-making. I've knowed forty of 'em go out together on a Sunday, and every man had a dog, and some two; and good dogs too – lots of 'em as you wouldn't buy for ten quid. They used to spread out like, and sweep the fields as clean as the crownd of your hat. Keepers weren't no good at all, and besides they never knowed which place us was going to make for. One of the chaps gave I a puppy, and he growed into the finest greyhound as you'd find in a day's walk. The first time I was took up before the bench I had to go to gaol, because the contractor had broke and the works was stopped, so that my mates hadn't no money to pay the fine.

'The dog was took away home to granny by my butty [comrade], but one of the gentlemen as seed it in the court sent his groom over and got it off the old woman for five pound. She thought if I hadn't the hound I should give it up, and she come and paid me out of gaol. It was a wonder as I didn't break her neck; only her was a good woman, you see, to I. But I wouldn't have parted with that hound for a quart-full of sovereigns. Many's a time I've seed his name – they changed his name, of course – in the papers for winning coursing matches. But we let that gent as bought him have it warm: we harried his pheasants and killed the most of 'em.

'After that I come home, and took to it regular. It ain't no use unless you do it regular. If a man goes out into the fields now and then chance-like he don't get much, and is most sure to be caught – very likely in the place of somebody else the keepers were waiting for and as didn't come. I goes to work every day the same as the rest, only I always take piece-work, which I can come to when I fancy, and stay as late in the evening as suits me with a good excuse. As I knows navigating, I do a main bit of draining and water-furrowing, and I gets good wages all the year round, and never wants for a job. You see, I knows more than the fellows as have never been at nothing but plough.

'The reason I gets on so well poaching is because I'm always at work out in the fields, except when I goes with the van. I watches everything as goes on, and marks the hares' tracks and the rabbit buries, and the double mounds and little copses as the pheasants wanders off to in the autumn. I keeps a 'nation good look out after the keeper and his men, and sees their dodges – which way they walks, and how they comes back sudden and unexpected on purpose. There's mostly one about with his eyes on me – when they see me working on a farm they puts a man special to look after me. I never does nothing close round where I'm at work, so he waits about a main bit for nothing.

'You see by going out piece-work I visits every farm in the parish. The other men they works for one farmer for two or three or maybe twenty years; but I goes very nigh all round the place – a fortnight here and a week there, and then a month somewhere else. So I knows every hare in the parish, and all his runs and all the double mounds and copses, and the little covers in the corners of the fields. When I be at work on one place I sets my wires about half a mile away on a farm as I ain't been working on for a month, and where the keeper don't keep no special look out now I be gone. As I goes all round, I knows the ways of all the farmers, and them as bides out late at night at their friends' and they as goes to bed early; and so I knows what paths to follow and what fields I can walk about in and never meet nobody.

'The dodge is to be always in the fields and to know everybody's ways. Then you may do just as you be a-mind. All of 'em knows I be a-poaching; but that don't make no difference for work; I can use my tools, and do it as well as any man in the country, and they be glad to get me on for 'em. They farmers as have got their shooting be sharper than the keepers, and you can't do much there; but they as haven't got the shooting don't take no notice. They sees my wires in the grass, and just looks the other way. If they sees I with a gun I puts un in the ditch till they be gone by, and they don't look among the nettles.

'Some of them as got land by the wood would like I to be there all day and night. You see, their clover and corn feeds the hares and pheasants; and then some day when they goes into the market and passes the poultry-shop there be four or five score pheasants a-hanging up with their long tails a-sweeping in the faces of them as fed 'em. The same with the hares and the rabbits; and so they'd just as soon as I had 'em – and a dalled deal sooner – out of spite. Lord bless you! if I was to walk through their courtyards at night with a sack over my shoulders full of you knows what, and met one of 'em, he'd tell his dog to stop that yowling, and go indoors rather than see me. As for the rabbits, they hates they worse than poison. They knocks a hare over now and then themselves on the quiet – bless you! I could tell tales on a main few, but I bean't such a fellow as that.

'But you see I don't run no risk except from the keeper hisself, the men as helps un, and two or three lickspittles as be always messing round after a ferreting job or some wood-cutting, and the Christmas charities. It be enough to make a man sick to see they. This yer parish be a very big un, and a be preserved very high, and I can do three times as much in he as in the next one, as ain't much preserved. So I sticks to this un.

'Of course they tried to drive I out of un, and wanted the cottage; but granny had all the receipts for the quit-rent, and my lard and all the lawyers couldn't shove us out, and there we means to bide. You have seed that row of oaks as grows in the hedge behind our house. One of 'em leaned over the roof, and one of the limbs was like to fall; but they wouldn't cut him, just to spite us, and the rain dripping spoilt the thatch. So I just had another chimney built at that end for an oven, and kept up the smoke till all the tree that side died. I've had more than one pheasant through them oaks, as draws 'em: I had one in a gin as I put in the ditch by my garden.

'They started a tale as 'twas I as stole the lambs a year or two ago, and they had me up for it; but they couldn't prove nothing agen me. Then they had me for unhinging the gates and drowning 'em in the water, but when they was going to try the case they two young farmers as you know of come and said as they did it when they was tight, and so I got off. They said as 'twas I that put the poison for the hounds when three on 'em took it and died while the hunt was on. It were the dalledest lie! I wouldn't hurt a dog not for nothing. The keeper hisself put that poison, I know, 'cause he couldn't bear the pack coming to upset the pheasants. Yes, they been down upon I a main bit, but I means to bide. All the farmers knows as I never touched no lamb, nor even pulled a turmot, and they never couldn't get no witnesses.

'After a bit I catched the keeper hisself and the policeman at it; and there be another as knows it, and who do you think that be? It be the man in town as got the licence to sell game as haves most of my hares: the keeper selled he a lot as the money never got to my lard's pocket and the steward never knowed of. Look at that now! So now he shuts his eye and axes me to drink, and give me the ferreting job in Longlands Mound; but, Lord bless 'ee, I bean't so soft as he thinks for.

'They used to try and get me to fight the keeper when they did catch me with a wire, but I knowed as hitting is transporting, and just put my hands in my pockets and let 'em do as they liked. *They* knows I bean't afraid of 'em in the road; I've threshed more than one of 'em, but I ain't going to jump into *that* trap. I've been before the bench, at one place and t'other, heaps of times, and paid the fine for trespass. Last time the chairman said to I, "So you be here again, Oby; we hear a good deal about you." I says, "Yes, my lard, I be here agen, but people never don't hear nothing about *you*." That shut the old duffer up. Nobody never heard nothing of he, except at rent-audit.

'However, they all knows me now – my lard and the steward, and the keeper and the bailies, and the farmers; and they don't take half the notice of I as they used to. The keeper he don't dare nor the policeman as I telled you, and the rest be got used to me and my ways. And I does very well one week with t'other. One week I don't take nothing, and the next I haves a good haul, chiefly hares and rabbits: 'cause of course I never goes into the wood, nor the plantations. It wants eight or ten with crape masks on for that job.

'I sets up about four wires, sometimes only two: if you haves so many it is a job to look after 'em. I stops the hare's other runs, so that she is sure to come along mine where I've got the turnpike up: the trick is to rub your hand along the runs as you want to stop, or spit on 'em, or summat like that; for a hare won't pass nothing of that sort. So pussy goes back and comes by the run as I've chose: if she comes quick she don't holler; if she comes slow she squeals a bit sometimes before the wire hangs her. Very often I bean't fur off and stops the squealing. That's why I can't use a gin – it makes 'em holler so. I ferrets a goodish few rabbits on bright nights in winter.

'As for the pheasants, I gets them mostly about acorn-time; they comes out of the plantations then. I keeps clear of the plantations, because, besides the men a-watching, they have got dogs chained up and alarm-guns as goes off if you steps on the spring; and some have got a string stretched along as you be pretty sure to kick against, and then, bang! and all the dogs sets up a yowling. Of course it's only powder, but it brings the keepers along. But when the acorns and the berries be ripe, the pheasants comes out along the hedges after 'em, and gets up at the haws and such like. They wanders for miles, and as they don't care to go all the way back to roost they bides in the little copses as I told you of. They come to the same copses every year, which is curious, as most of them as will come this year will be shot before next.

'If I can't get 'em the fust night, I just throws a handful or two of peas about the place, and they'll be sure to stay, and likely enough bring two or three more. I mostly shoots 'em with just a little puff of powder as you wouldn't hear across one field, especially if it's a windy night. I had a air-gun as was took from me, but he weren't much go: I likes a gun as throws the shot wide, but I never shoots any but roosters, unless I can catch 'em standing still.

'All as I can tell you is as the dodge is this: you watch everybody, and be always in the fields, and always work one parish till you knows every hare in un, and always work by yourself and don't have no mates.'

There were several other curious characters whom we frequently saw at work. The mouchers were about all the year round, and seemed to live in, or by the hedges, as much as the mice. These men probably see more than the most careful observer, without giving it a thought.

In January the ice that freezes in the ditches appears of a dark colour, because it lies without intervening water on the dead brown leaves. Their tint shows through the translucent crystal, but near the edge of the ice three white lines or bands run round. If by any chance the ice gets broken or upturned, these white bands are seen to be caused by flanges projecting from the under surface, almost like stands. They are sometimes connected in such a way that the parallel flanges appear like the letter 'h' with the two down-strokes much prolonged. In the morning the chalky rubble brought from the pits upon the Downs and used for mending gateways leading into the fields glistens brightly. Upon the surface of each piece of rubble there adheres a thin coating of ice: if this be lightly struck it falls off, and with it a flake of the chalk. As it melts, too, the chalk splits and crumbles; and thus in an ordinary gateway the same process may be seen that disintegrates the most majestic cliff.

The stubbles – those that still remain – are full of linnets, upon which the mouching fowler preys in the late autumn. And when at the end of January the occasional sunbeams give some faint hope of spring, he wanders through the lanes carrying a decoy bird in a darkened cage, and a few boughs of privet studded with black berries and bound round with rushes for the convenience of handling.

The female yellowhammers, whose hues are not so brilliant as those of the male birds, seem as winter approaches to flock together, and roam the hedges and stubble fields in bevies. Where loads of corn have passed through gates the bushes often catch some straws, and the tops of the gateposts, being decayed and ragged, hold others. These are neglected while the seeds among the stubble, the charlock and the autumn dandelion are plentiful and while the ears left by the gleaners may still be found. But in the shadowless winter days, hard and cold, each scattered straw is sought for.

A few days before the new year opened I saw a yellowhammer attacking, in a very ingenious manner, a straw that hung pendent, the ear downwards, from the post of a windy gateway. She fluttered up from the ground, clung to the ear, and outspread her wings, keeping them rigid. The draught acted on the wings just as the breeze does on a paper kite, and there the bird remained supported without an effort while the ear was picked. Now and then the balance was lost, but she was soon up again, and again, used the wind to maintain her position. The brilliant cock-birds return in the early spring, or at least appear to do so, for the habits of birds are sometimes quite local.

It is probable that in severe and continued frost many hedgehogs die. On January 19, in the midst of the sharp weather, a hedgehog came to the door opening on the garden at night, and was taken in. Though carefully tended, the poor creature died next day: it was so weak it could scarcely roll itself into a ball. As the vital heat declined the fleas deserted their host and issued from among the spines. In February, unless it be a mild season, the mounds are still bare; and then under the bushes the ground may be sometimes seen strewn with bulbous roots, apparently of the bluebell, lying thickly together and entirely exposed.

The moucher now carries a bill-hook, and as he shambles along the road keeps a sharp look-out for briars. When he sees one the roots of which are not difficult to get at, and whose tall upright stem is green – if dark it is too old – he hacks it off with as much of the root as possible. The lesser branches are cut, and, the stem generally trimmed; it is then sold to the gardeners as the stock on which to graft standard roses. In a few hours as he travels he will get together quite a bundle of such briars. He also collects moss, which is sold for the purpose of placing in flowerpots to hide the earth. The moss preferred is that growing on and round stoles.

The melting of the snow and the rains in February cause the ditches to overflow and form shallow pools in the level meadows. Into these sometimes the rooks wade as far as the length of their legs allows them, till the discoloured yellow water almost touches the lower part of the breast. The moucher searches for small shell snails, of which quantities are sold as food for cage birds, and cuts small 'turfs' a few inches square from the green by the roadside. These are in great request for larks, especially at this time of the year, when they begin to sing with all their might.

Large flocks of wood-pigeons are now in every field where the tender swede and turnip-tops are sprouting green and succulent. These 'tops' are the moucher's first great crop of the year. The time that they appear varies with the weather: in a mild winter some may be found early in January; if the frost has been severe there may be none till March. These the moucher gathers by stealth; he speedily fills a sack, and goes off with it to the nearest town. Turnip-tops are much more in demand now than formerly, and the stealing of them a more serious matter. This trade lasts some time, till the tops become too large and garden greens take their place.

In going to and fro the fields the moucher searches the banks and digs out primrose 'mars', and ferns with the root attached, which he hawks from door to door in the town. He also gathers quantities of spring flowers, as violets. This spring, owing to the severity of the season, there were practically none to gather, and when the weather moderated the garden flowers preceded those of the hedge. Till the 10th of March not a spot of colour was to be seen. About that time bright yellow flowers appeared suddenly on the clayey banks and waste places, and among the hard clay lumps of fields ploughed but not sown.

The brilliant yellow formed a striking contrast to the dull brown of the clods, there being no green leaf to moderate the extremes of tint. These were the blossoms of the coltsfoot, that sends up a stalk surrounded with faintly rosy scales. Several such stalks often spring from a single clod: lift the heavy clod, and you have half a dozen flowers, a whole bunch, without a single leaf. Usually the young grasses and the seed-leaves of plants have risen up and supply a general green; but this year the coltsfoot bloomed unsupported, studding the dark ground with gold.

Now the frogs are busy, and the land lizards come forth. Even these the moucher sometimes captures; for there is noth-

ing so strange but that some one selects it for a pet. The mad
March hares scamper about in broad daylight over the corn,
whose pale green blades rise in straight lines a few inches above
the soil. They are chasing their skittish loves, instead of soberly
dreaming the day away in a bunch of grass. The ploughman
walks in the furrow his share has made, and presently stops to
measure the 'lands' with the spud. His horses halt dead in the
tenth of a second at the sound of his voice, glad to rest for a
minute from their toil. Work there is in plenty, now, for stone-
picking, hoeing, and other matters must be attended to; but the
moucher lounges in the road decoying chaffinches, or perhaps
earns a shilling by driving some dealer's cattle home from fair
and market.

By April his second great crop is ready – the watercress; the
precise time of course varies very much, and at first the quantities are small. The hedges are now fast putting on the robe of
green that gradually hides the wreck of last year's growth. The
withered head of the teazle, black from the rain, falls and disappears. Great burdock stems lie prostrate. Thick and hard as
they are while the sap is still in them, in winter the wet ground
rots the lower part till the blast overthrows the stalk. The hollow 'gicks' too, that lately stood almost to the shoulder, is
down, or slanting, temporarily supported by some branch. Just
between the root and the stalk it has decayed till nothing but a
narrow strip connects the dry upper part with the earth. The
moucher sells the nests and eggs of small birds to townsfolk
who cannot themselves wander among the fields, but who love
to see something that reminds them of the green meadows.

As the season advances and the summer comes he gathers
vast quantities of dandelion leaves, parsley, sowthistle, clover,
and so forth, as food for the tame rabbits kept in towns. If his
haunt be not far from a river, he spends hours collecting bait –
worm and grub and fly – for the boatmen, who sell them again
to the anglers.

Again there is work in the meadows – the hay-making is
about, and the farmers are anxious for men. But the moucher
passes by and looks for quaking grass, bunches of which have
a ready sale. Fledgeling goldfinches and linnets, young rabbits,

young squirrels, even the nest of the harvest-trow mouse, and occasionally a snake, bring him in a little money. He picks the forget-me-nots from the streams and the 'blue-bottle' from the corn: bunches of the latter are sometimes sold in London at a price that seems extravagant to those who have seen whole fields tinted with its beautiful azure. By-and-by the golden wheat calls for an army of workers; bu the moucher passes on and gathers groundsel.

Then come the mushrooms: he knows the best places, and soon fills a basket full of 'buttons', picking them very early in the morning. These are then put in 'punnets' by the greengrocers and retailed at a high price. Later the blackberries ripen and form his third great crop; the quantity he brings in to the towns is astonishing, and still there is always a customer. The blackberry harvest lasts for several weeks, as the berries do not all ripen at once, but successively, and is supplemented by elderberries and sloes. The moucher sometimes sleeps on the heaps of disused tan in a tanyard: tanyards are generally on the banks of small rivers. The tan is said to possess the property of preserving those who sleep on it from chills and cold, though they may lie quite exposed to the weather.

There is generally at least one such a man as this about the outskirts of market towns, and he is an 'original' best defined by negatives. He is not a tramp, for he never enters the casual wards and never begs – that is, of strangers; though there are certain farmhouses where he calls once now and then and gets a slice of bread and cheese and a pint of ale. He brings to the farmhouse a duck's egg that has been dropped in the brook by some negligent bird, or carries intelligence of the nest made by some roaming goose in a distant withy-bed. Or once, perhaps, he found a sheep on its back in a narrow furrow, unable to get up and likely to die if not assisted, and by helping the animal to gain its legs earned a title to the owner's gratitude.

He is not a thief; apples and plums and so on are quite safe, though the turnip-tops are not: there is a subtle casuistry involved here – the distinction between the quasi-wild and the garden product. He is not a poacher in the sense of entering coverts, or even snaring a rabbit. If the pheasants are so numerous and so tame that passing carters have to whip them out of the way of the horses it is hardly wonderful if one should disappear now and then. Nor is he like the Running Jack that used to accompany the more famous packs of foxhounds, opening gates, holding horses, and a hundred other little services, and who kept up with the hunt by sheer fleetness of foot.

Yet he is fleet of foot in his way, though never seen to run; he *pads* along on naked feet like an animal, never straightening the leg, but always keeping the knee a little bent. With a basket of watercress slung at his back by a piece of tar-cord, he travels rapidly in this way; his feet go 'pad, pad' on the thick white dust, and he easily overtakes a good walker and keeps up the pace for miles without exertion. The watercress is a great staple, because it lasts for so many months. Seeing the nimble way in which he gathers it, thrusting aside the brook-lime, breaking off the coarser sprays, snipping away pieces of root, sorting and washing, and thinking of the amount of work to be got through before a shilling is earned, one would imagine that the slow, idling life of the labourer, with his regular wages, would be far more enticing.

Near the stream the ground is perhaps peaty; little black pools appear between tufts of grass, some of them streaked with a reddish or yellowish slime that glistens on the surface of the dark water; and as you step there is a hissing sound as the spongy earth yields, and a tiny spout is forced forth several yards distant. Some of the drier part of the soil the moucher takes to sell for use in gardens and flowerpots as peat.

The years roll on, and he grows old. But no feebleness of body or mind can induce him to enter the workhouse: he cannot quit his old haunts. Let it rain or sleet, or let the furious gale drive broken boughs across the road, he still sleeps in some shed or under a straw-rick. In sheer pity he is committed every now and then to prison for vagabondage – not for punishment, but in order to save him from himself. It is in vain: the moment he is out he returns to his habits. All he wants is a little beer – he is not a drunkard – and a little tobacco, and the hedges. Some chilly evening, as the shadows thicken, he shambles out of the town, and seeks the limekiln in the ploughed field, where, the substratum being limestone, the farmer burns it. Near the top of the kiln the ground is warm; there he reclines and sleeps.

The night goes on. Out from the broken blocks of stone now and again there rises a lambent flame, to shine like a meteor for a moment and then disappear. The rain falls. The moucher moves uneasily in his sleep; instinctively he rolls or crawls towards the warmth, and presently lies extended on the top of the kiln. The wings of the water-fowl hurtle in the air as they go over; by-and-by the heron utters his loud call.

Very early in the morning the quarryman comes to tend his fire, and starts to see on the now redhot and glowing stones, sunk below the rim, the presentment of a skeleton formed of the purest white ashes – a ghastly spectacle in the grey of the dawn, as the mist rises and the peewit plaintively whistles over the marshy meadow.

The Hunting Picture:
Its Defects and Difficulties

From Jefferies' note-book, April 1878
First collected in *Field and Farm*, 1957

Nothing passes so easily for a picture, nothing so difficult as a good one. Too ambitious, too many figures. Sketches in pencil are often the best, better than laboured productions. Locality: interesting to those who know it. Merging what does duty for a true thing they know: a brook they have jumped, or a huntsman they have followed. They are quite satisfied 'by Jove, isn't it good?' . . . Then again the fancy picture, fancy landscapes . . . To Hunting we owe no little knowledge of men and manners, social history. The stiffness and woodenness of the trees' impossible drawing. Chief characteristic, green ground and a grey horse. No one paints the foggy days, the southerly wind, the rain; the dead leaves; the soaking grass; the intense cold of the real hunt: its melancholy landscape. Why does not some one paint the natural hunt? The cottager and his billhook, looking up, and then the scarlet dulled by the rain or splashed by a fall, and the fence tearing the coat, and the forlorn four or five near the finish along the dusky hedge of the winter afternoon. Why these fancy horses going at full speed have not a speck of dust upon them, and where is the steam that rises from the hunter as he stands? No one has painted the waiting for the start in the cold. There is a romance in the rain, but no one has seized it yet. They have seized the humour, and they are the best. They have seized the local, they have not seized the artistic, and they have not seized the true natural.

PART TWO

NATURAL HISTORY WRITINGS
(1878–86)

Rooks Returning to Roost

First published in the *Pall Mall Gazette*, 1878
First collected in *Wild Life in a Southern County*, 1879

As evening approaches, and the rooks begin to wing their way homewards, sometimes a great number of them will alight upon the steep ascent close under the entrenchment on the Downs which has been described, and from whence the wood and beech trees where they sleep can be seen. They do not seem so much in search of food, of which probably there is not a great deal to be found in the short, dried-up herbage and hard soil, as to rest here, half-way home from arable fields. Sometimes they wheel and circle in fantastic flight over the very brow of the down, just above the rampart; occasionally, in the raw cold days of winter, they perch moping in disconsolate mood upon the bare branches of the clumps of trees on the ridge.

After the nesting time is over and they have got back to their old habits – which during that period are quite reversed – it is a sight to see from hence the long black stream in the air steadily flowing onwards to the wood below. They stretch from here to the roosting-trees, fully a mile and a half – literally as the crow flies; and backwards in the opposite direction the line reaches as far as the eye can see. It is safe to estimate that the aerial army's line of march extends over quite five miles in one unbroken corps. The breadth they occupy in the atmosphere varies – now twenty yards, now fifty, now a hundred, on an average say fifty yards; but rooks do not fly very close together like starlings, and the mass, it may be observed, fly on the same plane. Instead of three or four layers one above the other, the greater number pass by at the same height from the ground, side by side on a level, as soldiers would march upon a

road: not meaning, of course, an absolute, but a relative level.
This formation is more apparent from an elevation – as it were,
up among them – than from below; and looking along their
line towards the distant wood it is like glancing under a black
canopy.

Small outlying parties straggle from the line – now on one
side, now on the other; sometimes a few descend to alight on
trees in the meadows, where doubtless their nests were situated
in the spring. For it is a habit of theirs, months after the nesting
is over and also before it begins, to pay a flying visit to the trees
in the evening, calling *en route* to see that all is well and to
assert possession.

The rustling sound of these thousands upon thousands of
wings beating the air with slow steady stroke can hardly be
compared to anything else in its weird oppressiveness, so to
say: it is a little like falling water, but may be best likened, perhaps, to a vast invisible broom sweeping the sky. Every now
and then a rook passes with ragged wing – several feathers
gone, so that you can see daylight through it; sometimes the
feathers are missing from the centre, leaving a great gap, so
that it looks as if the bird had a large wing on this side and on
the other two narrow ones. There is a rough resemblance
between these and the torn sails of some of the old windmills
which have become dark in colour from long exposure to the
weather, and have been rent by the storms of years. Rooks can
fly with gaps of astonishing size in their wings, and do not seem
much incommoded by the loss – caused, doubtless, by a charge
of shot in the rook-shooting, or by the small sharp splinters of
flint with which the birdkeepers sometimes load their guns, not
being allowed to use shot.

Near their nesting-trees their black feathers may be picked
up by dozens in the grass; they beat them out occasionally
against the small boughs, and sometimes in fighting. If seen
from behind, the wings of the rook, as he spreads them and
glides, slowly descending, preparatory to alighting, slightly
turn up at the edges like the rim of a hat, but much less curved.
From a distance as he flies he appears to preserve a level course,
neither rising nor falling; but if observed nearer it will be seen

that with every stroke of the wings the body is lifted some inches, and sinks as much immediately afterwards.

As the black multitude floats past overhead with deliberate, easy flight, their trumpeters and buglemen, the jackdaws – two or three to every company – utter their curious chuckle; for the jackdaw is a bird which could not keep silence to save his life, but must talk after his fashion, while his grave, solemn companions move slowly onwards, rarely deigning to 'caw' him a reply. But away yonder at the wood, above the great beech trees, where so vast a congregation is gathered together, there is a mighty uproar and commotion: a seething and bubbling of the crowds, now settling on the branches, now rising in sable clouds, each calling to the other with all his might, the whole population delivering its opinions at once.

It is an assemblage of a hundred republics. We know how free States indulge in speech with their parliaments and congresses and senates, their public meetings, and so forth: here are a hundred such nations, all with perfect liberty of tongue holding forth unsparingly, and in a language which consists of two or three syllables indefinitely repeated. The din is wonderful – each republic as its forces arrive adding to the noise, and for a long time unable to settle upon their trees, but feeling compelled to wheel around and discourse. In spring each tribe has its special district, its own canton and city, in its own trees away in the meadows. Later on they all meet here in the evening. It is a full hour or more before the orations have all been delivered, and even then small bands rush up into the air still dissatisfied.

This great stream of rooks passing over the hills meets another great stream as it approaches the wood, crossing up from the meadows. From the rampart there may be seen, perhaps a mile and a half away, a dim black line crossing at right angles – converging on the wood, which itself stands on the edge of the table-land from which the steeper Downs arise. This second army is every whit as numerous, as lengthy, and as regular in its route as the first.

Every morning, from the beech trees where they have slept, safe at that elevation from all the dangers of the night, there set out these two vast expeditionary corps. Regularly the one flies steadily eastward over the Downs; as regularly the other flies steadily northwards over the vale and meadows. Doubtless in different country districts their habits in this respect vary; but here it is always east and always north. If any leave the wood for the south or the west, as probably they do, they go in small bodies and are quickly lost sight of. The two main divisions sail towards the sunrise and towards the north star.

They preserve their ranks for at least two miles from the wood; and then gradually first one and then another company falls out, and wheeling round, descends upon some favourite field, till by degrees, spreading out like a fan, the army melts away. In the evening the various companies, which may by that time have worked far to the right or to the left, gradually move into line. By-and-by the vanguard comes sweeping up, and each regiment rises from the meadow or the hill, and takes its accustomed place in the return journey.

So that although if you casually observe a flock of rooks in the daytime they seem to wander hither and thither just as fancy leads, or as they are driven by passers-by, in reality they have all their special haunts; they adhere to certain rules, and even act in concert, thousands upon thousands of them at once, as if in obedience to the word of command, and as if aware of the precise moment at which to move. They have their laws, from which there is no deviation: they are handed down unaltered from generation to generation. Tradition, indeed, seems to be their main guide, as it is with savage human tribes. They have their particular feeding grounds; and so you may notice that, comparing ten or a dozen fields, one or two will almost always be found to be frequented by rooks while the rest are vacant.

Here, for instance, is a meadow close to a farmstead – what is usually called the home-field, from its proximity to a house – here day after day rooks alight and spend hours in it, as much at their ease as the nag or the lambs brought up by hand. Another field, at a distance, which to the human eye appears so much more suitable, being retired, quiet, and apparently quite as full of food, is deserted; they scarcely come near it. The home-field itself is not the attraction, because other home-fields are not so favoured.

The tenacity with which rooks cling to localities is often illustrated near great cities where buildings have gradually closed in around their favourite haunts. Yet on the small waste spots covered with cinders and dustheaps, barren and unlovely, the rooks still alight: and you may see them, when driven up from such places, perching on the telegraph wires over the very steam of the locomotives as they puff into the station.

I think that neither considerations of food, water, shelter, nor convenience, are always the determining factors in the choice made by birds of the spots they frequent; for I have seen many cases in which all of these were evidently quite put on one side. Birds to ordinary observation seem so unfettered, to live so entirely without rhyme or reason, that it is difficult to convey the idea that the precise contrary is really the case.

Returning to these two great streams of rooks, which pour every evening in converging currents from the north and east upon the wood; why do they do this? Why not go forth to the west, or to the south, where there are hills and meadows and streams in equal number? Why not scatter abroad, and return according to individual caprice? Why, to go still further, do rooks manoeuvre in such immense numbers, and crows fly only in pairs? The simple truth is that birds, like men, have a history. They are unconscious of it, but its accomplished facts affect them still and shape the course of their existence. Without doubt, if we could trace that history back there are good and sufficient reasons why rooks prefer to fly in this particular locality, to the east and to the north. Something may perhaps be learnt by examining the routes along which they fly.

The second division – that which goes northwards, after flying little more than a mile in a straight line – passes over Wick Farm, and disperses gradually in the meadows surrounding and extending far below it. The rooks whose nests are placed in the elms of the Warren belong to this division, and, as their trees are the nearest to the great central roosting-place, they are the first to quit the line of march in the morning, descending to feed in the fields around their property. On the other hand, in the evening, as the army streams homewards, they are the last to rise and join the returning host.

So that there are often rooks in and about the Warren later in the evening after those whose habitations are farther away have gone by, for, having so short a distance to fly, they put off the movement till the last moment. Before watches became so common a possession, the labouring people used, they say, to note the passage overhead of the rooks in the morning in winter as one of their signs of time, so regular was their appearance; and if the fog hid them, the noise from a thousand black wings and throats could not be missed.

If, from the rising ground beyond the Warren or from the Downs beyond that, the glance is allowed to travel slowly over the vale northwards, instead of the innumerable meadows which are really there, it will appear to consist of one vast forest. Of the hamlet not far distant there is nothing visible but the white wall of a cottage, perhaps, shining in the sun, or the pale blue smoke curling upwards. This wooded appearance is caused by timber trees standing in the hedgerows, in the copses at the corners of the meadows, and by groups and detached trees in the middle of the fields.

Many hedges are full of elms, some have rows of oaks; some meadows have trees growing so thickly in all four hedges as to seem surrounded by a timber wall; one or two have a number of ancient spreading oaks dotted about in the field itself, or standing in rows. But there are not nearly so many trees as there used to be. Numerous hedges have been grubbed to make the fields larger.

Within the last thirty years two large falls of timber have taken place, when the elms especially were thrown wholesale. The old men, however, recall a much greater 'throw', as they term it, of timber, which occurred twice as long ago. Then before that they have a tradition that a still earlier 'throw' took place, when the timber chiefly went to the dockyards for the building of those wooden walls which held the world at bay. These traditions go back, therefore, some eighty or a hundred years. One field in particular is pointed out where stood a double row or avenue of great oaks leading to nothing but a farmstead of the ordinary sort, of which there is not the slightest record that it ever was anything but a farmhouse. Now avenues of great oaks are not planted to lead to farmsteads. Besides these, it is said, there were oaks in most of the fields – oaks that have long since disappeared, the prevalent tree being elm.

While all these 'throws' of timber have successively taken place, no attempt has been made to fill up the gaps; no planting of acorns, no shielding with rails the young saplings from the ravages of cattle. If a young tree could struggle up it could; if not, it perished. At the last two 'throws', especially, young trees which ought to have been saved were ruthlessly cut down. Yet even now the place is well timbered; so that it is easy to form some idea of the forest-like appearance it must have presented a hundred years ago, when rows of giant oaks led up to that farmhouse door.

Then there are archaeological reasons, which it would be out of place to mention, why in very ancient days a forest, in all probability, stood hereabouts. It seems reasonable to suppose that in one way or another the regular flight of the second army of rooks passing down into this district was originally attracted by the trees. Three suggestions arise out of the circumstances.

The wood in which both streams of rooks roost at night stands on the last slope of the Downs; behind it to the south extend the hills, and the open tilled upland plains; below it northwards are the meadows. It has, therefore, much the appearance of the last surviving remnant of the ancient forest. There has been a wood there time out of mind: there are references to the woods of the locality dating from the sixteenth century. Now if we suppose (and such seems to have been really the case) the unenclosed woodlands below gradually cleared of trees – thereby doubtless destroying many rookeries – the rooks driven away would naturally take refuge in the wood remaining. There the enclosure protected them, and there the trees, being seldom or never cut down, or if cut down felled with judgment and with a view to future timber, grew to great size and in such large groups as they prefer. But as birds are creatures of habit, their descendants in the fiftieth generation would still revisit the old places in the meadows.

Secondly, although so many successive 'throws' of timber thinned out the trees, yet there may still be found more groups and rows of elms and oak in this direction than in any other; that is, a line drawn northwards from the remaining wood passes through a belt of well-timbered country. On either side of this belt there is much less timber; so that the rooks that desired to build nests beyond the limits of the enclosed wood still found in the old places the best trees for their purpose. Here may be seen far more rookeries than in any other direction. Hardly a farmhouse lying near this belt but has got its rookery, large or small. Once these rookeries were established, an inducement to follow this route would arise in the invariable habit of the birds of visiting their nesting-trees even when the actual nesting time is past.

Thirdly, if the inquiry be carried still farther back, it is possible that the line taken by the rooks indicates the line of the first clearings in very early days. The clearing away of trees and underwood, by opening the ground and rendering it accessible, must be very attractive to birds, and rooks are particularly fond of following the plough. Now although the district is at present chiefly meadow land, numbers of these meadows were originally ploughed fields, of which there is evidence in the surface of the fields themselves, where the regular 'lands' and furrows are distinctly visible.

One or all of these suggestions may perhaps account for the course followed by the rooks. In any case it seems natural to look for the reason in the trees. The same idea applies to the other stream of rooks which leaves the wood for the eastward every morning, flying along the Downs. In describing the hill district, evidence was given of the existence of woods or forest land upon the Downs in the olden time. Detached copses and small woods are still to be found; and it happens that a part of this district, in the line of the eastward flight, belonged to a 'chase' of which several written notices are extant.

The habits of rooks seem more regular in winter than in summer. In winter the flocks going out in the morning or returning in the evening appear to pass nearly at the same hour day after day. But in summer they often stay about late. This last summer I noticed a whole flock, some hundreds in number, remaining out till late – till quite dusk – night after night, and always in the same place. It was an arable field, and there they stood close together on the ground, so close that in spots it was difficult to distinguish individuals. They were silent and still, making no apparent attempt at feeding. The only motion I observed was when a few birds arrived and alighted among them. Where they thus crowded together the earth was literally black.

It was about three-quarters of a mile from their nesting-trees, but nesting had been over for more than two months. This particular field had recently been ploughed by steam tackle, and was the only one for a considerable distance that had been ploughed for some time. There they stood motionless, side by side, as if roosting on the ground; possibly certain beetles were numerous just there (for it was noticeable that they chose the same part of the field evening after evening), and came crawling up out of the earth at night.

The jackdaws which – so soon as the rooks pack after nesting and fly in large flocks – are always with them, may be distinguished by their smaller size and the quicker beats of their wings, even when not uttering their well-known cry. Jackdaws will visit the hencoops if not close to the house, and help themselves to the food meant for the fowls. Poultry are often kept in rickyards, a field or two distant from the homestead, and it is then amusing to watch the impudent attempts of the jackdaws at robbery. Four or five will perch on the post and rails, intent on the tempting morsels: sitting with their heads a little on one side and peering over. Suddenly one thinks he sees an opportunity. Down he hops, and takes a peck, but before he has hardly seized it, a hen darts across, running at him with beak extended like lance in rest. Instantly he is up on the rail again, and the impetus of the hen's charge carries her right under him.

Then, while her back is turned, down hops a second and helps himself freely. Out rushes another hen, and up goes the jackdaw. A pause ensues for a few minutes: presently a third black rascal dashes right into the midst of the fowls, picks up a morsel, and rises again before they can attack him. The way in which the jackdaw dodges the hens though alighting among them, and as it were for the moment surrounded, is very clever: and it is laughable to see the cool impudence with which he perches again on the rail, and looks down demurely, not a whit abashed, on the feathered housewife he has just been doing his best to rob.

Wind-Anemones – The Fish Pond

First published in the *Pall Mall Gazette*, 1880
First collected in *Round About a Great Estate*, 1880

The only spot about the Chace where the wind-anemones grew
was in a small detached copse of ash-poles nearly a mile from
the great woods. Between the stoles, which were rather far
apart, the ground was quite covered in spring with dark-green
vegetation, so that it was impossible to walk there without
treading down the leaves of bluebells, anemones, and similar
woodland plants. But if you wished to see the anemones in
their full beauty it was necessary to visit the copse frequently;
for if you forgot it, or delayed a fortnight, very likely upon
returning you would find that their fleeting loveliness was over.
Their slender red stems rise but a few inches, and are surrounded with three leaves; the six white petals of the cup-shaped
flower droop a little and have a golden centre. Under the petal is
a tinge of purple, which is sometimes faintly visible through it.
The leaves are not only three in number, but are each cut deeply
thrice; they are hardy, but the flower extremely delicate.

On the banks dividing the copse from the meadows around
it the blue dog-violets, which have no perfume, often opened so
large and wide as to resemble pansies. They do not appear like
this till just as their flowering time is almost over. The meadows
by the copse were small, not more than two or three acres each.
One which was marshy was white for weeks together with the
lady's-smock or cuckoo-flower. The petals of these flowers are
silvery white in some places, in others tinted with lilac. The
hues of wild flowers vary with their situation: in shady woodlands the toadflax or butter-and-eggs is often pale – a sulphur
colour; upon the Downs it is a deep and beautiful yellow. In a
ditch of this marshy meadow was a great bunch of woodruff,

above whose green whorls the white flowers were lifted. Over them the brambles arched, their leaves growing in fives, and each leaf prickly. The bramble-shoots, as they touch the ground, take root and rise again, and thus would soon cross a field were they not cut down.

Pheasants were fond of visiting this copse, following the hedgerows to it from the Chace, and they always had one or more nests in it. A green woodpecker took it in his route, though he did not stay long, there not being many trees. These birds seem to have their regular rounds; there are some copses where they are scarcely ever heard. They prefer old trees; where there is much large and decaying timber, there the woodpeckers come. Such little meadows as these about the copse are the favourite resort of birds and the very home of flowers – more so than extensive woods like the Chace, or the open pastures and arable fields. Thick hedgerows attract birds, and behind such cover their motions may be watched. There is, too, more variety of bush and tree.

In one such hedgerow leading from the copse the maple-bushes in spring were hung with the green flowers which, though they depend in their season from so many trees, as the oak, are perhaps rarely observed. The elder-bushes in full white bloom scented the air for yards around both by night and day; the white bloom shows on the darkest evening. Besides several crab-stoles – the buds of the crab might be mistaken for thorns growing pointed at the extreme end of the twigs – there was a large crab tree, which bore a plentiful crop. The lads sharpen their knives by drawing the blade slowly to and fro through a crab-apple; the acid of the fruit eats the steel like aquafortis. They hide stores of these crabs in holes in the hayricks, suppos-ing them to improve by keeping. There, too, they conceal quantities of the apples from the old orchards, for the fruit in them is often almost as hard and not much superior in flavour to the crab. These apples certainly become more mellow after several months in the warm hay.

A wild 'plum', or bullace, grew in one place; the plum about twice the size of a sloe, with a bloom upon the skin like the cul-tivated fruit, but lacking its sweetness. Yet there was a distinct

difference of taste: the 'plum' had not got the extreme harshness of the sloe. A quantity of dogwood occupied a corner; in
summer it bore a pleasing flower; in the autumn, after the black
berries appeared upon it, the leaves became a rich bronze colour, and some when the first frosts touched them curled up at the
edge and turned crimson. There were two or three guelder-
rose bushes – the wild shrub – which were covered in June
with white bloom; not in snowy balls like the garden variety,
but flat and circular, the florets at the edge of the circle often
whitest, and those in the centre greenish. In autumn the slender
boughs were weighed down with heavy bunches of large purplish berries, so full of red juice as to appear on the point of
bursting. As these soon disappeared they were doubtless eaten
by birds.

Besides the hawthorn and briar there were several species of
willow – the snake-skin willow, so called because it sheds its
bark; the 'snap-willow', which is so brittle that every gale
breaks off its feeble twigs, and pollards. One of these, hollow
and old, had upon its top a crowd of parasites. A bramble had
taken root there, and hung over the side; a small currant-bush
grew freely – both, no doubt, unwittingly planted by birds –
and finally the bines of the noxious bitter-sweet or nightshade,
starting from the decayed wood, supported themselves among
the willow-branches, and in autumn were bright with red berries. Ash-stoles, the buds on whose boughs in spring are hidden
under black sheaths; nut-tree stoles, with ever-welcome nuts –
always stolen here, but on the Downs, where they are plentiful,
staying till they fall; young oak growing up from the butt of a
felled tree. On these oak-twigs sometimes, besides the ordinary
round galls, there may be found another gall, larger, and
formed, as it were, of green scales one above the other.

Where shall we find in the artificial and, to my thinking,
tasteless pleasure-grounds of modern houses so beautiful a
shrubbery as this old hedgerow? Nor were evergreens wanting,
for the ivy grew thickly, and there was one holly-bush – not
more, for the soil was not affected by holly. The tall cow-parsnip
or 'gicks' rose up through the bushes; the great hollow stem of
the angelica grew at the edge of the field, on the verge of the

grass, but still sheltered by the brambles. Some reeds early in spring thrust up their slender green tubes, tipped with two spear-like leaves. The reed varies in height according to the position in which it grows. If the hedge has been cut it does not reach higher than four or five feet; when it springs from a deep, hollow corner, or with bushes to draw it up, you can hardly touch its tip with your walking-stick. The leaders of the black bryony, lifting themselves above the bushes, and having just there nothing to cling to, twist around each other, and two bines thus find mutual support where one alone would fall of its own weight.

In the watery places the sedges send up their dark flowers, dusted with light yellow pollen, rising above the triangular stem with its narrow, ribbed leaf. The reed-sparrow or bunting sits upon the spray over the ditch with its carex grass and rushes; he is a graceful bird, with a crown of glossy black. Hops climb the ash and hang their clusters, which impart an aromatic scent to the hand that plucks them; broad burdock leaves, which the mouchers put on the top of their baskets to shield their freshly gathered watercresses from the sunshine; creeping avens, with buttercup-like flowers and long stems that straggle across the ditch, and in autumn are tipped with a small ball of soft spines; mints, strong-scented and unmistakable; yarrow, white and sometimes a little lilac, whose flower is perhaps almost the last that the bee visits. In the middle of October I have seen a wild bee on a last stray yarrow.

On the higher and drier bank some few slender square stems of betony, with leaves in pairs like wings, stand up tall and stiff as the summer advances. The labiate purplish flowers are all at the top; each flower is set in the cup by a curve at the lesser end, like a crook; the leaves and stalk are slightly rough, and have an aromatic bitter perfume when crushed. On the flower of a great thistle a moth has alighted, and hidden under its broad wing is a humble-bee, the two happy together and neither interfering with the other. Sometimes a bee will visit the white rose on the briar.

Near the gateway, on the edge of the trodden ground, grows a tall, stout, bushy plant, like a shrub, with pale greyish-green leaves, much lobed and divided: the top of each branch in

August is thick with small whitish-green flowers tipped with brown. These, if rubbed in the hand, emit a strong and peculiar scent, with a faint flavour of lavender, and yet quite different. This is the mugwort. Still later on, under the shade of the trees on the mound, there appear bunches of a pale herb, with greenish labiate flowers, and a scent like hops; it is the woodsage, and if tasted the leaf will be found extremely bitter.

In the mornings of autumn the webs of the spiders hang along the hedge bowed a little with dew, like hammocks of gossamer slung from thorn to thorn. Then the hedge-sparrows, perching on the topmost boughs of the hawthorn, cry 'peep-peep' mournfully; the heavy dew on the grass beneath arranges itself in two rows of drops along the edges of the blades. From the day when the first leaf appears upon the hardy woodbine, in the early year, to the time when the partridge finds the eggs in the ant-hill, and on again till the last harebell dies, there is always something beautiful or interesting in these great hedgerows. Indeed, it is impossible to exhaust them. I have omitted the wild geranium with its tiny red petals scarce seen in the mass of green, the mosses, the ferns, and have scarcely said a word about the living creatures that haunt it. But then one might begin to write a book about a hedgerow when a boy and find it incomplete in old age.

A much-neglected path led from the park through some fir plantations down to the fish pond. After the first turn of the narrow track the close foliage of the firs, through which nothing could be seen, shut out the world with green walls. The strip of blue sky visible above was wider than the path, because the trees sloped away somewhat, their branches shortening towards the top; still it was so contracted that a passing wood-pigeon was seen but for a second as he went over. Every step carried me into deeper silence – the sudden call of a jay was startling in its harsh contrast. Presently the path widened where the thickly planted firs were succeeded by sycamores, horse-chestnuts, alders, and aspen – trees which stand farther apart, and beneath which some underwood grew. Here there were thickets of hawthorn and bramble and elder bushes which can find no place among firs.

The ground now sloped rapidly down into a hollow, and upon this descent numbers of skeleton leaves were scattered. There was no other spot all over the Chace where they could be seen like this; you might walk for hours and not find one, yet here there were hundreds. Sometimes they covered the ground in layers, several leaves one on the other. In spring violets pushed up through them and bluebells – sweet hope rising over grey decay.

Lower down a large pond almost filled the hollow. It was surrounded on three sides by trees and thickets; on the fourth an irregular margin of marshy grass extended. Floating leaves of weeds covered the surface of the water; these weeds had not been disturbed for years, and there was no check to their growth except their own profusion, for they choked each other. The pond had long ceased to supply fish for the table. Before railways brought the sea so near, such ponds were very useful. At that time almost everything consumed came from the estate itself: the bread, the beef, the mutton, the venison, game, fish, all was supplied by the adjacent woods, the fields, or the water. The lord in old days hunted the deer on his own domain, brought down game with a crossbow or captured it with nets, and fished or netted his own streams and ponds. These great parks and chaces enclosed everything, so that it was within easy reach of his own door. Sometimes the lord and his visitors strolled out to see the fish ponds netted.

This pond had originally been one of a series, but the others had been drained and added to the meadows. It was said to be staked at the bottom to prevent illicit netting; but if so, the stakes by this time were probably rotten or buried in mud formed from the decaying weeds, the fallen leaves, and branches which were gradually closing it up. A few yards from the edge there was a mass of ivy through which a little brown thatch could be distinguished, and on approaching nearer this low roof was found to cover the entrance to a cave. It was an ice-house excavated in the sloping ground or bank, in which, 'when George the Third was King', the ice of the ponds had been preserved to cool the owner's wine in summer. Ice was then a luxury for the rich only; but when so large a supply arrived from America, a supply increased by freezing machines, the ice-house lost its importance. The door, once so jealously closed, was gone, and the dead leaves of last year had gathered in corners where the winds had whirled them.

The heat of a warm June day seemed still more powerful in this hollow. The sedges, into which two or three moorhens had retired at my approach, were still, and the leaves on the boughs overhanging the water were motionless. Where there was a space free from weeds – a deeper hole near the bank – a jack basked at the surface in the sunshine. High above on the hill stood a tall dead fir, from whose trunk the bark was falling; it had but one branch, which stood out bare and stark across the sky. There came a sound like distant thunder, but there were no clouds overhead, and it was not possible to see far round. Pushing gently through the hawthorn bushes and ash-stoles at the farther end of the pond, I found a pleasant little stream rushing swiftly over a clear chalky bottom, hastening away down to the larger brook.

Beyond it rose a mound and hedgerow, up to which came the meadows, where, from the noise, the cattle seemed racing to and fro, teased by insects. Tiny black flies alighting on my hands and face, irritated the skin; the haymakers call them 'thunder-flies'; but the murmur of the running water was so delicious that I sat down on a bulging tree-root, almost over the stream, and listened to the thrushes singing. Had it been merely warm they would have been silent. They do not sing in dry sunshine, but they knew what was coming; so that there is no note so hated by the haymaker as that of the thrush. The birds were not in the firs, but in the ash-trees along the course of the rill.

The voice of the thrush is the most 'cultivated', so to speak, of all our birds: the trills, the runs, the variations, are so numerous and contrasted. Not even the nightingale can equal it: the nightingale has not nearly such command: the thrush seems to know no limit. I own I love the blackbird best, but in excellence of varied music the thrush surpasses all. Few birds, except those that are formed for swimming, come to a still pond. They like a clear running stream; they visit the sweet running water

for drinking and bathing. Dreaming away the time, listening to
the rush of the water bubbling about the stones, I did not notice
that the sky had become overcast, till suddenly a clap of thunder near at hand awakened me. Some heavy drops of rain fell;
I looked up and saw the dead branch of the fir on the hill
stretched out like a withered arm across a black cloud.

Hastening back to the ice-house, I had barely entered the
doorway when the lightning, visible at noonday, flashed red
and threatening, the thunder crackled and snapped overhead,
and the rain fell in a white sheet of water. There were but two
of these overpowering discharges with their peculiar crack and
snap; the electricity passed on quickly, and the next clap roared
over the woods. But the rain was heavier than before, the fall
increased after every flash, however distant, and the surface of
the pond was threshed by the drops which bore down with
them many leaves weakened by blight.

Doubtless the mowers in the meadows had hidden the blades
of their scythes under the swathe, and the haymakers had placed
their prongs in the ditches: nothing is so likely to attract a shock
of lightning as a prong carried on the shoulder with the bright
steel points upwards. In the farmhouses the old folk would
cover up the looking-glasses lest the quicksilver should draw the
electric fluid. The haymakers will tell you that sometimes when
they have been standing under a hedge out of a storm a flash of
lightning has gone by with a distinct sound like 'swish', and
immediately afterwards the wet ground has sent forth a vapour,
or, as they say, smoked.

Wood-pigeons and many other birds seem to come home to
woods and copses before and during a storm. The wood-pigeon
is one of the freest of birds to all appearance: he passes over the
highest trees and goes straight away for miles. Yet, though it is
usual to speak of wild birds and of their freedom, the more you
watch their ways the more you feel that the wildest have their
routes and customs: that they do not act entirely from the
impulse of the moment, but have their unwritten laws. How do
the gnats there playing under the horse-chestnut boughs escape
being struck down by the heavy raindrops, each one of which
looks as if it would drown so small a creature? The numbers of

insects far exceed all that words can express: consider the clouds of midges that often dance over a stream. One day, chancing to glance at a steeple, I saw what looked like thin smoke issuing from the top of it. Now it shot out in a straight line from the gilded beak of the weathercock, now veered about, or declined from the vane. It was an innumerable swarm of insects, whose numbers made them visible at that height.

Some insects are much more powerful than would be supposed. A garden was enclosed with fresh palings formed of split oak so well seasoned (split oak is the hardest of wood) that it was difficult to train any creepers against them, for a nail could not be driven in without the help of a bradawl. Passing along the path one afternoon I heard a peculiar rasping sound like a very small saw at work, and found it proceeded from four wasps biting the oak for the materials of their nest. The noise they made was audible four or five yards away, and upon looking closer I found the palings all scored and marked in short shallow grooves. The scores and marks extended along that part of the palings where the sunshine usually fell; there were none on the shady side, the wasps preferring to work in the sunlight.

Soon the clouds began to break, and then the sun shone on innumerable raindrops. I at once started forth, knowing that such a storm is often followed by several lesser showers with brief intervals between. The deserted ice-house was rarely visited – only, perhaps, when some borage was wanted to put in summer drinks. For a thick growth of borage had sprung up by it, where perhaps a small garden patch had once been cultivated, for there was a pear-tree near. The plant, with its scent of cucumber, grew very strong; the blue flowers when fallen, if they had not been observed when growing, might be supposed to have been inserted exactly upside down to their real manner of attachment. In autumn the leaves of the pear-tree reddened, and afterwards, the ivy over the entrance to the ice-house flowered; then in the cold months of early spring the birds came for the ivy-berries.

A Brook – a London Trout

First published in the London *Standard*, 30 September 1880
First collected in *Nature Near London*, 1883

Some low wooden rails guarding the approach to a bridge over a brook one day induced me to rest under an aspen, with my back against the tree. Some horse-chestnuts, beeches, and alders grew there, fringing the end of a long plantation of willow stoles which extended in the rear following the stream. In front, southwards, there were open meadows and cornfields, over which shadow and sunshine glided in succession as the sweet westerly wind carried the white clouds before it.

The brimming brook, as it wound towards me through the meads, seemed to tremble on the verge of overflowing, as the crown of wine in a glass rises yet does not spill. Level with the green grass, the water gleamed as though polished where it flowed smoothly, crossed with the dark shadows of willows which leaned over it. By the bridge, where the breeze rushed through the arches, a ripple flashed back the golden rays. The surface by the shore slipped towards a side hatch and passed over in a liquid curve, clear and unvarying, as if of solid crystal, till shattered on the stones, where the air caught up and played with the sound of the bubbles as they broke.

Beyond the green slope of corn, a thin, soft vapour hung on the distant woods, and hid the hills. The pale young leaves of the aspen rustled faintly, not yet with their full sound; the sprays of the horse-chestnut, drooping with the late frosts, could not yet keep out the sunshine with their broad green. A white spot on the footpath yonder was where the bloom had fallen from a blackthorn bush.

The note of the tree-pipit came from over the corn – there were some detached oaks away in the midst of the field, and the birds were doubtless flying continually up and down between the wheat and the branches. A willow-wren sang plaintively in the plantation behind, and once a cuckoo called at a distance. How beautiful is the sunshine! The very dust of the road at my feet seemed to glow with whiteness, to be lit up by it, and to become another thing. This spot henceforward was a place of pilgrimage.

Looking that morning over the parapet of the bridge, down stream, there was a dead branch at the mouth of the arch, it had caught and got fixed while it floated along. A quantity of aquatic weeds coming down the stream had drifted against the branch and remained entangled in it. Fresh weeds were still coming and adding to the mass, which had attracted a water-rat.

Perched on the branch the little brown creature bent forward over the surface, and with its two forepaws drew towards it the slender thread of a weed, exactly as with hands. Holding the thread in the paws, it nibbled it, eating the sweet and tender portion, feeding without fear though but a few feet away, and precisely beneath me.

In a minute the surface of the current was disturbed by larger ripples. There had been a ripple caused by the draught through the arch, but this was now increased. Directly afterwards a moorhen swam out, and began to search among the edge of the tangled weeds. So long as I was perfectly still the bird took no heed, but at a slight movement instantly scuttled back under the arch. The water-rat, less timorous, paused, looked round, and returned to feeding.

Crossing to the other side of the bridge, up stream, and looking over, the current had scooped away the sand of the bottom by the central pier, exposing the brickwork to some depth – the same undermining process that goes on by the piers of bridges over great rivers. Nearer the shore the sand has silted up, leaving it shallow, where water-parsnip and other weeds joined, as it were, the verge of the grass and the stream. The sunshine reflected from the ripples on this, the southern side, continually ran with a swift, trembling motion up the arch.

Penetrating the clear water, the light revealed the tiniest stone at the bottom: but there was no fish, no water-rat, or moorhen on this side. Neither on that nor many succeeding mornings could anything be seen there; the tail of the arch was evidently the favourite spot. Carefully looking over that side again, the moorhen who had been out rushed back; the water-rat was gone. Were there any fish? In the shadow the water was difficult to see through, and the brown scum of spring that lined the bottom rendered everything uncertain.

By gazing steadily at a stone my eyes presently became accustomed to the peculiar light, the pupils adjusted themselves to it, and the brown tints became more distinctly defined. Then sweeping by degrees from a stone to another, and from thence to a rotting stick embedded in the sand, I searched the bottom inch by inch. If you look, as it were at large – at everything at once – you see nothing. If you take some object as a fixed point, gaze all around it, and then move to another, nothing can escape.

Even the deepest, darkest water (not, of course, muddy) yields after a while to the eye. Half close the eyelids, and while gazing into it let your intelligence rather wait upon the corners of the eye than on the glance you cast straight forward. For some reason when thus gazing the edge of the eye becomes exceedingly sensitive, and you are conscious of slight motions or of a thickness – not a defined object, but a thickness which indicates an object – which is otherwise quite invisible.

The slow feeling sway of a fish's tail, the edges of which curl over and grasp the water, may in this manner be identified without being positively seen, and the dark outline of its body known to exist against the equally dark water or bank. Shift, too, your position according to the fall of the light, just as in looking at a painting. From one point of view the canvas shows little but the presence of paint and blurred colour, from another at the side the picture stands out.

Sometimes the water can be seen into best from above, sometimes by lying on the sward, now by standing back a little way, or crossing to the opposite shore. A spot where the sunshine sparkles with dazzling gleam is perhaps perfectly inpenetrable till you get the other side of the ripple, when the same rays that just now baffled the glance light up the bottom as if thrown from a mirror for the purpose. I convinced myself that there was nothing here, nothing visible at present – not so much as a stickleback.

Yet the stream ran clear and sweet, and deep in places. It was too broad for leaping over. Down the current sedges grew thickly at a curve; up the stream the young flags were rising; it had an inhabited look, if such a term may be used, and moor-hens and water-rats were about but no fish. A wide furrow came along the meadow and joined the stream from the side. Into this furrow, at flood time, the stream overflowed farther up, and irritated the level sward.

At present it was dry, its course, traced by the yellowish and white hue of the grasses in it only recently under water, contrasting with the brilliant green of the sweet turf around. There was a marsh marigold in it, with stems a quarter of an inch thick; and in the grass on the verge, but just beyond where the flood reached, grew the lilac-tinted cuckoo flowers, or cardamine.

The side hatch supplied a pond, which was only divided from the brook by a strip of sward not more than twenty yards across. The surface of the pond was dotted with patches of scum that had risen from the bottom. Part at least of it was shallow, for a dead branch blown from an elm projected above the water, and to it came a sedge-reedling for a moment. The sedge-reedling is so fond of sedges, and reeds, and thick undergrowth, that though you hear it perpetually within a few yards it is not easy to see one. On this bare branch the bird was well displayed, and the streak by the eye was visible; but he stayed there for a second or two only, and then back again to the sedges and willows.

There were fish I felt sure as I left the spot and returned along the dusty road, but where were they?

On the sward by the wayside, among the nettles and under the bushes, and on the mound the dark green arum leaves grew everywhere, sometimes in bunches close together. These bunches varied – in one place the leaves were all spotted with black irregular blotches; in another the leaves were without such markings. When the root leaves of the arum first push up they are closely rolled together in a pointed spike.

This, rising among the dead and matted leaves of the autumn, occasionally passes through holes in them. As the spike grows it lifts the dead leaves with it, which hold it like a ring and prevent it from unfolding. The force of growth is not sufficiently strong to burst the bond asunder till the green leaves have attained considerable size.

A little earlier in the year the chattering of magpies would have been heard while looking for the signs of spring, but they were now occupied with their nests. There are several within a short distance, easily distinguished in winter, but somewhat hidden now by the young leaves. Just before they settled down to housekeeping there was a great chattering and fluttering and excitement, as they chased each other from elm to elm.

Four or five were then often in the same field, some in the trees, some on the ground, their white and black showing distinctly on the level brown earth recently harrowed or rolled. On such a surface birds are visible at a distance; but when the blades of the corn begin to reach any height such as alight are concealed. In many districts of the country that might be called wild and lonely, the magpie is almost extinct. Once now and then a pair may be observed, and those who know their haunts can, of course, find them, but to a visitor passing through, there seems none. But here, so near the metropolis, the magpies are common, and during an hour's walk their cry is almost sure to be heard. They have, however, their favourite locality, where they are much more frequently seen.

Coming to my seat under the aspen by the bridge week after week, the burdocks by the wayside gradually spread their leaves, and the procession of the flowers went on. The dandelion, the lesser celandine, the marsh marigold, the coltsfoot, all yellow, had already led the van, closely accompanied by the purple ground-ivy, the red dead-nettle, and the daisy; this last a late comer in the neighbourhood. The blackthorns, the horse-chestnut, and the hawthorn came, and the meadows were golden with the buttercups.

Once only had I noticed any indication of fish in the brook; it was on a warm Saturday afternoon, when there was a labourer a long way up the stream, stooping in a peculiar manner near the edge of the water with a stick in his hand. He was, I felt sure, trying to wire a spawning jack, but did not succeed. Many weeks had passed, and now there came (as the close time for coarse fish expired) a concourse of anglers to the almost stagnant pond fed by the side hatch.

Well-dressed lads with elegant and finished tackle rode up on their bicycles, with their rods slung at their backs. Hoisting the bicycles over the gate into the meadow, they left them leaning against the elms, fitted their rods and fished in the pond. Poorer boys, with long wands cut from the hedge and ruder lines, trudged up on foot, sat down on the sward and watched their corks by the hour together. Grown men of the artisan class, covered with the dust of many miles' tramping, came with their luncheons in a handkerchief, and set about their sport with a quiet earnestness which argued long if desultory practice.

In fine weather there were often a dozen youths and four or five men standing, sitting, or kneeling on the turf along the shore of the pond, all intent on their floats, and very nearly silent. People driving along the highway stopped their traps, and carts, and vans a minute or two to watch them: passengers on foot leaned over the gate, or sat down and waited expectantly.

Sometimes one of the more venturesome anglers would tuck up his trousers and walk into the shallow water, so as to be able to cast his bait under the opposite bank, where it was deep. Then an ancient and much battered punt was discovered aground in a field at some distance, and dragged to the pond. One end of the punt had quite rotted away, but by standing at the other, so as to depress it there and lift the open end above the surface, two, or even three, could make a shift to fish from it.

The silent and motionless eagerness with which these anglers dwelt upon their floats, grave as herons, could not have been exceeded. There they were day after day, always patient and always hopeful. Occasionally a small catch – a mere 'bait' – was handed round for inspection; and once a cunning fisherman, acquainted with all the secrets of his craft, succeeded in drawing forth three perch, perhaps a quarter of a pound each, and one slender eel. These made quite a show, and were greatly admired; but I never saw the same man there again. He was satisfied.

As I sat on the white rail under the aspen, and inhaled the scent of the beans flowering hard by, there was a question which suggested itself to me, and the answer to which I never could supply. The crowd about the pond all stood with their backs to the beautiful flowing brook. They had before them the muddy banks of the stagnant pool, on whose surface patches of scum floated.

Behind them was the delicious stream, clear, and limpid, bordered with sedge and willow and flags, and overhung with branches. The strip of sward between the two waters was certainly not more than twenty yards; there was no division hedge, or railing, and evidently no preservation, for the mouchers came and washed their watercress which they had gathered in the ditches by the side hatch, and no one interfered with them.

There was no keeper or water bailiff, not even a notice board. Policemen, on foot and mounted, passed several times daily, and, like everybody else, paused to see the sport, but said not a word. Clearly, there was nothing whatever to prevent any of those present from angling in the stream; yet they one and all, without exception, fished in the pond. This seemed to me a very remarkable fact.

After a while I noticed another circumstance; nobody ever even looked into the stream or under the arches of the bridge. No one spared a moment from his float amid the scum of the pond, just to stroll twenty paces and glance at the swift current. It appeared from this that the pond had a reputation for fish, and the brook had not. Everybody who had angled in the pond recommended his friends to go and do likewise. There were fish in the pond.

So every fresh comer went and angled there, and accepted the fact that there were fish. Thus the pond obtained a traditionary reputation, which circulated from lip to lip round about. I need not enlarge on the analogy that exists in this respect between the pond and various other things.

By implication it was evidently as much understood and accepted on the other hand that there was nothing in the stream. Thus I reasoned it out, sitting under the aspen, and yet somehow the general opinion did not satisfy me. There must be something in so sweet a stream. The sedges by the shore, the flags in the shallow slowly swaying from side to side with the current, the sedge-reedlings calling, the moorhens and water-rats, all gave an air of habitation.

One morning, looking very gently over the parapet of the bridge (down stream) into the shadowy depth beneath, just as my eyes began to see the bottom, something like a short thick dark stick drifted out from the arch, somewhat sideways. Instead of proceeding with the current, it had hardly cleared the arch when it took a position parallel to the flowing water and brought up. It was thickest at the end that faced the stream; at the other there was a slight motion as if caused by the current against a flexible membrane, as it sways a flag. Gazing down intently into the shadow the colour of the sides of the fish appeared at first not exactly uniform, and presently these indistinct differences resolved themselves into spots. It was a trout, perhaps a pound and a half in weight.

His position was at the side of the arch, out of the rush of the current, and almost behind the pier, but where he could see anything that came floating along under the culvert. Immediately above him but not over was the mass of weeds tangled in the dead branch. Thus in the shadow of the bridge and in the darkness under the weeds he might easily have escaped notice. He was, too, extremely wary. The slightest motion was enough to send him instantly under the arch; his cover was but a foot distant, and a trout shoots twelve inches in a fraction of time.

The summer advanced, the hay was carted, and the wheat ripened. Already here and there the reapers had cut portions of the more forward corn. As I sat from time to time under the aspen, within hearing of the murmuring water, the thought did rise occasionally that it was a pity to leave the trout there till some one blundered into the knowledge of his existence.

There were ways and means by which he could be withdrawn without any noise or publicity. But, then, what would be the pleasure of securing him, the fleeting pleasure of an hour, compared to the delight of seeing him almost day by day? I watched him for many weeks, taking great precautions that no one should observe how continually I looked over into the water there. Sometimes after a glance I stood with my back to the wall as if regarding an object on the other side. If any one was following me, or appeared likely to peer over the parapet, I carelessly struck the top of the wall with my stick in such a manner that it should project, an action sufficient to send the fish under the arch. Or I raised my hat as if heated, and swung it so that it should alarm him.

If the coast was clear when I had looked at him still I never left without sending him under the arch in order to increase his alertness. It was a relief to know that so many persons who went by wore tall hats, a safeguard against their seeing anything, for if they approached the shadow of the tall hat reached out beyond the shadow of the parapet, and was enough to alarm him before they could look over. So the summer passed, and, though never free from apprehensions, to my great pleasure without discovery.

The sword-flags are rusting at their edges, and their sharp points are turned. On the matted and entangled sedges lie the scattered leaves which every rush of the October wind hurries from the boughs. Some fall on the water and float slowly with the current, brown and yellow spots on the dark surface. The grey willows bend to the breeze; soon the osier beds will look reddish as the wands are stripped by the gusts. Alone the thick polled alders remain green, and in their shadow the brook is still darker. Through a poplar's thin branches the wind sounds as in the rigging of a ship; for the rest, it is silence.

The thrushes have not forgotten the frost of the morning, and will not sing at noon; the summer visitors have flown and the moorhens feed quietly. The plantation by the brook is silent, for the sedges, though they have drooped and become entangled, are not dry and sapless yet to rustle loudly. They will rustle dry enough next spring, when the sedge-birds come. A long withey-bed borders the brook and is more resorted to by sedge-reedlings, or sedge-birds, as they are variously called, than any place I know, even in the remotest country.

Generally it has been difficult to see them, because the withey is in leaf when they come, and the leaves and sheaves of innumerable rods hide them, while the ground beneath is covered by a thick growth of sedges and flags, to which the birds descend. It happened once, however, that the withey stoles had been polled, and in the spring the boughs were short and small. At the same time, the easterly winds checked the sedges, so that they were hardly half their height, and the flags were thin, and not much taller, when the sedge-birds came, so that they for once found but little cover, and could be seen to advantage.

There could not have been less than fifteen in the plantation, two frequented some bushes beside a pond near by, some stayed in scattered willows farther down the stream. They sang so much they scarcely seemed to have time to feed. While approaching one that was singing by gently walking on the sward by the roadside, or where thick dust deadened the footsteps, suddenly another would commence in the low thorn hedge on a branch, so near that it could be touched with a walking-stick. Yet though so near the bird was not wholly visible – he was partly concealed behind a fork of the bough. This is a habit of the sedge-birds. Not in the least timid, they chatter at your elbow, and yet always partially hidden.

If in the withey, they choose a spot where the rods cross or bunch together. If in the sedges, though so close it seems as if you could reach forward and catch him, he is behind the stalks. To place some obstruction between themselves and any one passing is their custom; but that spring, as the foliage was so thin, it only needed a little dexterity in peering to get a view. The sedge-bird perches aside, on a sloping willow rod, and, slightly raising his head, chatters, turning his bill from side to side. He is a very tiny bird, and his little eye looks out from under a yellowish streak. His song at first sounds nothing but chatter.

After listening a while the ear finds a scale in it – an arrangement and composition – so that, though still a chatter, it is a

tasteful one. At intervals he intersperses a chirp, exactly the
same as that of the sparrow, a chirp with a tang in it. Strike a
piece of metal, and besides the noise of the blow, there is a
second note, or tang. The sparrow's chirp has such a note
sometimes, and the sedge-bird brings it in – tang, tang, tang.
This sound has given him his country name of brook-sparrow,
and it rather spoils his song. Often the moment he has concluded he starts for another willow stole, and as he flies begins
to chatter when halfway across, and finishes on a fresh branch.

But long before this another bird has commenced to sing in
a bush adjacent; a third takes it up in the thorn hedge; a fourth
in the bushes across the pond; and from farther down the
stream comes a faint and distant chatter. Ceaselessly the competing gossip goes on the entire day and most of the night;
indeed, sometimes all night through. On a warm spring morning, when the sunshine pours upon the willows, and even the
white dust of the road is brighter, bringing out the shadows in
clear definition, their lively notes and quick motions make a
pleasant commentary on the low sound of the stream rolling
round the curve.

A moorhen's call comes from the hatch. Broad yellow petals
of marsh-marigold stand up high among the sedges rising from
the greyish-green ground, which is covered with a film of
sun-dried aquatic grass left dry by the retiring waters. Here and
there are lilac-tinted cuckoo-flowers, drawn up on taller stalks
than those that grow in the meadows. The black flowers of the
sedges are powdered with yellow pollen; and dark green
sword-flags are beginning to spread their fans. But just across
the road, on the topmost twigs of birch poles, swallows twitter
in the tenderest tones to their loves. From the oaks in the meadows on that side titlarks mount above the highest bough and
then descend, sing, sing, singing, to the grass.

A jay calls in a circular copse in the midst of the meadow;
solitary rooks go over to their nests in the elms on the hill;
cuckoos call, now this way and now that, as they travel round.
While leaning on the grey and lichen-hung rails by the brook,
the current glides by, and it is the motion of the water and its
low murmur which renders the place so idle; the sunbeams

brood, the air is still but full of song. Let us, too, stay and watch the petals fall one by one from a wild apple and float down on the stream.

But now in autumn the haws are red on the thorn, the swallows are few as they were in the earliest spring; the sedge-birds have flown, and the redwings will soon be here. The sharp points of the sword-flags are turned, their edges rusty, the forget-me-nots are gone. October's winds are too searching for us to linger beside the brook, but still it is pleasant to pass by and remember the summer days. For the year is never gone by; in a moment we can recall the sunshine we enjoyed in May, the roses we gathered in June, the first wheatear we plucked as the green corn filled. Other events go by and are forgotten, and even the details of our own lives, so immensely important to us at the moment, in time fade from the memory till the date we fancied we should never forget has to be sought in a diary. But the year is always with us; the months are familiar always; they have never gone by.

So with the red haws around and the rustling leaves it is easy to recall the flowers. The withey plantation here is full of flowers in summer; yellow iris flowers in June when midsummer comes, for the iris loves a thunder-shower. The flowering flag spreads like a fan from the root, the edges overlap near the ground, and the leaves are broad as sword-blades, indeed the plant is one of the largest that grows wild. It is quite different from the common flag with three grooves – bayonet shape – which appears in every brook. The yellow iris is much more local, and in many country streams may be sought for in vain, so that so fine a display as may be seen here seemed almost a discovery to me.

They were finest in the year of rain, 1879, that terrible year which is fresh in the memory of all who have any interest in out-of-door matters. At midsummer the plantation was aglow with iris bloom. The large yellow petals were everywhere high above the sedge; in one place a dozen, then two or three, then one by itself, then another bunch. The marsh was a foot deep in water, which could only be seen by parting the stalks of the sedges, for it was quite hidden under them. Sedges and flags grew so thick that everything was concealed except the yellow bloom above.

One bunch grew on a bank raised a few inches above the flood which the swollen brook had poured in, and there I walked among them; the leaves came nearly up to the shoulder, the golden flowers on the stalks stood equally high. It was a thicket of iris. Never before had they risen to such a height; it was like the vegetation of tropical swamps, so much was everything drawn up by the continual moisture. Who could have supposed that such a downpour as occurred that summer would have had the effect it had upon flowers? Most would have imagined that the excessive rain would have destroyed them; yet never was there such floral beauty as that year. Meadow-orchis, buttercups, the yellow iris, all the spring flowers came forth in extraordinary profusion. The hay was spoiled, the farmers ruined, but their fields were one broad expanse of flower.

As that spring was one of the wettest, so that of the year in present view was one of the driest, and hence the plantation between the lane and the brook was accessible, the sedges and flags short, and the sedge-birds visible. There is a beech in the plantation standing so near the verge of the stream that its boughs droop over. It has a number of twigs around the stem – as a rule the beech-bole is clear of boughs, but some which are of rather stunted growth are fringed with them. The leaves on the longer boughs above fall off and voyage down the brook, but those on the lesser twigs beneath, and only a little way from the ground, remain on, and rustle, dry and brown, all through the winter.

Under the shelter of these leaves, and close to the trunk, there grew a plant of flag – the tops of the flags almost reached to the leaves – and all the winter through, despite the frosts for which it was remarkable, despite the snow and the bitter winds which followed, this plant remained green and fresh. From this beech in the morning a shadow stretches to a bridge across the brook, and in that shadow my trout used to lie. The bank under the drooping boughs forms a tiny cliff a foot high, covered with moss, and here I once observed shrew mice diving and racing about. But only once, though I frequently passed the spot; it is curious that I did not see them afterwards.

Just below the shadow of the beech there is a sandy, oozy shore, where the footprints of moorhens are often traceable. Many of the trees of the plantation stand in water after heavy rain; their leaves drop into it in autumn, and, being away from the influence of the current, stay and soak, and lie several layers thick. Their edges overlap, red, brown, and pale yellow, with the clear water above and shadows athwart it, and dry white grass at the verge. A horse-chestnut drops its fruit in the dusty road; high above its leaves are tinted with scarlet.

It was at the tail of one of the arches of the bridge over the brook that my favourite trout used to lie. Sometimes the shadow of the beech came as far as his haunts, that was early in the morning, and for the rest of the day the bridge itself cast a shadow. The other parapet faces the south, and looking down from it the bottom of the brook is generally visible, because the light is so strong. At the bottom a green plant may be seen waving to and fro in summer as the current sways it. It is not a weed or flag, but a plant with pale green leaves, and looks as if it had come there by some chance; this is the water-parsnip.

By the shore on this, the sunny side of the bridge, a few forget-me-nots grow in their season, water crow's-foot flowers, flags lie along the surface and slowly swing from side to side like a boat at anchor. The breeze brings a ripple, and the sunlight sparkles on it; the light reflected dances up the piers of the bridge. Those that pass along the road are naturally drawn to this bright parapet where the brook winds brimming full through green meadows. You can see right to the bottom; you can see where the rush of the water has scooped out a deeper channel under the arches, but look as long as you like there are no fish.

The trout I watched so long, and with such pleasure, was always on the other side, at the tail of the arch, waiting for whatever might come through to him. There in perpetual shadow he lay in wait, a little at the side of the arch, scarcely ever varying his position except to dart a yard up under the bridge to seize anything he fancied, and drifting out again to bring up at his anchorage. If people looked over the parapet that side they did not see him; they could not see the bottom there for the shadow, or if the summer noonday cast a strong beam even then it seemed to cover the surface of the water with a film of light which could not be seen through. There are some aspects from which even a picture hung on the wall close at hand cannot be seen. So no one saw the trout; if any one more curious leant over the parapet he was gone in a moment under the arch.

Folk fished in the pond about the verge of which the sedge-birds chattered, and but a few yards distant; but they never looked under the arch on the northern and shadowy side, where the water flowed beside the beech. For three seasons this continued. For three summers I had the pleasure to see the trout day after day whenever I walked that way, and all that time, with fishermen close at hand, he escaped notice, though the place was not preserved. It is wonderful to think how difficult it is to see anything under one's very eyes, and thousands of people walked actually and physically right over the fish.

However, one morning in the third summer, I found a fisherman standing in the road and fishing over the parapet in the shadowy water. But he was fishing at the wrong arch, and only with paste for roach. While the man stood there fishing, along came two navvies; naturally enough they went quietly up to see what the fisherman was doing, and one instantly uttered an exclamation. He had seen the trout. The man who was fishing with paste had stood so still and patient that the trout, reassured, had come out, and the navvy – trust a navvy to see anything of the kind – caught sight of him.

The navvy knew how to see through water. He told the fisherman, and there was a stir of excitement, a changing of hooks and bait. I could not stay to see the result, but went on, fearing the worst. But he did not succeed; next day the wary trout was there still, and the next, and the next. Either this particular fisherman was not able to come again, or was discouraged; at any rate, he did not try again. The fish escaped, doubtless more wary than ever.

In the spring of the next year the trout was still there, and up to the summer I used to go and glance at him. This was the fourth season, and still he was there; I took friends to look at this wonderful fish, which defied all the loafers and poachers, and above all, surrounded himself not only with the shadow of the bridge, but threw a mental shadow over the minds of passers-by, so that they never thought of the possibility of such a thing as trout. But one morning something happened. The brook was dammed up on the sunny side of the bridge, and the water let off by a side hatch, that some accursed main or pipe or other horror might be laid across the bed of the stream somewhere far down.

Above the bridge there was a brimming broad brook, below it the flags lay on the mud, the weeds drooped, and the channel was dry. It was dry up to the beech tree. There, under the drooping boughs of the beech, was a small pool of muddy water, perhaps two yards long, and very narrow – a stagnant muddy pool, not more than three or four inches deep. In this I saw the trout. In the shallow water, his back came up to the surface (for his fins must have touched the mud sometimes) – once it came above the surface, and his spots showed as plain as if you had held him in your hand. He was swimming round to try and find out the reason of this sudden stinting of room.

Twice he heaved himself somewhat on his side over a dead branch that was at the bottom, and exhibited all his beauty to the air and sunshine. Then he went away into another part of the shallow and was hidden by the muddy water. Now under the arch of the bridge, his favourite arch, close by there was a deep pool, for, as already mentioned, the scour of the current scooped away the sand and made a hole there. When the stream was shut off by the dam above this hole remained partly full. Between this pool and the shallow under the beech there was sufficient connection for the fish to move into it.

My only hope was that he would do so, and as some showers fell, temporarily increasing the depth of the narrow canal between the two pools, there seemed every reason to believe that he had got to that under the arch. If now only that accursed pipe or main, or whatever repair it was, could only be finished quickly, even now the trout might escape! Every day my anxiety increased, for the intelligence would soon get about that the brook was dammed up, and any pools left in it would be sure to attract attention.

Sunday came, and directly the bells had done ringing four men attacked the pool under the arch. They took off shoes and stockings and waded in, two at each end of the arch. Stuck in the mud close by was an eel-spear. They churned up the mud, wading in, and thickened and darkened it as they groped under. No one could watch these barbarians longer.

Is it possible that he could have escaped? He was a wonderful fish, wary and quick. Is it just possible that they may not even have known that a trout was there at all; but have merely hoped for perch, or tench, or eels? The pool was deep and the fish quick – they did not bale it, might he have escaped? Might they even, if they did find him, have mercifully taken him and placed him alive in some other water nearer their homes? Is it possible that he may have almost miraculously made his way down the stream into other pools?

There was very heavy rain one night, which might have given him such a chance. These 'mights', and 'ifs', and 'is it possible' even now keep alive some little hope that some day I may yet see him again. But that was in the early summer. It is now winter, and the beech has brown spots. Among the limes the sedges are matted and entangled, the sword-flags rusty; the rooks are at the acorns, and the plough is at work in the stubble. I have never seen him since. I never failed to glance over the parapet into the shadowy water. Somehow it seemed to look colder, darker, less pleasant than it used to do. The spot was empty, and the shrill winds whistled through the poplars.

Mind Under Water

First published in *Graphic*, 19 May 1883
First collected in *The Life of the Fields*, 1884

The thud, thud of a horse's hoof does not alarm fish. Basking
in the sun under the bank, a jack or pike lying close to the surface of the water will remain unmoved, however heavy the
sound may be. The vibrations reach the fish in several ways.
There is what we should ourselves call the noise as conveyed by
the air, and which in the case of a jack actually at the surface
may be supposed to reach him direct. Next there is the vibration passing through the water, which is usually pronounced to
be a good medium. Lastly, there is the bodily movement of the
substance of the water. When the bank is hard and dry this latter amounts only to a slight shaking, but it frequently happens
that the side of a brook or pond is soft, and 'gives' under a
heavy weight. Sometimes the edge is even pushed into the
water, and the brook in a manner squeezed. You can see this
when cattle walk by the margin; the grassy edge is pushed out,
and in a minute way they may be said to contract the stream. It
is in too small a degree to have the least apparent effect upon
the water, but it is different with the sense of hearing, which is
so delicate that the bodily movement thus caused may be reasonably believed to be very audible indeed to the jack. The wire
fences which are now so much used round shrubberies and
across parks give a very good illustration of the conveyance of
sound. Strung tight by a spanner, the strands of twisted wire
resemble a stringed instrument. If you place your hand on one
of the wires and get a friend to strike it with his stick, say, thirty
or forty yards away, you will distinctly feel it vibrate. If the ear
is held close enough you will hear it, vibration and sound being
practically convertible terms. To the basking jack three such

wires extend, and when the cart-horse in the meadow puts down his heavy hoof he strikes them all at once. Yet, though fish are so sensitive to sound, the jack is not in the least alarmed, and there can be little doubt that he knows what it is. A whole herd of cattle feeding and walking about does not disturb him, but if the light step – light in comparison – of a man approach, away he goes. Poachers, therefore, unable to disguise their footsteps, endeavour to conceal them, and by moving slowly to avoid vibrating the earth, and through it the water.

In poaching, the intelligence of the man is backed against the intelligence of the fish or animal, and the poacher tries to get himself into the ways of the creature he means to snare. That is what really takes place as seen by us as lookers-on; to the poacher himself, in nine out of ten cases, it is merely an acquired knack learned from watching others, and improved by practice. But to us, as lookers-on, this is what occurs: the man fits himself to the ways of the creature, and for the time it becomes a struggle between them. It is the same with the Red Indians, and the white trappers and hunters in wild regions, who depend much more on their knowledge of the ways and habits of the fur-bearing animals than upon their skill with the rifle. A man may be an excellent shot with gun or rifle, and yet be quite incapable of coping on comparatively equal terms with wild creatures. He is a sportsman, depending on skill, quick sight, and ready hand – not a hunter. Perhaps the nearest approach to it in legitimate English sport is in fly-fishing and salmon fishing, when the sportsman relies upon his own unassisted efforts. Deer-stalking, where the sportsman has to reckon on the wind, and its curious twists and turns in valleys and round rocks, would be a very near approach to it did the stalker stalk alone. But all this work is usually done for him by an attendant, a native Highlander; and this man really does pit his intelligence against that of the stag. The Highlander actually is a Red Indian, or hunter, and in this sense struggles with the wild animal. The poacher is the hunter on illegitimate ground, and with arts which it has been mutually agreed shall not be employed.

Considered in this sense it is interesting to observe to what extent the intelligence even of a fish reaches – and I think upon reflection it will be found that the fish is as clever as any creature could be in its position. I deny altogether that the cold-blooded fish – looked on with contempt so far as its intellectual powers are concerned – is stupid, or slow to learn. On the contrary, fish are remarkably quick, not only under natural conditions, but quick at accommodating themselves to altered circumstances which they could not foresee, and the knowledge how to meet which could not have been inherited. The basking jack is not alarmed at the cart-horse's hoofs, but remains quiet, let them come down with ever so heavy a thud. He has observed that these vibrations never cause him any injury. He hears them at all periods of the day and night, often with long intervals of silence and with every possible vibration. Never once has the sound been followed by injury or by anything to disturb his peace. So the rooks have observed that passing trains are harmless, and will perch on the telegraph wires or poles over the steam of the roaring locomotive. Observation has given them confidence. Thunder of wheels and immense weight in motion, the open furnace and glaring light, the faces at the long tier of windows – all these terrors do not ruffle a feather. A little boy with a wooden clapper can set a flock in retreat immediately. Now the rooks could not have acquired this confidence in the course of innumerable generations; it is not hereditary; it is purely what we understand by intelligence. Why are the rooks afraid of the little boy with the clapper? Because they have noticed his hostile intent. Why is the basking jack off the instant he hears the light step of a man?

He has observed that after this step there have often followed attempts to injure him; a stone has been flung at him, a long pole thrust into the water; he has been shot at, or felt the pinch of a wire. He remembers this, and does not wait for the attempt to be repeated, but puts himself into safety. If he did not realize that it was a man – and a possible enemy – he would not trouble. The object consequently of the tricks of the poacher is to obliterate himself. If you can contrive to so move, and to so conduct yourself that the fish shall not recognize you as his enemy, you can do much as you please with him, and in varying degrees it is the same with animals. Think a moment by what tokens a fish recognizes a man. First, his light, and, compared with other animals, brisk step – a two-step instead of a four-step, remember; two feet, not four hoofs. There is a difference at once in the rhythm of the noise. Four hoofs can by no possibility produce the same sound, or succession of sounds, as is made even by four feet – that is, by two men. The beats are not the same. Secondly, by his motions, and especially the brisk motions of the arms. Thirdly, by this briskness itself; for most animals, except man, move with a slow motion – paradox as it may seem – even when they are going along fast. With them it is usually repose in action. Fourthly – and this is rather curious – experience seems to show that fish, and animals and birds certainly, recognize man by his hat or cap, to which they have a species of superstitious dislike.

Hats are generally of a different hue to the rest of the suit, for one thing; and it was noted, a century ago, that wild creatures have a particular objection to a black hat. A covering to the head at all is so opposite to their own ideas that it arouses suspicion, for we must remember that animals look on our clothes as our skin. To have a black skin over the hair of the head is somewhat odd. By all these signs a fish knows a man immediately, and as certainly as any creature moving on land would know him. There is no instinctive or hereditary fear of man at all – it is acquired by observation (which a thousand facts demonstrate); so that we are quite justified in believing that a fish really does notice some or all of these attributes of its enemy. What the poacher or wild hunter has to do is to conceal these attributes. To hide the two-step, he walks as slowly as possible, not putting the foot down hard, but feeling the ground first, and gradually pressing it. In this way progress may be made without vibration. The earth is not shaken, and does not communicate the sound to the water. This will bring him to the verge of the place where the fish is basking.

Very probably not only fish, but animals and some birds hear as much by the vibration of the earth as by the sound travelling in the atmosphere, and depend as much upon their immediate perception of the slightest tremor of the earth as upon recognition by the ear in the manner familiar to ourselves. When rabbits, for instance, are out feeding in the grass, it is often possible to get quite close to them by walking in this way, extremely slowly, and carefully placing the foot by slow degrees upon the ground. The earth is then merely pressed, and not stepped upon at all, so that there is no jar. By doing this I have often moved up within gunshot of rabbits without the least aid from cover. Once now and then I have walked across a field straight at them. Something, however, depends on the direction of the wind, for then the question of scent comes in. To some degree it is the same with hares. It is certainly the case with birds, as wood-pigeons, a flock of them, will remain feeding only just the other side of the hedge; but, if you stamp the earth, will rise instantly. So will rooks, though they will not fly far if you are not armed. Partridges certainly secure themselves by their attention to the faint tremor of the ground. Pheasants do so too, and make off, running through the underwood long before any one is in sight. The most sensitive are landrails, and it is difficult to get near them, for this reason. Though the mowing-grass must conceal an approaching person from them as it conceals them from him, these birds change their positions, no matter how quietly he walks. Let him be as cunning as he will, and think to cut off corners and cross the landrail's retreat, the bird baffles him nine times in ten. That it is advised of the direction the pursuer takes by the vibration of the surface is at least probable. Other birds sit, and hope to escape by remaining still, till they detect the tremor coming direct towards them, when they rise.

Rain and dry weather change the susceptibility of the surface to vibrate, and may sometimes in part account for the wildness or apparent tameness of birds and animals. Should any one doubt the existence of such tremors, he has only to lie on the ground with his ear near the surface; but, being unused to the experiment, he will at first only notice the heavier sounds, as of a waggon or a cart-horse. In recent experiments with most delicate instruments devised to show the cosmic vibration of the earth, the movements communicated to it by the tides, or by the 'pull' of the sun and moon, it has been found almost impossible as yet to carry out the object, so greatly are these movements obscured by the ceaseless and inexplicable vibrations of the solid earth. There is nothing unreasonable in the supposition that, if an instrument can be constructed to show these, the ears of animals and birds – living organisms, and not iron and steel – should be able to discover the tremors of the surface.

The wild hunter can still further check or altogether prevent observation by moving on hands and knees, when his weight is widely distributed. In the particular instance of a fish he endeavours to come to the margin of the water at the rear of the fish, whose eyes are so placed that it can see best in front. When he has arrived at the margin, and has to rear himself up, if from hands and knees, or, if already upright, when he commences his work, he tries to conceal his arms, or, rather, to minimize their peculiar appearance as much as practicable by keeping them close to his sides. All this time I am supposing that you are looking at the poacher from the fish. To a fish or any wild animal the arms of a man are suspicious. No other creature that they know possesses these singular appurtenances, which move in almost any direction, and yet have nothing to do with locomotion. You may be sure that this great difference in the anatomical construction of a man is recognized by all wild animals once they are compelled for their own safety to observe him. Arms are so entirely opposite to all the varieties of limb possessed by the varieties of living creatures.

Can you put yourselves in the position of either of these creatures – moving on all-fours, on wings, or by the aid of a membraneous tail and fins, and without arms, and imagine how strange the arms of a man must look? Suppose yourself with your arms tucked to your sides under the fur of an animal; something of the idea may be gathered by putting on a cloak without sleeves or armholes. At once it will be apparent how helpless all creatures are in comparison with man. It is true that apes are an exception; yet their arms are also legs, and they are deficient in the power of the thumb. Man may be defined as an animal with arms. While the creatures of the field or the water have no cause to fear him they do not observe him, but the moment they learn that he is bent on their destruction they watch him narrowly, and his arms are, above all, the part which alarms them. To them these limbs are men's weapons – his tusks, and tusks which strike and wound afar. From these proceed an invisible force which can destroy where it would seem the intervening distance alone would afford safety. The sharp shot, the keen hook, the lacerating wire, the spear – everything which kills or wounds, comes in some manner or other from the arms, down to the stone or the primitive knobkerrie. Consequently animals, birds, and fishes not only in our own, but in the wildest countries, have learned to watch and to dread man's arms. He raises his arms, and in an instant there shoots forth a bright flash of flame, and before the swift wings can bear the air again the partridge is dashed to the ground.

So long as a gun is carried under the arm – that is, with the arms close to the sides – many birds will let the sportsman approach. Rabbits will do the same. Rabbits have one advantage (and perhaps only one): being numerous and feeding out by daylight, all kinds of experiments can be tried on them, while hares are not so easily managed. Suppose a rabbit feeding, and any one with a gun creeping up beside the hedge, while the gun is kept down and the arms down the rabbit remains still; the instant the arms are lifted to point the gun, up he sits, or off he goes. You have only to point your arm at a rook, without any gun, to frighten him. Bird-keepers instinctively raise their arms above their heads, when shouting, to startle birds. Every creature that has ever watched man knows that his arms are dangerous. The poacher or wild hunter has to conceal his arms by reducing their movements to a minimum, and by conducting those movements as slowly as possible.

To thoroughly appreciate the importance which animals of all kinds put on the motions of the upper limbs, and to put one's self quite in their position, one has only to recall to mind the well-known trick of the Australian bushrangers. 'Bail up!' is their order when they suddenly produce their revolvers; 'Bail up!' they shout to the clerks of the bank they are about to sack, to the inmates of a house, or to the travellers they meet on the road. 'Hold your arms above your head' is the meaning; and, if it is not immediately obeyed, they fire. They know that every man has a pistol in his pocket or belt; but he cannot use it if compelled to keep his arms high over his head. One or more of the band keep a sharp look-out on the upheld arms while the rest plunder; and, if any are lowered – bang! Like the animals, they know the extreme danger to be apprehended from movements of the human arms. So long as the human arms are 'bailed' (though in this case in an opposite direction, i.e. held down), animals are not afraid. Could they make us 'bail up', we should be helpless to injure them. Moving his arms as gently as possible, with the elbows close to his sides, the poacher proceeds to slowly push his rod and wire loop towards the basking jack. If he were going to shoot partridges at roost on the ground, he would raise his gun in an equally slow and careful manner. As a partridge is a small bird, and stands at about a shilling in the poacher's catalogue, he does not care to risk a shot at one, but likes to get several at once. This he can do in the spring, when the birds have paired and remain so near together, and again in the latter part of the summer, when the coveys are large, not having yet been much broken up by the sportsmen. These large coveys, having enjoyed an immunity from disturbance all through the summer, wandering at their own will among clover and corn, are not at all difficult to approach, and a shot at them through a gap in a hedge will often bring down four or five. Later on the poacher takes them at roost. They roost on the ground in a circle, heads outwards, much in the same position as the eggs of a lapwing. The spot is marked; and at night, having crept up near enough, the poacher fires at the spot itself rather than at the birds, with a gun loaded with a moderate charge of powder, but a large quantity of shot, that it may spread wide. On moderately light nights he can succeed at this game. It is in raising the arms to point the gun that the risk of alarming the birds has to be met; and so with a hare sitting in a form in daytime. Lift your arms suddenly, and away she goes; keep your arms still, and close to your side, and she will sit till you have crept up actually to her very side, and can pounce on her if you choose.

Sometimes, where fish have not been disturbed by poachers, or loafers throwing stones and otherwise annoying them, they will not heed a passer-by, whose gentle walk or saunter does not affright them with brisk motion, especially if the saunterer, on espying them, in no degree alters his pace or changes his manner. That wild creatures immediately detect a change of manner, and therefore of mood, any one may demonstrate for himself. They are as quick to see it as the dog, who is always with his master, and knows by the very way he puts a book on the table what temper he is in. When a book goes with a bang on the table the dog creeps under it. Wild creatures, too, catch their manners from man. Walk along a lane with your hands in your pockets, and you will see twice as much of the birds and animals, because they will not set themselves to steadfastly watch you. A quick movement sets wings quickly beating. I have noticed that even horses in stables do not like visitors with jerky, brisk, angular ways of moving. A stranger entering in a quiet, easy manner is not very objectionable, but if he comes in in a bustling, citizen-like style, it is quite probable that one or other horse will show a wicked white corner in his eye. It roughs them up the wrong way. Especially all wild creatures dislike the shuffling, mincing step so common in towns. That alone will disturb everything. Indeed, I have often thought that a good and successful wild hunter – like the backwoodsman, or the sportsman in African bush or Indian jungle – is really made as much by his feet as his eyes or hands. Unconsciously he feels with his feet; they come to know the exact time to move, whether a long or short stride be desirable, and where to put down, not to rustle or cause a cracking sound, and accommodate themselves to the slope of the ground, touching it and holding it like hands. A great many people seem to have no feet; they have boots, but no feet. They stamp or clump, or swing their boots along and knock the ground at every step; this matters not in most callings, but if a man wish to become what I have called a wild hunter, he must let his feet learn. He must walk with hands in his boots. Now and then a person walks like this naturally, and he will come in and tell you that he has seen a fish basking, a partridge, a hare, or what not, when another never gets near anything. This is where they have not been much disturbed by loafers, who are worse than poachers.

As a rule, poachers are intermittent in their action, and they do not want to disturb the game, as it makes it wild and interferes with their profits. Loafers are not intermittent – they are always about, often in gangs, and destroy others' sport without having any themselves. Near large towns there are places where the fish have to be protected with hurdles thrown across the stream on poles, that the stones and brick-bats hurled by every rascal passing may not make their very life a burden. A rural poacher is infinitely preferable. The difference in the ways of fish when they have been much disturbed and when they have been let alone is at once discerned. No sooner do you approach a fish who has been much annoyed and driven than he strikes, and a quick-rotating curl on the surface shows with what vehemence his tail was forced against it. In other places, if a fish perceives you, he gives himself so slight a propulsion that the curl hardly rises, and you can see him gliding slowly into the deeper or overshadowed water. If in terror he would go so quickly as to be almost invisible. In places where the fish have been much disturbed the poacher, or any one who desires to watch their habits, has to move as slowly as the hands of a clock, and even then they will scarcely bear the very sight of a man, sometimes not at all. The least briskness of movement would send them into the depths out of sight. Cattle, to whom they are accustomed, walk slowly, and so do horses left to themselves in the meads by water. The slowest man walking past has quicker, perhaps because shorter, movements than those of cattle and horses, so that, even when bushes intervene and conceal his form, his very ways often proclaim him.

Most people will only grant a moderate degree of intelligence to fish, linking coldness of blood to narrowness of intellect, and convinced that there can be but little brain in so small a compass as its head. That the jack can compete with the dog, of course, is out of the question; but I am by no means prepared to admit that fish are so devoid of sense as supposed. Not long since an experiment was tried with a jack, an account of which appeared in the papers. The jack was in a tank, and after awhile the tank was partly divided by inserting a plate of glass. He was then hunted round, and notes taken of the number of times he bumped his head against the plate of glass, and how long it took him to learn that there was something to obstruct his path. Further statistics were kept as to the length of his memory when he had learnt the existence of the glass – that is, to see if he would recollect it several days afterwards. The fish was some time learning the position of the glass; and then, if much alarmed, he would forget its position and dash against it. But he did learn it, and retained his memory some while. It seems to me that this was a very hard and unfair test. The jack had to acquire the idea of something transparent, and yet hard as wood. A moment's thought will show how exactly opposite the qualities of glass are to anything either this particular fish or his ancestors could have met with – no hereditary intelligence to aid him, no experience bearing, however slightly, upon the subject.

Accustomed all his life to transparent water, he had also been accustomed to find it liquid, and easily parted. Put suddenly face to face with the transparent material which repelled him, what was he to think? Much the same effect would be produced if you or I, having been accustomed, of course, all our lives, to the fluidity of air, which opens for our passage, were opposed by a solid block of transparent atmosphere. Imagine any one running for a train, and striking his head with all his might against such a block. He would rise, shake himself together, and endeavour to pursue his journey, and be again repelled. More than likely he would try three times before he became convinced that it really was something in the air itself which stopped him. Then he would thrust with his stick and feel, more and more astounded every moment, and scarcely able to believe his own senses. During the day, otherwise engaged, he would argue himself into the view that he had made a mistake, and determine to try again, though more cautiously. But so strong is habit that if a cause for alarm arose, and he started running, he might quite probably go with tremendous force up to the solid block of transparent air, to be hurled back as the jack was.

These are no mere suppositions, for quite recently I heard of a case which nearly parallels the conduct of the jack. A messenger was despatched by rail to a shop for certain articles, and was desired to return by a certain time. The parcel was made up, the man took it, heard an engine whistle, turned to run, and in his haste dashed himself right through a plate-glass window into the street. He narrowly escaped decapitation, as the great pieces of glass fell like the knife of a guillotine. Cases of people injuring themselves by walking against plate-glass are by no means uncommon; when the mind is preoccupied it takes much the same place as the plate of glass in the water and the jack. Authorities on mythology state that some Oriental nations had not arrived at the conception of a fluid heaven – of free space; they thought the sky was solid, like a roof. The fish was very much in the same position. The reason why fish swim round and round in tanks, and do not beat themselves against the glass walls, is evidently because they can see where the water ends. A distinction is apparent between it and the air outside; but when the plate of glass was put inside the tank the jack saw water beyond it, or through it. I never see a fish in a tank without remembering this experiment and the long train of reflections it gives rise to. To take a fish from his native brook, and to place him suddenly in the midst of such, to him, inconceivable conditions, is almost like watching the actual creation of mind. His mind has to be created anew to meet it, and that it did ultimately meet the conditions shows that even the fish – the cold-blooded, the narrow-brained – is not confined to the grooves of hereditary knowledge alone, but is capable of wider and novel efforts. I thought the jack came out very well indeed from the trial, and I have mentioned the matter lest some should think I have attributed too much intelligence to fish.

Other creatures besides fish are puzzled by glass. One day I observed a robin trying to get in at the fanlight of a hall door. Repeatedly he struck himself against it, beat it with his wings, and struggled to get through the pane. Possibly there was a spider inside which tempted him; but allowing that temptation, it was remarkable that the robin should so strive in vain. Always about houses, he must have had experience of the properties of glass, and yet forgot it so soon. His ancestors for many generations must have had experience of glass, still it did

not prevent him making many trials. The slowness of the jack
to learn the impenetrable nature of the glass plate and its position is not the least indication of lack of intelligence. In daily
life we constantly see people do things they have observed
injure them, and yet, in spite of experience, go and do the same
again.

The glass experiment proves to me that the jack, like all
other creatures, really has a latent power of intelligence beyond
that brought into play by the usual circumstances of existence.
Consider the conditions under which the jack exists – the jack
we have been approaching so carefully. His limits are the
brook, the ponds it feeds, and the ditches that enter it. He can
only move a short distance up the stream because there is a
high hatch, nor can he go far down because of a mill; if he
could, the conditions would be much the same; but, as a matter
of fact, the space he has at his command is not much. The running water, the green flags, the lesser fishes, the water-rats, the
horses and cattle on the bank – these are about all the things
that he is likely to be interested in. Of these only the water, the
lesser fishes, the flags, and the bottom or sides of the brook, are
actually in his touch and complete understanding. As he is
unable to live out of water, the horse on the bank, in whose
very shadow he sometimes lies, might be a mile away for aught
it concerns him. By no possible means can he discover anything
about it. The horse may be itself nothing more than a shadow,
unless in a shallow place he steps in and splashes. Night and
day he knows, the cool night, and the sunbeams in which he
basks; but he has no way of ascertaining the nature of anything
outside the water. Centuries spent in such conditions could add
but little to his experience.

Does he hear the stream running past him? Do the particles
of water, as they brush his sides and fins, cause a sound, as the
wind by us? While he lurks beneath a weed in the still pool,
suddenly a shoal of roach rush by with a sound like a flock of
birds whose wings beat the air. The smooth surface of the still
water appears to cover an utter silence, but probably to the fish
there are ceaseless sounds. Water-fowl feeding in the weedy
corners, whose legs depend down into the water and disturb it;

water-rats diving and running along the bottom; water-beetles moving about; eels in the mud; the lower parts of flags and aquatic grasses swinging as the breeze ruffles their tips; the thud, thud of a horse's hoofs, and now and then the more distant roll of a hay-laden waggon. And thunder – how does thunder sound under the surface? It seems reasonable to suppose that fish possess a wide gamut of hearing since their other senses are necessarily somewhat curtailed, and that they are peculiarly sensitive to vibratory movements is certain from the destruction a charge of dynamite causes if exploded under water. Even in the deep sea the discharge of a torpedo will kill thousands of herrings. They are as it were killed by noise. So that there are grounds for thinking that my quiet jack in the pool, under the bank of the brook, is most keenly alive by his sense of hearing to things that are proceeding both out and in the water. More especially, no doubt, of things in the water itself. With all this specialized power of hearing he is still circumscribed and limited to the groove of the brook. The birds fly from field to field, from valley to mountain, and across the sea. Their experience extends to whole countries, and their opportunities are constant. How much more fortunate in this respect than the jack! A small display of intelligence by the fish is equivalent to a large display by the bird.

When the jack has been much disturbed no one can do more than obtain a view of him, however skilfully he may conceal himself. The least sign of further proceedings will send the jack away; sometimes the mere appearance of the human form is sufficient. If less suspicious, the rod with the wire attached – or if you wish to make experiments, the rod without the wire – can be placed in the water, and moved how you choose.

The Modern Thames

First published in the *Pall Mall Gazette*,
6 September 1884
First collected in *The Open Air*, 1885

The wild red deer can never again come down to drink at the
Thames in the dusk of the evening as once they did. While
modern civilization endures, the larger fauna must necessarily
be confined to parks or restrained to well-marked districts; but
for that very reason the lesser creatures of the wood, the field,
and the river should receive the more protection. If this applies
to the secluded country, far from the stir of cities, still more
does it apply to the neighbourhood of London. From a sportsman's point of view, or from that of a naturalist, the state of the
river is one of chaos. There is no order. The Thames appears
free even from the usual rules which are in force upon every
highway. A man may not fire a gun within a certain distance of
a road under a penalty – a law enacted for the safety of passengers, who were formerly endangered by persons shooting
small birds along the hedges bordering roads. Nor may he
shoot at all, not so much as fire off a pistol (as recently publicly
proclaimed by the Metropolitan police to restrain the use of
revolvers), without a licence. But on the river people do as they
choose, and there does not seem to be any law at all – or at
least there is no authority to enforce it, if it exists. Shooting
from boats and from the towing-path is carried on in utter defi-
ance of the licensing law, of the game law (as applicable to wild
fowl), and of the safety of persons who may be passing. The
moorhens are shot, the kingfishers have been nearly extermi-
nated or driven away from some parts, the once common
black-headed bunting is comparatively scarce in the more frequented reaches, and if there is nothing else to shoot at, then

the swallows are slaughtered. Some have even taken to shooting at the rooks in the trees or fields by the river with small-bore
rifles – a most dangerous thing to do. The result is that the
osier-beds on the eyots and by the backwaters – the copses of
the river – are almost devoid of life. A few moorhens creep
under the aquatic grasses and conceal themselves beneath the
bushes, water-voles hide among the flags, but the once extensive host of water-fowl and river life has been reduced to the
smallest limits. Water-fowl cannot breed because they are shot
on the nest, or their eggs taken. As for rarer birds, of course
they have not the slightest chance.

The fish have fared better because they have received the
benefit of close seasons, enforced with more or less vigilance all
along the river. They are also protected by regulations making
it illegal to capture them except in a sportsmanlike manner;
snatching, for instance, is unlawful. Riverside proprietors preserve some reaches, piscatorial societies preserve others, and
the complaint indeed is that the rights of the public have been
encroached upon. The too exclusive preservation of fish is in a
measure responsible for the destruction of water-fowl, which
are cleared off preserved places in order that they may not help
themselves to fry or spawn. On the other hand, the societies
may claim to have saved parts of the river from being entirely
deprived of fish, for it is not long since it appeared as if the
stream would be quite cleared out. Large quantities of fish have
also been placed in the river taken from ponds and bodily
transported to the Thames. So that upon the whole the fish
have been well looked after of recent years.

The more striking of the aquatic plants – such as white
water-lilies – have been much diminished in quantity by the
constant plucking, and injury is said to have been done by careless navigation. In things of this kind a few persons can do a
great deal of damage. Two or three men with guns, and indifferent to the interests of sport or natural history, at work every
day, can clear a long stretch of river of water-fowl, by scaring if
not by actually killing them. Imagine three or four such gentry
allowed to wander at will in a large game preserve – in a week
they would totally destroy it as a preserve. The river, after all,

is but a narrow band as it were, and is easily commanded by a gun. So, too, with fish poachers; a very few men with nets can quickly empty a good piece of water: and flowers like water-lilies, which grow only in certain spots, are soon pulled or spoiled. This aspect of the matter – the immense mischief which can be effected by a very few persons – should be carefully borne in mind in framing any regulations. For the mischief done on the river is really the work of a small number, a mere fraction of the thousands of all classes who frequent it. Not one in a thousand probably perpetrates any intentional damage to fish, fowl, or flowers.

As the river above all things is, and ought to be, a place of recreation, care must be particularly taken that in restraining these practices the enjoyment of the many be not interfered with. The rational pleasure of 999 people ought not to be checked because the last of the thousand acts as a blackguard. This point, too, bears upon the question of steam-launches. A launch can pass as softly and quietly as a skiff floating with the stream. And there is a good deal to be said on the other side, for the puntsmen stick themselves very often in the way of every one else; and if you analyse fishing for minnows from a punt you will not find it a noble sport. A river like the Thames, belonging as it does – or as it ought – to a city like London, should be managed from the very broadest standpoint. There should be pleasure for all, and there certainly is no real difficulty in arranging matters to that end. The Thames should be like a great aquarium, in which a certain balance of life has to be kept up. When aquaria first came into favour such things as snails and weeds were excluded as eyesores and injurious. But it was soon discovered that the despised snails and weeds were absolutely necessary; an aquarium could not be maintained in health without them, and now the most perfect aquarium is the one in which the natural state is most completely copied. On the same principle it is evident that too exclusive preservation must be injurious to the true interests of the river. Fish enthusiasts, for instance, desire the extinction of water-fowl – there is not a single aquatic bird which they do not accuse of damage to fry, spawn, or full-grown fish; no, not one, from the heron down to the tiny grebe. They are nearly as bitter against animals; the poor water-vole (or water-rat) even is denounced and shot. Any one who chooses may watch the water-rat feeding on aquatic vegetation; never mind, shoot him because he's there. There is no other reason. Bitterest, harshest, most envenomed of all is the outcry and hunt directed against the otter. It is as if the otter were a wolf – as if he were as injurious as the mighty boar whom Meleager and his companions chased in the days of dim antiquity. What, then, has the otter done? Has he ravaged the fields? Does he threaten the homesteads? Is he at Temple Bar? Are we to run, as the old song says, from the Dragon? The fact is, the ravages attributed to the otter are of a local character. They are chiefly committed in those places where fish are more or less confined. If you keep sheep close together in a pen the wolf who leaps the hurdles can kill the flock if he chooses. In narrow waters, and where fish are maintained in quantities out of proportion to extent, an otter can work doleful woe. That is to say, those who want too many fish are those who give the otter his opportunity.

In a great river like the Thames a few otters cannot do much or lasting injury except in particular places. The truth, is, that the otter is an ornament to the river, and more worthy of preservation than any other creature. He is the last and largest of the wild creatures who once roamed so freely in the forests which enclosed Londinium, that fort in the woods and marshes – marshes which to this day, though drained and built over, enwrap the nineteenth-century city in thick mists. The red deer are gone, the boar is gone, the wolf necessarily destroyed – the red deer can never again drink at the Thames in the dusk of the evening while our civilization endures. The otter alone remains – the wildest, the most thoroughly self-supporting of all living things left – a living link going back to the days of Cassivelaunus. London ought to take the greatest interest in the otters of its river. The shameless way in which every otter that dares to show itself is shot, trapped, beaten to death and literally battered out of existence, should rouse the indignation of every sportsman and every lover of nature. The late Rev. John Russell, who, it will be admitted, was a true sportsman, walked three thousand miles to see an otter. That was a different spirit, was it not?

That is the spirit in which the otter in the Thames should be regarded. Those who offer money rewards for killing Thames otters ought to be looked on as those who would offer rewards for poisoning foxes in Leicestershire. I suppose we shall not see the ospreys again; but I should like to. Again, on the other side of the boundary, in the tidal waters, the same sort of ravenous destruction is carried on against everything that ventures up. A short time ago a porpoise came up to Mortlake; now, just think, a porpoise up from the great sea – that sea to which Londoners rush with such joy – past Gravesend, past Greenwich, past the Tower, under London Bridge, past Westminster and the Houses of Parliament, right up to Mortlake. It is really a wonderful thing that a denizen of the sea, so large and interesting as a porpoise, should come right through the vast City of London. In an aquarium, people would go to see it and admire it, and take their children to see it. What happened? Some one hastened out in a boat, armed with a gun or a rifle, and occupied himself with shooting at it. He did not succeed in killing it, but it was wounded. Some difference here to the spirit of John Russell. If I may be permitted to express an opinion, I think that there is not a single creature, from the sand-marten and the black-headed bunting to the broad-winged heron, from the water-vole to the otter, from the minnow on one side of the tidal boundary to the porpoise on the other – big and little, beasts and birds (of prey or not) – that should not be encouraged and protected on this beautiful river, morally the property of the greatest city in the world.

The Water-Colley

First published in the *Manchester Guardian*,
31 August 1883
First collected in *The Life of the Fields*, 1884

The sweet grass was wet with dew as I walked through a meadow
in Somerset to the river. The cuckoo sang, the pleasanter perhaps
because his brief time was nearly over, and all pleasant things
seem to have a deeper note as they draw towards an end. Dew
and sweet green grass were the more beautiful because of the
knowledge that the high hills around were covered by sun-dried,
wiry heather. Riverside mead, dew-laden grass, and sparkling
stream were like an oasis in the dry desert. They refreshed the
heart to look upon as water refreshes the weary. The shadows
were more marked and defined than they are as day advances,
the hues of the flowers brighter, for the dew was to shadow and
flower as if the colours of the artist were not yet dry. Humble-bees
went down with caution into the long grass, not liking to wet
their wings. Butterflies and the brilliant moths of a hot summer's
morn alight on a dry heated footpath till the dew is gone. A great
rock rising from the grass by the river's edge alone looked arid,
and its surface already heated, yet it also cast a cool shadow. By
a copse, two rabbits – the latest up of all those which had sported
during the night – stayed till I came near, and then quietly moved
in among the ferns and foxgloves.

In the narrowest part of the wood between the hedge and
the river a corncrake called his loudest 'crake, crake', incessantly. The corncrake or landrail is difficult even to see, so
closely does he conceal himself in the tall grasses, and his call
echoed and re-echoed deceives those who try to find him. Yet
by great patience and watchful skilfulness the corncrake is
sometimes caught by hand. If tracked, and if you can see him –

the most difficult part – you can put your hand on him. Now
and then a corncrake is caught in the same way by hand while
sitting on her nest on the ground. It is not, however, as easy as
it reads. Walking through the grass, and thinking of the dew
and the beautiful morning sunshine, I scarcely noticed the quantity of cuckoo-flowers, or cardamine, till presently it occurred to
me that it was very late in the season for cuckoo-flowers; and
stooping I picked one, and in the act saw it was an orchis – the
early purple. The meadow was coloured, or rather tinted, with
the abundance of the orchis, palest of pale, dotted with red, the
small narrow leaves sometimes with black spots. They grew in
the pasture everywhere, from the river's side in the deep valley
to the top of the hill by the wood.

As soon as the surface of the river was in sight I stood and
watched, but no ripple or ring of wavelets appeared; the trout
were not feeding. The water was so low that the river consisted
of a series of pools, connected by rapids descending over ledges of
stones and rocky fragments. Illumined to the very bottom, every
trout was visible, even those under the roots of trees and the
hollow of the bank. A cast with the fly there was useless; the
line would be seen; there was no ripple to hide it. As the trout,
too, were in the pools, it might be concluded that those worth
taking had fed, and only the lesser fish would be found in the
eddies, where they are permitted by the larger fish to feed after
they have finished. Experience and reason were all against the
attempt, yet so delightful is the mere motion and delicate touch
of the fly-line on the water that I could not but let myself enjoy
that at least. The slender lancewood rod swayed, the line
swished through the air, and the fly dropped a few inches too
high up the rapid among the stones – I had meant it to fall farther across in the dark backwater at the foot of the fall. The
swift rush of the current carried the fly instantly downwards,
but not so quick as to escape a troutlet; he took it, and was
landed immediately. But to destroy these under-sized fish was
not sport, and as at that moment a water-colley passed I determined to let the trout alone, and observe his ways.

Colley means a blackbird; water-colley, the water-blackbird
or water-ousel – called the dipper in the North. In districts

where the bird is seldom seen it is occasionally shot and preserved as a white blackbird. But in flight and general appearance the water-colley is almost exactly like a starling with a white neck. His colour is not black or brown – it is a rusty, undecided brown, at a distance something the colour of a young starling, and he flies in a straight line, and yet clumsily, as a young starling does. His very cry, too, sounds immature, pettish, and unfinished, as if from a throat not capable of a full note. There are usually two together, and they pass and re-pass all day as you fish, but if followed are not to be observed without care. I came on the colley too suddenly the first time, at a bend of the river; he was beneath the bank towards me, and flew out from under my feet, so that I did not see him till he was on the wing. Away he flew with a call like a young bird just tumbled out of its nest, following the curves of the stream. Presently I saw him through an alder bush which hid me; he was perched on a root of alder under the opposite bank. Worn away by the stream the dissolved earth had left the roots exposed, the colley was on one of them; in a moment he stepped on to the shore under the hollow, and was hidden behind the roots under a moss-grown stole. When he came out he saw me, and stopped feeding.

He bobbed himself up and down as he perched on the root in the oddest manner, bending his legs so that his body almost touched his perch, and rising again quickly, this repeated in quick succession as if curtsying. This motion with him is a sign of uncertainty – it shows suspicion; after he had bobbed to me ten times off he went. I found him next on a stone in the middle of the river; it stood up above the surface of a rapid connecting two pools. Like the trout, the colley always feeds at the rapids, and flies as they swim, from fall to fall. He was bobbing up and down, his legs bent, and his rusty brown body went up and down, but as I was hidden by a hedge he gained confidence, suspended his curtsying, and began to feed. First he looked all round the stone, and then stepped to another similar island in the midst of the rushing water, pushing his head over the edge into it. Next he stepped into the current, which, though shallow, looked strong enough to sweep him away. The water checked against him rose to the white mark on his breast. He waded up the rapid, every now and then thrusting his head completely under the water; sometimes he was up to his neck, sometimes not so deep; now and then getting on a stone, searching right and left as he climbed the cascade. The eddying water shot by his slender legs, but he moved against it easily, and soon ascended the waterfall. At the summit a second colley flew past, and he rose and accompanied his friend.

Upon a ledge of rock I saw him once more, but there was no hedge to hide me, and he would not feed; he stood and curtsied, and at the moment of bobbing let his wings too partly down, his tail drooping at the same time. Calling in an injured tone, as if much annoyed, he flew, swept round the meadow, and so to the river behind me. His friend followed. On reaching the river at a safe distance down, he skimmed along the surface like a kingfisher. They find abundance of insect life among the stones at the falls, and everywhere in shallow water. Some accuse them of taking the ova of trout, and they are shot at trout nurseries; but it is doubtful if they are really guilty, nor can they do any appreciable injury in an open stream, not being in sufficient numbers. It is the birds and other creatures peculiar to the water that render fly-fishing so pleasant; were they all destroyed, and nothing left but the mere fish, one might as well stand and fish in a stone cattle-trough. I hope all true lovers of sport will assist in preserving rather than in killing them.

Trees About Town

First published in the London *Standard*, 28 September 1881
First collected in *Nature Near London*, 1883

Just outside London there is a circle of fine, large houses, each
standing in its own grounds, highly rented, and furnished with
every convenience money can supply. If any one will look at the
trees and shrubs growing in the grounds about such a house,
chosen at random for an example, and make a list of them, he
may then go round the entire circumference of Greater London,
mile after mile, many days' journey, and find the list ceaselessly
repeated.

There are acacias, sumachs, cedar deodaras, araucarias, laurels, planes, beds of rhododendrons, and so on. There are various
other foreign shrubs and trees whose names have not become
familiar, and then the next grounds contain exactly the same,
somewhat differently arranged. Had they all been planted by
Act of Parliament, the result could scarcely have been more
uniform.

If, again, search were made in these enclosures for English
trees and English shrubs, it would be found that none have
been introduced. The English trees, timber trees, that are there,
grew before the house was built; for the rest, the products of
English woods and hedgerows have been carefully excluded.
The law is, 'Plant planes, laurels, and rhododendrons; root up
everything natural to this country.'

To those who have any affection for our own woodlands
this is a pitiful spectacle, produced, too, by the expenditure of
large sums of money. Will no one break through the practice,
and try the effect of English trees? There is no lack of them, and
they far excel anything yet imported in beauty and grandeur.

Though such suburban grounds mimic the isolation and

retirement of ancient country houses surrounded with parks, the distinctive feature of the ancient houses is omitted. There are no massed bodies, as it were, of our own trees to give a substance to the view. Are young oaks ever seen in those grounds so often described as park-like? Some time since it was customary for the builder carefully to cut down every piece of timber on the property before putting in the foundations.

Fortunately, the influence of a better taste now preserves such trees as chance to be growing on the site at the moment it is purchased. These remain, but no others are planted. A young oak is not to be seen. The oaks that are there drop their acorns in vain, for if one takes root it is at once cut off; it would spoil the laurels. It is the same with elms; the old elms are decaying, and no successors are provided.

As for ash, it is doubtful if a young ash is anywhere to be found; if so, it is an accident. The ash is even rarer than the rest. In their places are put more laurels, cedar deodaras, various evergreens, rhododendrons, planes. How tame and insignificant are these compared with the oak! Thrice a year the oaks become beautiful in a different way.

In spring the opening buds give the tree a ruddy hue; in summer the great head of green is not to be surpassed; in autumn, with the falling leaf and acorn, they appear buff and brown. The nobility of the oak casts the pitiful laurel into utter insignificance. With elms it is the same; they are reddish with flower and bud very early in the year, the fresh leaf is a tender green; in autumn they are sometimes one mass of yellow.

Ashes change from almost black to a light green, then a deeper green, and again light green and yellow. Where is the foreign evergreen in the competition? Put side by side, competition is out of the question; you have only to get an artist to paint the oak in its three phases to see this. There is less to be said against the deodara than the rest, as it is a graceful tree; but it is not English in any sense.

The point, however, is that the foreigners oust the English altogether. Let the cedar and the laurel, and the whole host of invading evergreens, be put aside by themselves, in a separate and detached shrubbery, maintained for the purpose of exhibiting strange growths. Let them not crowd the lovely English trees out of the place. Planes are much planted now, with ill effect; the blotches where the bark peels, the leaves which lie on the sward like brown leather, the branches wide apart and giving no shelter to birds – in short, the whole ensemble of the plane is unfit for our country.

It was selected for London plantations, as the Thames Embankment, because its peeling bark was believed to protect it against the deposit of sooty particles, and because it grows quickly. For use in London itself it may be preferable; for semi-country seats, as the modern houses surrounded with their own grounds assume to be, it is unsightly. It has no association. No one has seen a plane in a hedgerow, or a wood, or a copse. There are no fragments of English history clinging to it as there are to the oak.

If trees of the plane class be desirable, sycamores may be planted, as they have in a measure become acclimatized. If trees that grow fast are required, there are limes and horse-chestnuts; the lime will run a race with any tree. The lime, too, has a pale yellow blossom, to which bees resort in numbers, making a pleasant hum, which seems the natural accompaniment of summer sunshine. Its leaves are put forth early.

Horse-chestnuts, too, grow quickly and without any attention, the bloom is familiar, and acknowledged to be fine, and in autumn the large sprays of leaves take orange and even scarlet tints. The plane is not to be mentioned beside either of them. Other trees as well as the plane would have flourished on the Thames Embankment, in consequence of the current of fresh air caused by the river. Imagine the Embankment with double rows of oaks, elms, or beeches; or, if not, even with limes or horse-chestnuts! To these certainly birds would have resorted – possibly rooks, which do not fear cities. On such a site the experiment would have been worth making.

If in the semi-country seats fast-growing trees are needed, there are, as I have observed, the lime and horse-chestnut; and if more variety be desired, add the Spanish chestnut and the walnut. The Spanish chestnut is a very fine tree, the walnut, it is true, grows slowly. If as many beeches as cedar deodaras and

laurels and planes were planted in these grounds, in due course
of time the tap of the woodpecker would be heard: a sound
truly worth ten thousand laurels. At Kew, far closer to town
than many of the semi-country seats are now, all our trees
flourish in perfection.

Hardy birches, too, will grow in thin soil. Just compare the
delicate drooping boughs of birch – they could not have been
more delicate if sketched with a pencil – compare these with
the gaunt planes!

Of all the foreign shrubs that have been brought to these
shores, there is not one that presents us with so beautiful a
spectacle as the bloom of the common old English hawthorn in
May. The mass of blossom, the pleasant fragrance, its divided
and elegant leaf, place it far above any of the importations.
Besides which, the traditions and associations of the May give
it a human interest.

The hawthorn is a part of natural English life – country life.
It stands side by side with the Englishman, as the palm tree is
pictured side by side with the Arab. You cannot pick up an old
play, or book of the time when old English life was in the prime,
without finding some reference to the hawthorn. There is nothing of this in the laurel, or any shrub whatever that may be
thrust in with a ticket to tell you its name; it has a ticket because
it has no interest, or else you would know it.

For use there is nothing like hawthorn; it will trim into a
thick hedge, defending the enclosure from trespassers, and
warding off the bitter winds; or it will grow into a tree. Again,
the old hedge-crab – the common, despised crab-apple – in
spring is covered with blossom, such a mass of blossom that it
may be distinguished a mile. Did any one ever see a plane or a
laurel look like that?

How pleasant, too, to see the clear white flower of the blackthorn come out in the midst of the bitter easterly breezes! It is
like a white handkerchief beckoning to the sun to come. There
will not be much more frost; if the wind is bitter to-day, the sun
is rapidly gaining power. Probably, if a blackthorn bush were by
any chance discovered in the semi-parks or enclosures alluded
to, it would at once be rooted out as an accursed thing. The very

brambles are superior; there is the flower, the sweet berry, and afterwards the crimson leaves – three things in succession.

What can the world produce equal to the June rose? The common briar, the commonest of all, offers a flower which, whether in itself, or the moment of its appearance at the juncture of all sweet summer things, or its history and associations, is not to be approached by anything a millionaire could purchase. The labourer casually gathers it as he goes to his work in the field, and yet none of the rich families whose names are synonymous with wealth can get anything to equal it if they ransack the earth.

After these, fill every nook and corner with hazel, and make filbert walks. Up and down such walks men strolled with rapiers by their sides while our admirals were hammering at the Spaniards with culverin and demi-cannon, and looked at the sun-dial and adjourned for a game at bowls, wishing that they only had a chance to bowl shot instead of peaceful wood. Fill in the corners with nut-trees, then, and make filbert walks. All these are like old story books, and the old stories are always best.

Still, there are others for variety, as the wild guelder rose, which produces heavy bunches of red berries; dogwood, whose leaves when frost-touched take deep colours; barberry, yielding a pleasantly acid fruit; the wayfaring tree; not even forgetting the elder, but putting it at the outside, because, though flowering, the scent is heavy, and because the elder was believed of old time to possess some of the virtue now attributed to the blue gum, and to neutralize malaria by its own odour.

For colour add the wild broom and some furze. Those who have seen broom in full flower, golden to the tip of every slender bough, cannot need any persuasion, surely, to introduce it. Furze is specked with yellow when the skies are dark and the storms sweep around, besides its prime display. Let wild clematis climb wherever it will. Then laurels may come after these, put somewhere by themselves, with their thick changeless leaves, unpleasant to the touch; no one ever gathers a spray.

Rhododendrons it is unkind to attack, for in themselves they afford a rich flower. It is not the rhododendron, but the abuse

of it, which must be protested against. Whether the soil suits or
not – and, for the most part, it does not suit – rhododendrons
are thrust in everywhere. Just walk in amongst them – behind
the show – and look at the spindly, crooked stems, straggling
how they may, and then look at the earth under them, where
not a weed even will grow. The rhododendron is admirable in
its place, but it is often overdone and a failure, and has no right
to exclude those shrubs that are fitter. Most of the foreign
shrubs about these semi-country seats look exactly like the stiff
and painted little wooden trees that are sold for children's toys,
and, like the toys, are the same colour all the year round.

Now, if you enter a copse in spring the eye is delighted with
cowslips on the banks where the sunlight comes, with bluebells,
or earlier with anemones and violets, while later the ferns rise.
But enter the semi-parks of the semi-country seat, with its
affected assumption of countryness, and there is not one of these.
The fern is actually purposely eradicated – just think! Purposely!
Though indeed they would not grow, one would think, under
rhododendrons and laurels, cold-blooded laurels. They will
grow under hawthorn, ash, or beside the bramble bushes.

If there chance to be a little pond or 'fountain', there is no
such thing as a reed, or a flag, or a rush. How the rushes would
be hastily hauled out and hurled away with execrations!

Besides the greater beauty of English trees, shrubs, and
plants, they also attract the birds, without which the grandest
plantation is a vacancy, and another interest, too, arises from
watching the progress of their growth and the advance of the
season. Our own trees and shrubs literally keep pace with the
stars which shine in our northern skies. An astronomical floral
almanac might almost be constructed, showing how, as the
constellations marched on by night, the buds and leaves and
flowers appeared by day.

The lower that brilliant Sirius sinks in the western sky after
ruling the winter heavens, and the higher that red Arcturus
rises, so the buds thicken, open, and bloom. When the Pleiades
begin to rise in the early evening, the leaves are turning colour,
and the seed vessels of the flowers take the place of the petals.
The coincidences of floral and bird life, and of these with the

movements of the heavens, impart a sense of breadth to their observation.

It is not only the violet or the anemone, there are the birds coming from immense distances to enjoy the summer with us; there are the stars appearing in succession, so that the most distant of objects seems brought into connection with the nearest, and the world is made one. The sharp distinction, the line artificially drawn between things, quite disappears when they are thus associated.

Birds, as just remarked, are attracted by our own trees and shrubs. Oaks are favourites with rooks and wood-pigeons; blackbirds whistle in them in spring; if there is a pheasant about in autumn he is sure to come under the oak; jays visit them. Elms are resorted to by most of the larger birds. Ash plantations attract wood-pigeons and turtle-doves. Thrushes are fond of the ash, and sing much on its boughs. The beech is the woodpecker's tree so soon as it grows old – birch one of the missel-thrush's.

In blackthorn the long-tailed tit builds the domed nest every one admires. Under the cover of brambles whitethroats build. Nightingales love hawthorn, and so does every bird. Plant the hawthorn, and almost every bird will come to it, from the wood-pigeon down to the wren. Do not clear away the fallen branches and brown leaves, sweeping the plantation as if it were the floor of a ball-room, for it is just the tangle and the wilderness that brings the birds, and they like the disarray.

If evergreens are wanted, there are the yew, the box, and holly – all three well sanctioned by old custom. Thrushes will come for the yew berries, and birds are fond of building in the thick cover of high box hedges. Notwithstanding the prickly leaves, they slip in and out of the holly easily. A few bunches of rushes and sedges, with some weeds and aquatic grasses, allowed to grow about a pond, will presently bring moorhens. Bare stones – perhaps concrete – will bring nothing.

If a bough falls into the water, let it stay; sparrows will perch on it to drink. If a sandy drinking-place can be made for them the number of birds that will come in the course of the day will be surprising.

Kind-hearted people, when winter is approaching, should have two posts sunk in their grounds, with planks across at the top; a raised platform with the edges projecting beyond the posts, so that cats cannot climb up, and of course higher than a cat can spring. The crumbs cast out upon this platform would gather crowds of birds; they will come to feel at home, and in spring-time will return to build and sing.

Nightingales

First published in the *St James's Gazette*, 10 April 1886
First collected in *Chronicles of the Hedges*, 1948

The nightingales have arrived. They have already been heard, and early notice of the fact has been duly and promptly made. There is always some one ready to chronicle this event, and many who believe that the precise period is of importance. Scientific men seem now to have decided that no peculiar significance is to be attached to early or late arrivals. Head winds are quite sufficient to explain a delay of a few days, which is the greatest interval between an early and a very early return. A family of the name of Massham, living in the neighbourhood of Norwich, kept for four generations a chronicle of the dates of arrival. The first entry was made in the spring of 1736, and the series was left unbroken till April 1810, after which it was allowed to drop. It was, however, resumed in 1836, and the returns duly entered up to 1874. These 110 cases give every variety of premature and belated arrival of the nightingales, and showed that the dates were quite useless as a weather guide.

As a general rule the nightingales reach us about the middle of April, and the cocks come first. A fantastic idea was once cherished that the males started first and sang day and night until the females arrived. The truth seems to be that they all start together; but the cocks, being the stronger, arrive first. The fact, as a fact, obtained curious commercial recognition. It is hard to tell a hen-bird from a cock; for there is not much difference either in size or in plumage. A few years ago, before the Wild Birds Protection Act had been passed, the first nightingales of the season were sold for considerably more than the later arrivals; the presumption being that they were of the singing sex. Scarcely any bird that visits us and breeds in our country is more shy and at the same time more stupid. In the 'good old days of bird-catching' it was child's play to snare them. A couple of roughs would come down from town and silence a whole grove. The nightingale would watch the trap being laid, and pounce on the alluring meal-worm as soon as the trapper was out of sight. It would be quite as much curiosity as gluttony that led to its fate; and the fate was a sad one. These birds are so shy that it is nearly impossible to keep them alive. They literally beat themselves to death against their prison wires. So for the first fortnight of captivity the wings were tied, and the bird was kept caged in the dark. Light was gradually let in – at first by a few pinholes in the paper that covered the cage. The captive would peck and peck at these till a rent was made and in time the paper could come away. The mortality was pitiable. Seventy per cent of these little creatures that were singing a week before in full-throated ease in the Surrey lanes would be flung out into the gutters of Seven Dials or Whitechapel. You might buy a fresh-caught bird for two or three shillings; a few weeks later the same bird, if alive, would be worth thirty. Now, of course, by the Act of 1880, they are protected through April, May, and June; and, in fact, such nightingales as can be bought in London are for the most part imports from Germany.

In the nightingale nothing is more remarkable than its constancy and its caprice. Year after year it will return to the same copse, and be heard at the end of each succeeding April, though it will have spent the winter in Africa or the Holy Land. The French naturalist Maupertuis mentions that in 1736 he discovered a nest on Arusaxa, a hill in Finland notable as the most southern point where the midnight sun could be seen. Birds were found in the same spot again in 1799 by Skjoldebrand; and from 1835 to 1865 they continued to breed there without any interval. But though it is faithful to the district it selects, its caprice in making choice is really quite incalculable. The bird is as capricious as a prima donna. It seems, for instance, to have as great a dislike to Scotland as Dr Johnson himself. This is not on account of the cold; for it visits much colder countries.

Indeed, climate has much less influence with it than one might expect in the case of the summer immigrant. It chooses rather to ignore Devonshire and Cornwall, and seems to hold, with the great lexicographer, that Ireland is worth seeing but not worth going to see. It rarely goes there, though it is not correct to say that it is never to be met with. Its appreciation of Yorkshire is extremely arbitrary. In some parts it is often to be met with; in others its occurrence is very rare. A few years ago a nightingale came to a wood in the neighbourhood of one of the large manufacturing towns. The intelligence was soon noised about, and the wood got to be so popular that an enterprising omnibus proprietor started a vehicle that took passengers 'to the Nightingale', at sixpence a head. The bird soon left that wood, and a little boy who got up into a tree and imitated it, was very near being stoned in the moonlight by some angry passengers who were disappointed at the failure of their excursion.

Sir John Sinclair tried to overcome the bird's antipathy to Scotland and failed. He knew that in its case, as in that of most immigrants, there is a persistency of return to old breeding places. Accordingly, a London dealer had directions to procure as many nightingale's eggs as he could at the liberal terms of twelve shillings a dozen. A considerable quantity was obtained, and they were packed in wool and sent up by mail to Scotland. In the meantime, all the robin's nests in the district had been discovered and protected. As the batches of eggs arrived the robin's nests were robbed and refurnished with nightingale's eggs. The experiment was carried out over a wide area. The hen robins reared these precious foster-children, and so far the experiment succeeded. For that year there were plenty of nightingales in that part of the country. Then came September, the time of migration. The young birds all flew away, and they never returned.

It is curious that there does not seem to be any appreciable increase in the number of nightingales since the Act of 1880. No doubt, however, its operation must have largely assisted their preservation. Even before the Act, England – considering its latitude and the density of its population – was a very favourite breeding-place with the bird; but this was owing partly to the character of the English landscape. The nightingale, with all its shyness, seems to love the neighbourhood of man, or the homes of man. It is not so much a bird of the woods as of the shrubbery. It is mentioned in the *Spectator* that Sir Roger de Coverley stopped to listen to the nightingales in Vauxhall. They were heard last year in Kensington Gardens, and till lately – again this year for aught we know – they sang regularly within half-a-dozen yards of the highway that passes the Star and Garter at Richmond.

The Hovering of the Kestrel

First published in the *St James's Gazette*, 22 February 1883
First collected in *The Life of the Fields*, 1884

There has lately been some discussion about the hovering of kestrels: the point being whether the bird can or cannot support itself in the air while stationary, without the assistance of one or more currents of air. The kestrel is the commonest hawk in the southern parts of England, so that many opportunities occur to observe his habits; and there ought not to be any doubt in the matter. It is even alleged that it will go far to decide the question of the possibility of flight or of the construction of an aerial machine. Without entering into this portion of the discussion, let us examine the kestrel's habits.

This hawk has a light easy flight, usually maintaining an altitude a little lower than the tallest elms, but higher than most trees. He will keep this particular altitude for hours together, and sweep over miles of country, with only occasional variations – excluding, of course, descents for the purpose of taking mice. It is usually at this height that a kestrel hovers, though he is capable of doing it at a much greater elevation. As he comes gliding through the atmosphere, suddenly he shoots up a little (say, roughly, two or three feet), and then stops short. His tail, which is broader than it looks, is bent slightly downwards; his wings beat the air, at the first glance, just as if he was progressing. Sometimes he seems to oscillate to one side, sometimes to the other; but these side movements do not amount to any appreciable change of position. If there be little or no wind (note this) he remains beating the air, to the eye at least perfectly stationary, perhaps as much as half a minute or more. He then seems to slip forward about half a yard, as if a pent-up force was released, but immediately recovers himself and hovers again. This alternate hovering and slipping forward may be repeated two or three times: it seems to depend on the bird's judgment as to the chance of prey. If he does not think a mouse is to be had, at the first slip he allows himself to proceed. If the spot be likely, or (what is still more tempting) if it is near a place where he has taken prey previously, he will slip and bring up several times. Now and then he will even fetch a half-circle when his balance or impetus (or both) is quite exhausted, and so return to the same spot and recommence. But this is not often, as a rule, after two or three slips he proceeds on his voyage. He will repeat the same round day after day, if undisturbed, and, if the place be at all infested with mice, he will come to it three or four times a day. There is, therefore, every chance of watching him, if you have once found his route. Should he spy a mouse, down he comes, quick but steady, and very nearly straight upon it. But kestrels do not always descend upon prey actually in view. Unless I am much mistaken, they now and then descend in a likely spot and watch like a cat for a minute or two for mice or beetles. For rest they always seek a tree.

Now, having briefly sketched his general manner, let us return and examine the details. In the first place, he usually rises slightly, with outstretched wings, as if about to soar at the moment of commencing hovering. The planes of the wings are then inclined, and meet the air. At the instant of stopping, the tail is depressed. It appears reasonable to conjecture that the slight soaring is to assist the tail in checking his onward course, and to gain a balance. Immediately the wings beat rapidly, somewhat as they do in ordinary flight but with a more forward motion, and somewhat as birds do when about to perch on an awkward ledge, as a swallow at an incomplete nest under an eave. The wings look more, in front, as if attached to his neck. In an exaggerated way ducks beat the air like this, with no intention of rising at all, merely to stretch their wings. The duck raises himself as he stands on the ground, stretches himself to his full height, and flaps his wings horizontally. The kestrel's wings strike downwards and a very little forwards, for his natural tendency is to slip forwards, and the object of slightly reversing his vanes is to prevent this and yet at the same time to support him. His shape is such that if he were rigid with outstretched wings he would glide ahead, just as a ship in a calm slowly forges ahead because of her lines, which are drawn for forward motion. The kestrel's object is to prevent his slip forwards, and the tail alone will not do it. It is necessary for him to 'stroke' the air in order to keep up at all; because the moment he pauses gravitation exercises a force much greater than when he glides.

While hovering there are several forces balanced: first, the original impetus onwards; secondly, that of the depressed tail dragging and stopping that onward course; thirdly, that of the wing beating downwards; and fourthly, that of the wing a very little reversed beating forwards, like backing water with a scull. When used in the ordinary way the shape of the wing causes it to exert a downward and backward pressure. His slip is when he loses balance: it is most obviously a loss of balance; he quite oscillates sometimes when it occurs; and now and then I have seen a kestrel unable to catch himself, and obliged to proceed some distance before he could hover again. Occasionally, in the slip he loses a foot or so of elevation, but not always. While actually hovering, his altitude does not vary an inch. All and each of these movements and the considerations to which they give rise show conclusively that the act of hovering is nothing more or less than an act of balancing; and when he has his balance he will rest a moment with outstretched wings kept still. He uses his wings with just sufficient force neither to rise nor fall, and prevents progress by a slightly different stroke.

The next point is, Where does he hover? He hovers any and everywhere, without the slightest choice. He hovers over meadows, cornfields; over the tops of the highest Downs, sometimes at the very edge of a precipice or above a chalk quarry; over gardens, waste ground; over the highway; over summer and other ricks and thatched sheds, from which he sometimes takes his prey; over stables, where mice abound. He has no preference for one side of a hedge or grove, and cares not the least on which the wind blows. His hovering is entirely determined by his judgment as to the chance of prey. I have seen a kestrel hover over every variety of dry ground that is to be found.

Next, as to the wind. If any one has read what has preceded

upon his manner of preserving his balance, it must be at once apparent that, supposing a kestrel were hovering in a calm and a wind arose, he would at once face it, else his balance could not be kept. Even on the ground almost all birds face the wind by choice; but the hovering kestrel has no choice. He must hover facing the wind, or it would upset him: just as you may often see a rook flung half aback by a sudden gust. Hence has arisen the supposition that a kestrel cannot hover without a wind. The truth is, he can hover in a perfect calm, and no doubt could do so in a room if it were large enough. He requires no current of any kind, neither a horizontal breeze nor an ascending current. A kestrel can and does hover in the dead calm of summer days, when there is not the faintest breath of wind. He will and does hover in the still, soft atmosphere of early autumn, when the gossamer falls in showers, coming straight down as if it were raining silk. If you puff up a ball of thistledown it will languish on your breath and sink again to the sward. The reapers are sweltering in the wheat, the keeper suffocates in the wood, the carter walks in the shadow cast by his load of corn, the countryside stares all parched and cracked and gasps for a rainy breeze. The kestrel hovers just the same. Could he not do so, a long calm would half starve him, as that is his manner of preying. Having often spent hours in trees for the purpose of a better watch upon animals and birds, I can vouch for it that ascending currents are not frequent – rare, in fact, except in a gale. In a light air or calm there is no ascending current, or it is imperceptible and of no use to the kestrel. Such currents, when they do exist, are very local; but the kestrel's hover is not local: he can hover anywhere. He can do it in the face of a stiff gale, and in a perfect calm. The only weather he dislikes is heavy thunder, rain, or hail, during which he generally perches on a tree; but he can hover in all ordinary rain. He effects it by sheer power and dexterity of wing. Therefore if the fact has any bearing upon the problem of flight, the question of currents may be left out altogether. His facing the wind is, as has been pointed out, only a proof that he is keeping his balance.

The kestrel is not the only bird that hovers. The sparrowhawk can. So can all the finches, more or less, when taking

seeds from a plant which will not bear their weight or which they
cannot otherwise get at; also when taking insects on the wing.
Sparrows do the same. Larks hover in their mating season, uttering a short song, not the same as when they soar. Numerous
insects can hover: the great dragon-fly will stop dead short in his
rapid flight, and stay suspended till it suits him to advance. None
of these require any current or wind. I do not think that hovering
requires so much strength of wing or such an exercise of force as
when birds rise almost straight up. Snipes do it, and woodcocks;
so also pheasants, rocketing with tremendous effort; so also a
sparrow in a confined court, rising almost straight to the slates.
Evidently this needs great power. Hovering is very interesting;
but not nearly so mysterious as at least one other power possessed by birds.

Out of Doors in February

First published in *Good Words*, February 1882
First collected in *The Open Air*, 1885

The cawing of the rooks in February shows that the time is coming when their nests will be re-occupied. They resort to the trees, and perch above the old nests to indicate their rights; for in the rookery possession is the law, and not nine-tenths of it only. In the slow dull cold of winter even these noisy birds are quiet, and as the vast flocks pass over, night and morning, to and from the woods in which they roost, there is scarcely a sound. Through the mist their black wings advance in silence, the jackdaws with them are chilled into unwonted quiet, and unless you chance to look up the crowd may go over unnoticed. But so soon as the waters begin to make a sound in February, running in the ditches and splashing over stones, the rooks commence the speeches and conversations which will continue till late into the following autumn.

The general idea is that they pair in February, but there are some reasons for thinking that the rooks, in fact, choose their mates at the end of the preceding summer. They are then in large flocks, and if only casually glanced at appear mixed together without any order or arrangement. They move on the ground and fly in the air so close, one beside the other, that at the first glance or so you cannot distinguish them apart. Yet if you should be lingering along the by-ways of the fields as the acorns fall, and the leaves come rustling down in the warm sunny autumn afternoons, and keep an observant eye upon the rooks in the trees, or on the fresh-turned furrows, they will be seen to act in couples. On the ground couples alight near each other, on the trees they perch near each other, and in the air fly side by side. Like soldiers each has his comrade. Wedged in the

ranks every man looks like his fellow, and there seems no tie
between them but a common discipline. Intimate acquaintance
with barrack or camp life would show that every one had his
friend. There is also the mess, or companionship of half a
dozen, a dozen, or more, and something like this exists part of
the year in the armies of the rooks. After the nest time is over
they flock together, and each family of three or four flies in concert. Later on they apparently choose their own particular
friends, that is the young birds do so. All through the winter
after, say October, these pairs keep together, though lost in the
general mass to the passing spectator. If you alarm them while
feeding on the ground in winter, supposing you have not got a
gun, they merely rise up to the nearest tree, and it may then be
observed that they do this in pairs. One perches on a branch
and a second comes to him. When February arrives, and they
resort to the nests to look after or seize on the property there,
they are in fact already paired, though the almanacs put down
St Valentine's day as the date of courtship.

There is very often a warm interval in February, sometimes
a few days earlier and sometimes later, but as a rule it happens
that a week or so of mild sunny weather occurs about this time.
Released from the grip of the frost, the streams trickle forth
from the fields and pour into the ditches, so that while walking
along the footpath there is a murmur all around coming from
the rush of water. The murmur of the poets is indeed louder in
February than in the more pleasant days of summer, for then
the growth of aquatic grasses checks the flow and stills it,
whilst in February, every stone, or flint, or lump of chalk divides
the current and causes a vibration. With this murmur of water,
and mild time, the rooks caw incessantly, and the birds at large
essay to utter their welcome of the sun. The wet furrows reflect
the rays so that the dark earth gleams, and in the slight mist
that stays farther away the light pauses and fills the vapour
with radiance. Through this luminous mist the larks race after
each other twittering, and as they turn aside, swerving in their
swift flight, their white breasts appear for a moment. As while
standing by a pool the fishes come into sight, emerging as they

swim round from the shadow of the deeper water, so the larks dart over the low hedge, and through the mist, and pass before you, and are gone again. All at once one checks his pursuit, forgets the immediate object, and rises, singing as he soars. The notes fall from the air over the dark wet earth, over the dank grass, and broken withered fern of the hedges, and listening to them it seems for a moment spring. There is sunshine in the song: the lark and the light are one. He gives us a few minutes of summer in February days. In May he rises before as yet the dawn is come, and the sunrise flows down to us under through his notes. On his breast, high above the earth, the first rays fall as the rim of the sun edges up at the eastward hill. The lark and the light are as one, and wherever he glides over the wet furrows the glint of the sun goes with him. Anon alighting he runs between the lines of the green corn. In hot summer, when the open hill-side is burned with bright light, the larks are then singing and soaring. Stepping up the hill laboriously, suddenly a lark starts into the light and pours forth a rain of unwearied notes over-head. With bright light, and sunshine, and sunrise, and blue skies the bird is so associated in the mind, that even to see him in the frosty days of winter, at least assures us that summer will certainly return.

Ought not winter, in allegorical designs, the rather to be rep-resented with such things that might suggest hope than such as convey a cold and grim despair? The withered leaf, the snow-flake, the hedging bill that cuts and destroys, why these? Why not rather the dear larks for one? They fly in flocks, and amid the white expanse of snow (in the south) their pleasant twitter or call is heard as they sweep along seeking some grassy spot cleared by the wind. The lark, the bird of the light, is there in the bitter short days. Put the lark then for winter, a sign of hope, a certainty of summer. Put, too, the sheathed bud, for if you search the hedge you will find the buds there, on tree and bush, carefully wrapped around with the case which protects them as a cloak. Put, too, the sharp needles of the green corn; let the wind clear it of snow a little way, and show that under cold clod and colder snow the green thing pushes up, knowing

that summer must come. Nothing despairs but man. Set the
sharp curve of the white new moon in the sky: she is white in
true frost, and yellow a little if it is devising change. Set the new
moon as something that symbols an increase. Set the shepherd's
crook in a corner as a token that the flocks are already enlarged
in number. The shepherd is the symbolic man of the hardest
winter time. His work is never more important than then.
Those that only roam the fields when they are pleasant in May,
see the lambs at play in the meadow, and naturally think of
lambs and May flowers. But the lamb was born in the adversity
of snow. Or you might set the morning star, for it burns and
burns and glitters in the winter dawn, and throws forth beams
like those of metal consumed in oxygen. There is nought that I
know by comparison with which I might indicate the glory of
the morning star, while yet the dark night hides in the hollows.
The lamb is born in the fold. The morning star glitters in the sky.
The bud is alive in its sheath; the green corn under the snow;
the lark twitters as he passes. Now these to me are the allegory
of winter.

These mild hours in February check the hold which winter
has been gaining, and as it were, tear his claws out of the earth,
their prey. If it has not been so bitter previously, when this Gulf
stream or current of warmer air enters the expanse it may bring
forth a butterfly and tenderly woo the first violet into flower.
But this depends on its having been only moderately cold
before, and also upon the stratum, whether it is backward clay,
or forward gravel and sand. Spring dates are quite different
according to the locality, and when violets may be found in one
district, in another there is hardly a woodbine-leaf out. The
border line may be traced, and is occasionally so narrow, one
may cross over it almost at a step. It would sometimes seem as
if even the nut-tree bushes bore larger and finer nuts on the
warmer soil, and that they ripened quicker. Any curious in the
first of things, whether it be a leaf, or flower, or a bird, should
bear this in mind, and not be discouraged because he hears
some one else has already discovered or heard something.

A little note taken now at this bare time of the kind of earth
may lead to an understanding of the district. It is plain where

the plough has turned it, where the rabbits have burrowed and thrown it out, where a tree has been felled by the gales, by the brook where the bank is worn away, or by the sediment at the shallow places. Before the grass and weeds, and corn and flowers have hidden it, the character of the soil is evident at these natural sections without the aid of a spade. Going slowly along the footpath – indeed you cannot go fast in moist February – it is a good time to select the places and map them out where herbs and flowers will most likely come first. All the autumn lies prone on the ground. Dead dark leaves, some washed to their woody frames, short grey stalks, some few decayed hulls of hedge fruit, and among these the mars or stocks of the plants that do not die away, but lie as it were on the surface waiting. Here the strong teazle will presently stand high; here the ground-ivy will dot the mound with bluish-purple. But it will be necessary to walk slowly to find the ground-ivy flowers under the cover of the briers. These bushes will be a likely place for a blackbird's nest; this thick close hawthorn for a bullfinch; these bramble thickets with remnants of old nettle stalks will be frequented by the whitethroat after a while. The hedge is now but a lattice-work which will before long be hung with green. Now it can be seen through, and now is the time to arrange for future discovery. In May everything will be hidden, and unless the most promising places are selected beforehand, it will not be easy to search them out. The broad ditch will be arched over, the plants rising on the mound will meet the green boughs drooping, and all the vacancy will be filled. But having observed the spot in winter you can almost make certain of success in spring.

It is this previous knowledge which invests those who are always on the spot, those who work much in the fields or have the care of woods, with their apparent prescience. They lead the new comer to a hedge, or the corner of a copse, or a bend of the brook, announcing beforehand that they feel assured something will be found there; and so it is. This, too, is one reason why a fixed observer usually sees more than one who rambles a great deal and covers ten times the space. The fixed observer who hardly goes a mile from home is like the man who sits still by the edge of a crowd, and by-and-by his lost companion returns to him. To walk about in search of persons in a crowd is well known to be the worst way of recovering them. Sit still and they will often come by. In a far more certain manner this is the case with birds and animals. They all come back. During a twelvemonth probably every creature would pass over a given locality: every creature that is not confined to certain places. The whole army of the woods and hedges marches across a single farm in twelve months. A single tree – especially an old tree – is visited by four-fifths of the birds that ever perch in the course of that period. Every year, too, brings something fresh, and adds new visitors to the list. Even the wild sea birds are found inland, and some that scarce seem able to fly at all are cast far ashore by the gales. It is difficult to believe that one would not see more by extending the journey, but, in fact, experience proves that the longer a single locality is studied the more is found in it. But you should know the places in winter as well as in tempting summer, when song and shade and colour attract every one to the field. You should face the mire and slippery path. Nature yields nothing to the sybarite. The meadow glows with buttercups in spring, the hedges are green, the woods lovely; but these are not to be enjoyed in their full significance unless you have traversed the same places when bare, and have watched the slow fulfilment of the flowers.

The moist leaves that remain upon the mounds do not rustle, and the thrush moves among them unheard. The sunshine may bring out a rabbit, feeding along the slope of the mound, following the paths or runs. He picks his way, he does not like wet. Though out at night in the dewy grass of summer, in the rain-soaked grass of winter, and living all his life in the earth, often damp nearly to his burrows, no time, and no succession of generations can make him like wet. He endures it, but he picks his way round the dead fern and the decayed leaves. He sits in the bunches of long grass, but he does not like the drops of rain or dew on it to touch him. Water lays his fur close, and mats it, instead of running off and leaving him sleek. As he hops a little way at a time on the mound he chooses his route almost as we pick ours in the mud and pools of February. By the shore of the ditch there still stand a few dry, dead dock stems, with some dry reddish-brown seed adhering. Some dry brown nettle stalks remain; some grey and broken thistles; some teazles leaning on the bushes. The power of winter has reached its upmost now, and can go no farther. These bines which still hang in the bushes are those of the greater bindweed, and will be used in a month or so by many birds as conveniently curved to fit about their nests. The stem of wild clematis, grey and bowed, could scarcely look more dead. Fibres are peeling from it, they come off at the touch of the fingers. The few brown feathers that perhaps still adhere where the flowers once were are stained and discoloured by the beating of the rain. It is not dead: it will flourish again ere long. It is the sturdiest of creepers, facing the ferocious winds of the hills, the tremendous rains that blow up from the sea, and bitter frost, if only it can get its roots into soil that suits it. In some places it takes the place of the hedge proper and becomes itself the hedge. Many of the trunks of the elms are swathed in minute green vegetation which has flourished in the winter, as the clematis will in the summer. Of all, the brambles bear the wild works of winter best. Given only a little shelter, in the corner of the hedges or under trees and copses they retain green leaves till the buds burst again. The frosts tint them in autumn with crimson, but not all turn colour or fall. The brambles are the bowers of the birds; in these still leafy bowers they do the courting of the spring, and under the brambles the earliest arum, and cleaver, or avens, push up. Round about them the first white nettle flowers, not long now; latest too, in the autumn. The white nettle sometimes blooms so soon (always according to locality), and again so late, that there seems but a brief interval between, as if it flowered nearly all the year round. So the berries on the holly if let alone often stay till summer is in, and new berries begin to appear shortly afterwards. The ivy, too, bears its berries far into the summer. Perhaps if the country be taken at large there is never a time when there is not a flower of some kind out, in this or that warm southern nook. The sun never sets, nor do the flowers ever die. There is life always, even in the dry fir-cone that looks so brown and sapless.

The path crosses the uplands where the lapwings stand on the parallel ridges of the ploughed field like a drilled company; if they rise they wheel as one, and in the twilight move across the fields in bands, invisible as they sweep near the ground, but seen against the sky in rising over the trees and the hedges. There is a plantation of fir and ash on the slope, and a narrow waggon-way enters it, and seems to lose itself in the wood. Always approach this spot quietly, for whatever is in the wood is sure at some time or other to come to the open space of the track. Wood-pigeons, pheasants, squirrels, magpies, hares, everything feathered or furred, down to the mole, is sure to seek the open way. Butterflies flutter through the copse by it in summer, just as you or I might use the passage between the trees. Towards the evening the partridges may run through to join their friends before roost-time on the ground. Or you may see a covey there now and then, creeping slowly with humped backs, and at a distance not unlike hedgehogs in their motions. The spot therefore should be approached with care; if it is only a thrush out it is a pleasure to see him at his ease and, as he deems, unobserved. If a bird or animal thinks itself noticed it seldom does much, some will cease singing immediately they are looked at. The day is perceptibly longer already. As the sun goes down, the western sky often takes a lovely green tint in this month, and one stays to look at it, forgetting the dark and miry way homewards. I think the moments when we forget the mire of the world are the most precious. After a while the green corn rises higher out of the rude earth.

Pure colour almost always gives the idea of fire, or rather it is perhaps as if a light shone through as well as colour itself. The fresh green blade of corn is like this, so pellucid, so clear and pure in its green as to seem to shine with colour. It is not brilliant – not a surface gleam or an enamel, – it is stained through. Beside the moist clods the slender flags arise filled with the sweetness of the earth. Out of the darkness under –

that darkness which knows no day save when the ploughshare opens its chinks – they have come to the light. To the light they have brought a colour which will attract the sunbeams from now till harvest. They fall more pleasantly on the corn, toned, as if they mingled with it. Seldom do we realize that the world is practically no thicker to us than the print of our footsteps on the path. Upon that surface we walk and act our comedy of life, and what is beneath is nothing to us. But it is out from that under-world, from the dead and the unknown, from the cold moist ground, that these green blades have sprung. Yonder a steam-plough pants up the hill, groaning with its own strength, yet all that strength and might of wheels, and piston, and chains, cannot drag from the earth one single blade like these. Force cannot make it; it must grow – an easy word to speak or write, in fact full of potency. It is this mystery of growth and life, of beauty, and sweetness, and colour, starting forth from the clods that gives the corn its power over me. Somehow I identify myself with it; I live again as I see it. Year by year it is the same, and when I see it I feel that I have once more entered on a new life. And I think the spring, with its green corn, its violets, and hawthorn-leaves, and increasing song, grows yearly dearer and more dear to this our ancient earth. So many centuries have flown! Now it is the manner with all natural things to gather as it were by smallest particles. The merest grain of sand drifts unseen into a crevice, and by-and-by another; after a while there is a heap; a century and it is a mound, and then every one observes and comments on it. Time itself has gone on like this; the years have accumulated, first in drifts, then in heaps, and now a vast mound, to which the mountains are knolls, rises up and overshadows us. Time lies heavy on the world. The old, old earth is glad to turn from the cark and care of drifted centuries to the first sweet blades of green.

There is sunshine to-day after rain, and every lark is singing. Across the vale a broad cloud-shadow descends the hillside, is lost in the hollow, and presently, without warning, slips over the edge, coming swiftly along the green tips. The sunshine follows – the warmer for its momentary absence. Far, far down in a grassy coomb stands a solitary cornrick, conical roofed, casting a lonely shadow – marked because so solitary, and beyond it on the rising slope is a brown copse. The leafless branches take a brown tint in the sunlight; on the summit above there is furze; then more hill lines drawn against the sky. In the tops of the dark pines at the corner of the copse, could the glance sustain itself to see them, there are finches warming themselves in the sunbeams. The thick needles shelter them from the current of air, and the sky is bluer above the pines. Their hearts are full already of the happy days to come, when the moss yonder by the beech, and the lichen on the fir-trunk, and the loose fibres caught in the fork of an unbending bough, shall furnish forth a sufficient mansion for their young. Another broad cloud-shadow, and another warm embrace of sunlight. All the serried ranks of the green corn bow at the word of command as the wind rushes over them.

There is largeness and freedom here. Broad as the down and free as the wind, the thought can roam high over the narrow roofs in the vale. Nature has affixed no bounds to thought. All the palings, and walls, and crooked fences deep down yonder are artificial. The fetters and traditions, the routine, the dull roundabout which deadens the spirit like the cold moist earth, are the merest nothings. Here it is easy with the physical eye to look over the highest roof. The moment the eye of the mind is filled with the beauty of things natural an equal freedom and width of view come to it. Step aside from the trodden footpath of personal experience, throwing away the petty cynicism born of petty hopes disappointed. Step out upon the broad down beside the green corn, and let its freshness become part of life.

The wind passes, and it bends – let the wind, too, pass over the spirit. From the cloud-shadow it emerges to the sunshine – let the heart come out from the shadow of roofs to the open glow of the sky. High above, the songs of the larks fall as rain – receive it with open hands. Pure is the colour of the green flags, the slender-pointed blades – let the thought be pure as the light that shines through that colour. Broad are the Downs and open the aspect – gather the breadth and largeness of view. Never can that view be wide enough and large enough, there will always be room to aim higher. As the air of the hills enriches the blood, so let the presence of these beautiful things enrich the inner sense. One memory of the green corn, fresh beneath the sun and wind, will lift up the heart from the clods.

Haunts of the Lapwing: Winter

First published in *Good Words*, January 1883
First collected in *The Open Air*, 1885

Coming like a white wall the rain reaches me, and in an instant
everything is gone from sight that is more than ten yards distant. The narrow upland road is beaten to a darker hue, and
two runnels of water rush along at the sides, where, when the
chalk-laden streamlets dry, blue splinters of flint will be exposed
in the channels. For a moment the air seems driven away by the
sudden pressure, and I catch my breath and stand still with one
shoulder forward to receive the blow. Hiss, the land shudders
under the cold onslaught; hiss, and on the blast goes, and the
sound with it, for the very fury of the rain, after the first second,
drowns its own noise. There is not a single creature visible, the
low and stunted hedgerows, bare of leaf, could conceal nothing;
the rain passes straight through to the ground. Crooked and
gnarled, the bushes are locked together as if in no other way
could they hold themselves against the gales. Such little grass
as there is on the mounds is thin and short, and could not hide
a mouse. There is no finch, sparrow, thrush, blackbird. As the
wave of rain passes over and leaves a hollow between the waters,
that which has gone and that to come, the ploughed lands on
either side are seen to be equally bare. In furrows full of water,
a hare would not sit, nor partridge run; the larks, the patient
larks which endure almost everything, even they have gone.
Furrow on furrow with flints dotted on their slopes, and chalk
lumps, that is all. The cold earth gives no sweet petal of flower,
nor can any bud of thought or bloom of imagination start
forth in the mind. But step by step, forcing a way through the
rain and over the ridge, I find a small and stunted copse down
in the next hollow. It is rather a wide hedge than a copse, and

stands by the road in the corner of a field. The boughs are bare; still they break the storm, and it is a relief to wait a while there and rest. After a minute or so the eye gets accustomed to the branches and finds a line of sight through the narrow end of the copse. Within twenty yards – just outside the copse – there are a number of lapwings, dispersed about the furrows. One runs a few feet forward and picks something from the ground; another runs in the same manner to one side; a third rushes in still a third direction. Their crests, their green-tinted wings, and white breasts are not disarranged by the torrent. Something in the style of the birds recalls the wagtail, though they are so much larger. Beyond these are half a dozen more, and in a straggling line others extend out into the field. They have found some slight shelter here from the sweeping of the rain and wind, and are not obliged to face it as in the open. Minutely searching every clod they gather their food in imperceptible items from the surface.

Sodden leaves lie in the furrows along the side of the copse; broken and decaying burdocks still uphold their jagged stems, but will be soaked away by degrees; dank grasses droop outwards; the red seed of a dock is all that remains of the berries and fruit, the seeds and grain of autumn. Like the hedge, the copse is vacant. Nothing moves within, watch as carefully as I may. The boughs are blackened by wet and would touch cold. From the grasses to the branches there is nothing any one would like to handle, and I stand apart even from the bush that keeps away the rain. The green plovers are the only things of life that save the earth from utter loneliness. Heavily as the rain may fall, cold as the saturated wind may blow, the plovers remind us of the beauty of shape, colour, and animation. They seem too slender to withstand the blast – they should have gone with the swallows – too delicate for these rude hours; yet they alone face them.

Once more the wave of rain has passed, and yonder the hills appear; these are but uplands. The nearest and highest has a green rampart, visible for a moment against the dark sky, and then again wrapped in a toga of misty cloud. So the chilled Roman drew his toga around him in ancient days as from that spot he looked wistfully southwards and thought of Italy. Wee-ah-wee! Some chance movement has been noticed by the nearest bird, and away they go at once as if with the same wings, sweeping overhead, then to the right, then to the left, and then back again, till at last lost in the coming shower. After they have thus vibrated to and fro long enough, like a pendulum coming to rest, they will alight in the open field on the ridge behind. There in drilled ranks, well closed together, all facing the same way, they will stand for hours. Let us go also and let the shower conceal them. Another time my path leads over the hills.

It is afternoon, which in winter is evening. The sward of the down is dry under foot, but hard, and does not lift the instep with the springy feel of summer. The sky is gone, it is not clouded, it is swathed in gloom. Upwards the still air thickens, and there is no arch or vault of heaven. Formless and vague, it seems some vast shadow descending. The sun has disappeared, and the light there still is, is left in the atmosphere enclosed by the gloomy mist as pools are left by a receding tide. Through the sand the water slips, and through the mist the light glides away. Nearer comes the formless shadow, and the visible earth grows smaller. The path has faded, and there are no means on the open Downs of knowing whether the direction pursued is right or wrong, till a boulder (which is a landmark) is perceived. Thence the way is down the slope, the last and limit of the hills there. It is a rough descent, the paths worn by sheep may at any moment cause a stumble. At the foot is a waggon-track beside a low hedge, enclosing the first arable field. The hedge is a guide, but the ruts are deep, and it still needs slow and careful walking. Wee-ah-wee! Up from the dusky surface of the arable field springs a plover, and the notes are immediately repeated by another. They can just be seen as darker bodies against the shadow as they fly overhead. Wee-ah-wee! The sound grows fainter as they fetch a longer circle in the gloom.

There is another winter resort of plovers in the valley where a barren waste was ploughed some years ago. A few furze bushes still stand in the hedges about it, and the corners are full

of rushes. Not all the grubbing of furze and bushes, the deep
ploughing and draining, has succeeded in rendering the place
fertile like the adjacent fields. The character of a marsh adheres
to it still. So long as there is a crop, the lapwings keep away, but
as soon as the ploughs turn up the ground in autumn they
return. The place lies low, and level with the waters in the
ponds and streamlets. A mist hangs about it in the evening, and
even when there is none, there is a distinct difference in the
atmosphere while passing it. From their hereditary home the
lapwings cannot be entirely driven away. Out of the mist comes
their plaintive cry; they are hidden, and their exact locality is
not to be discovered. Where winter rules most ruthlessly, where
darkness is deepest in daylight, there the slender plovers stay
undaunted.

PART THREE

LATE ESSAYS
(1882–7)

Notes on Landscape Painting

First published in the *Magazine of Art*, March 1882
First collected in *The Life of the Fields*, 1884

The earth has a way of absorbing things that are placed upon it, of drawing from them their stiff individuality of newness, and throwing over them something of her own antiquity. As the furrow smoothes and brightens the share, as the mist eats away the sharpness of the iron angles, so, in a larger manner, the machines sent forth to conquer the soil are conquered by it, become a part of it, and as natural as the old, old scythe and reaping-hook. Thus already the new agriculture has grown hoar.

The oldest of the modern implements is the threshing-machine, which is historic, for it was once the cause of rural war. There are yeomanry-men still living who remember how they rode about at night after the rioters, guided by the blazing bonfires kindled to burn the new-fangled things. Much blood – of John Barleycorn – was spilt in that campaign; and there is many a farmer yet hearty who recollects the ale-barrels being rolled up into the rickyards and there broached in cans and buckets, that the rebels, propitiated with plentiful liquor, might forbear to set fire to the ricks or sack the homestead. Such memories read strange to the present generation, proving thereby that the threshing-machine has already grown old. It is so accepted that the fields would seem to lack something if it were absent. It is as natural as the ricks: things grow old so soon in the fields.

On the fitful autumn breeze, with brown leaves whirling and grey grass rustling in the hedges, the hum of the fly-wheel sounds afar, travelling through the mist which hides the hills. Sometimes the ricks are in the open stubble, up the Down side, where the wind comes in a long, strong rush, like a tide, carrying away the smoke from the funnel in a sweeping trail; while the brown canvas, stretched as a screen, flaps and tears, and the folk at work can scarce hear each other speak, any more than you can by the side of the sea. Vast atmospheric curtains – what else can you call them? – roll away, opening a view of the stage of hills a moment, and, closing again, reach from heaven to earth around. The dark sky thickens and lowers as if it were gathering thunder, as women glean wheatears in their laps. It is not thunder; it is as if the wind grew solid and hurled itself – as a man might throw out his clenched fist – at the hill. The inclined plane of the mist-clouds again reflects a grey light, and, as if swept up by the fierce gale, a beam of sunshine comes. You see it first long, as it is at an angle; then overhead it shortens, and again lengthens after it has passed, somewhat like the spoke of a wheel. In the second of its presence a red handkerchief a woman wears on the ricks stands out, the brass on the engine glows, the water in the butt gleams, men's faces brighten, the cart-horse's coat looks glossy, the straw a pleasant yellow. It is gone, and lights up the backs of the sheep yonder as it runs up the hill swifter than a hare. Swish! The north wind darkens the sky, and the fly-wheel moans in the gloom; the wood-pigeons go a mile a minute on the wind, hardly using their wings; the brown woods below huddle together, rounding their shoulders to the blast; a great air-shadow, not mist, a shadow of thickness in the air looms behind a tiled roof in the valley. The vast profound is full of the rushing air.

These are days of autumn; but earlier than this, when the wheat that is now being threshed was ripe, the reaping-machine went round and round the field, beginning at the outside by the hedges. Red arms, not unlike a travelling windmill on a small scale, sweep the corn as it is cut and leave it spread on the ground. The bright red fans, the white jacket of the man driving, the brown and iron-grey horses, and yellow wheat are toned – melted together at their edges – with warm sunlight. The machine is lost in the corn, and nothing is visible, but the colours, and the fact that it is the reaping, the time of harvest, dear to man these how many thousand years! There is nothing new in it; it is all old as the hills. The straw covers over the knives, the rims of the wheels sink into pimpernel, convolvulus, veronica; the dry earth powders them, and so all beneath is concealed. Above the sunlight (and once now and then the shadow of a tree) throws its mantle over, and, like the hand of an enchanter softly waving, surrounds it with a charm. So the cranks, and wheels, and knives, and mechanism do not exist – it was a machine in the workshop, but it is not a machine in the wheat-field. For the wheat-field you see is very, very old, and the air is of old time, and the shadow, the flowers, and the sunlight, and that which moves among them becomes of them. The solitary reaper alone in the great field goes round and round, the red fans striking beside him, alone with the sunlight, and the blue sky, and the distant hills; and he and his reaper are as much of the cornfield as the long-forgotten sickle or the reaping-hook.

The sharp rattle of the mowing-machine disturbs the corn-crake in the meadow. Crake! crake! for many a long day since the grass began to grow fast in April till the cowslips flowered, and white parsley flourished like a thicket, blue scabious came up, and yonder the apple trees drop their bloom. Crake! crake! nearly day and night; but now the rattle begins, and the bird must take refuge in the corn. Like the reaper, the mowing-machine is buried under the swathe it cuts, and flowers fall over it – broad ox-eye daisies and red sorrel. Upon the hedge June roses bloom; blackbirds whistle in the oaks; now and again come the soft hollow notes of the cuckoo. Angles and wheels, cranks and cogs, where are they? They are lost; it is not these we see, but the flowers and the pollen on the grass. There is an odour of new-made hay; there is the song of birds, and the trees are beautiful.

As for the drill in spring-time, it is ancient indeed, and ancients follow it – aged men stepping after over the clods, and watching it as if it were a living thing, that the grains may fall each in its appointed place. Their faces, their gait, nay, the very planting of their heavy shoes' stamp on the earth, are full of the importance of this matter. On this the year depends, and the harvest, and all our lives, that the sowing be accomplished in good order, as is meet. Therefore they are in the earnest, and do not turn aside to gaze at strangers, like those do who hoe, being of no account. This is a serious matter, needing men of days, little of speech, but long of experience. So the heavy drill, with its hanging rows of funnels, travels across the field well tended, and there is not one who notes the deep azure of the March sky above the elms.

Still another step, tracing the seasons backwards, brings in the steam-plough. When the spotted arum leaves unfold on the bank, before the violets or the first celandine, while the 'pussies' hang on the hazel, the engines roll into the field, pressing the earth into barred ruts. The massive wheels leave their imprint, the footsteps of steam, behind them. By the hedges they stand, one on either side, and they hold the field between them with their rope of iron. Like the claws of some pre-historic monster, the shares rout up the ground; the solid ground is helpless before them; they tear and rend it. One engine is under an oak, dark yet with leafless boughs, up through which the black smoke rises; the other overtops a low hedge, and is in full profile. By the panting, and the humming, and the clanking as the drum revolves, by the smoke hanging in the still air, by the trembling of the monster as it strains and tugs, by the sense of heat, and effort, and pent-up energy bubbling over in jets of steam that struggle through crevices somewhere, by the straightened rope and the jerking of the plough as it comes, you know how mighty is the power that thus in narrow space works its will upon the earth. Planted broadside, its four limbs – the massive wheels – hold the ground like a wrestler drawing to him the unwilling opponent. Humming, panting, trembling, with stretched but irresistible muscles, the iron creature conquers, and the plough approaches. All the field for the minute seems concentrated in this thing of power. There are acres and acres, scores of acres around, but they are surface only. This is the central spot: they are nothing, mere matter. This is force – Thor in another form. If you are near you cannot take your eyes off the sentient iron, the wrestler straining. But now the plough has come over, and the signal given reverses its way. The lazy monotonous clanking as the drum unwinds on this side, the rustling of the rope as it is dragged forth over the clods, the quiet rotation of the fly-wheel – these sounds let the excited thought down as the rotating fly-wheel works off the maddened steam. The combat over, you can look round.

It is the February summer that comes, and lasts a week or so between the January frosts and the east winds that rush through the thorns. Some little green is even now visible along the mound where seed-leaves are springing up. The sun is warm, and the still air genial, the sky only dotted with a few white clouds. Wood-pigeons are busy in the elms, where the ivy is thick with ripe berries. There is a feeling of spring and of growth; in a day or two we shall find violets; and listen, how sweetly the larks are singing! Some chase each other, and then hover fluttering above the hedge. The stubble, whitened by exposure to the weather, looks lighter in the sunshine, and the distant view is softened by haze. A water-tank approaches, and the cart-horse steps in the pride of strength. The carter's lad goes to look at the engine and to wonder at the uses of the gauge. All the brazen parts gleam in the bright sun, and the driver presses some waste against the piston now it works slowly, till it shines like polished silver. The red glow within, as the furnace-door is opened, lights up the lad's studious face beneath like sunset. A few brown leaves yet cling to one bough of the oak, and the rooks come over cawing happily in the unwonted warmth. The low hum and the monotonous clanking, the rustling of the wire rope, give a sense of quiet. Let us wander along the hedge, and look for signs of spring. This is to-day. To-morrow, if we come, the engines are half-hidden from afar by driving sleet and scattered snow-flakes fleeting aslant the field. Still sternly they labour in the cold and gloom. A third time you may find them, in September or bright October, with acorns dropping from the oaks, the distant sound of the gun, and perhaps a pheasant looking out from the corner. If the moon be full and bright they work on an hour or so by her light, and the vast shadows of the engines are thrown upon the stubble.

Walks in the Wheat-fields

First published in the *English Illustrated Magazine*,
July and August 1887
First collected in *Field and Hedgerow*, 1889

If you will look at a grain of wheat you will see that it seems
folded up: it has crossed its arms and rolled itself up in a cloak,
a fold of which forms a groove, and so gone to sleep. If you
look at it some time, as people in the old enchanted days used
to look into a mirror, or the magic ink, until they saw living
figures therein, you can almost trace a miniature human being
in the oval of the grain. It is narrow at the top, where the head
would be, and broad across the shoulders, and narrow again
down towards the feet; a tiny man or woman has wrapped
itself round about with a garment and settled to slumber. Up in
the far north, where the dead ice reigns, our arctic explorers
used to roll themselves in a sleeping-bag like this, to keep the
warmth in their bodies against the chilliness of the night. Down
in the south, where the heated sands of Egypt never cool, there
in the rock-hewn tombs lie the mummies wrapped and lapped
and wound about with a hundred yards of linen, in the hope, it
may be, that spices and balm might retain within the sarcopha-
gus some small fragment of human organism through endless
ages, till at last the gift of life revisited it. Like a grain of wheat
the mummy is folded in its cloth. And I do not know really
whether I might not say that these little grains of English corn
do not hold within them the actual flesh and blood of man.
Transubstantiation is a fact there.

Sometimes the grains are dry and shrivelled and hard as shot,
sometimes they are large and full and have a juiciness about
them, sometimes they are a little bit red, others are golden,
many white. The sack stands open in the market – you can

thrust your arm in it a foot deep, or take up a handful and let it run back like a liquid stream, or hold it in your palm and balance it, feeling the weight. They are not very heavy as they lie in the palm, yet these little grains are a ponderous weight that rules man's world. Wherever they are there is empire. Could imperial Rome have only grown sufficient wheat in Italy to have fed her legions Caesar would still be master of three-fourths of the earth. Rome thought more in her latter days of grapes and oysters and mullets, that change colour as they die, and singing girls and flute-playing, and cynic verse of Horace – anything rather than corn. Rome is no more, and the lords of the world are they who have mastership of wheat. We have the mastership at this hour by dint of our gold and our hundred-ton guns, but they are telling our farmers to cast aside their corn, and to grow tobacco and fruit and anything else that can be thought of in preference. The gold is slipping away. These sacks in the market open to all to thrust their hands in are not sacks of corn but of golden sovereigns, half-sovereigns, new George and the dragon, old George and the dragon, Sydney mint sovereigns, Napoleons, half Napoleons, Belgian gold, German gold, Italian gold; gold scraped and scratched and gathered together like old rags from door to door. Sacks full of gold, verily I may say that all the gold poured out from the Australian fields, every pennyweight of it, hundreds of tons, all shipped over the sea to India, Australia, South Africa, Egypt, and, above all, America, to buy wheat. It was said that Pompey and his sons covered the great earth with their bones, for each one died in a different quarter of the world; but now he would want two more sons for Australia and America, the two new quarters which are now at work ploughing, sowing, reaping, without a month's intermission, growing corn for us. When you buy a bag of flour at the baker's you pay fivepence over the counter, a very simple transaction. Still you do not expect to get even that little bag of flour for nothing, your fivepence goes over the counter in somebody else's till. Consider now the broad ocean as the counter and yourself to represent thirty-five millions of English people buying sixteen, seventeen, or eighteen million quarters of wheat from the nations opposite, and paying for it shiploads of gold.

So that these sacks of corn in the market are truly filled with gold dust; and how strange it seems at first that our farmers, who are for ever dabbling with their hands in these golden sands, should be for ever grumbling at their poverty! 'The nearer the church the farther from God' is an old country proverb; the nearer to wheat the farther from mammon, I may construct as an addendum. Quite lately a gentleman told me that while he grew wheat on his thousand acres he lost just a pound an acre per annum, i.e. a thousand a year out of capital, so that if he had not happily given up this amusement he would now have been in the workhouse munching the putty there supplied for bread.

The rag and bone men go from door to door filling an old bag with scraps of linen, and so innumerable agents of bankers and financiers, vampires that suck gold, are for ever prowling about collecting every golden coin they can scent out and shipping it over sea. And what does not go abroad is in consequence of this great drain sharply locked up in the London safes as reserves against paper, and cannot be utilized in enterprises or manufacture. Therefore trade stands still, and factories are closed, and ship-yards are idle, and beautiful vessels are stored up doing nothing by hundreds in dock; coal mines left to be filled with water, and furnaces blown out. Therefore there is bitter distress and starvation, and cries for relief works, and one meal a day for Board school children, and the red flag of Socialism is unfurled. All because of these little grains of wheat.

They talked of bringing artillery, with fevered lips, to roar forth shrapnel in Trafalgar Square; why not Gatling guns? The artillery did not come for very shame, but the Guards did, and there were regiments of infantry in the rear, with glittering bayonets to prod folk into moving on. All about these little grains of wheat.

These thoughts came into my mind in the winter afternoon at the edge of a level cornfield, with the copper-sheathed spire of the village church on my right, the sun going down on the left. The copper did not gleam, it was dull and brown, no better than discoloured wood, patched with pieces of later date and another shade of dullness. I wish they would glitter, some of these steeples or some of our roofs, and so light up the reddish brown of the elms and the grey lichened oaks. The very rooks are black, and the starlings and the wintry fieldfares and red-wings have no colour at a distance. They say the metal roofs and domes gleam in Russia, and even in France, and why not in our rare sunshine? Once now and then you see a gilded weather-cock shine like a day-star as the sun goes down three miles away, over the dark brown field, where the plough has been going to and fro through the slow hours. I can see the plough and the horses very well at three miles, and know what they are doing.

I wish the trees, the elms, would grow tall enough and thick enough to hide the steeples and towers which stand up so stiff and stark, and bare and cold, some of them blunted and squab, some of them sharp enough to impale, with no more shape than a walking-stick, ferrule upwards – every one of them out of proportion and jarring to the eye. If by good fortune you can find a spot where you cannot see a steeple or a church tower, where you can see only fields and woods, you will find it so much more beautiful, for nature has made it of its kind perfect. The dim sea is always so beautiful a view because it is not dis-figured by these buildings. In the ships men live; in the houses among the trees they live; these steeples and towers are empty, and no spirit can dwell in that which is out of proportion. Scarcely any one can paint a picture of the country without sticking in one of these repellent structures. The oast-houses, whose red cones are so plentiful in Kent and Sussex, have quite a different effect; they have some colour, and by a curious feli-city the builders have hit upon a good proportion, so that the shape is pleasant; these, too, have some use in the world.

Westward the sun was going down over the sea, and a wild west wind, which the glow of the sun as it touched the waves seemed to heat into fury, brought up the distant sound of the billows from the beach. A line of dark Spanish oaks from which the sharp pointed acorns were dropping, darkest green oaks, shut out the shore. A thousand starlings were flung up into the air out of these oaks, as if an impatient hand had cast them into the sky; then down they fell again, with a ceaseless whistling and clucking; up they went and down they came, lost in the deep green foliage as if they had dropped in the sea. The long level of the wheat-field plain stretched out from my feet towards the far-away Downs, so level that the first hedge shut off the fields beyond; and every now and then over these hedges there rose up the white forms of sea-gulls drifting to and fro among the elms. White sea-gulls – birds of divination, you might say – a good symbol of the times, for now we plough the ocean. The barren sea! In the Greek poets you may find constant reference to it as that which could not be reaped or sowed. Ulysses, to betoken his madness, took his plough down to the shore and drew furrows in the sand – the sea that even Demeter, great goddess, could not sow nor bring to any fruition. Yet now the ocean is our wheat-field and ships are our barns. The sea-gull should be painted on the village tavern sign instead of the golden wheatsheaf.

There could be no more flat and uninteresting surface than this field, a damp wet brown, water slowly draining out of the furrows, not a bird that I can see. No hare certainly, or partridge, or even a rabbit – nothing to sit or crouch – on that cold surface, tame and level as the brown cover of a book. They like something more human and comfortable; just as we creep into nooks and corners of rooms and into cosy arm-chairs, so they like tufts or some growth of shelter, or mounds that are dry, between hedges where there is a bite for them. I can trace nothing on this surface, so heavily washed by late rain. Let now the harriers come, and instantly the hounds' second sense of smell picks up the invisible sign of the hare that has crossed it in the night or early dawn, and runs it as swiftly as if he were lifting a clue of thread. The dull surface is all written over with hieroglyphics to the hound, he can read and translate to us in joyous tongue. Or the foxhounds carry a bee-line straight from hedge to hedge, and after them come the hoofs, prospecting deeply into the earth, dashing down fibre and blade, crunching up the tender wheat and battering it to pieces. It will rise again all the fresher and stronger, for there is something human in wheat, and the more it is trampled on the better it grows. Despots grind half the human race, and despots stronger than man –

plague, pestilence, and famine – grind the whole; and yet the world increases, and the green wheat of the human heart is not to be trampled out.

The starlings grew busier and busier in the dark green Spanish oaks, thrown up as if a shell had burst among them; suddenly their clucking and whistling ceased, the speeches of contention were over, a vote of confidence had been passed in their Government, and the House was silent. The pheasants in the park shook their wings and crowed 'kuck, kuck – kow', and went to roost; the water in the furrows ceased to reflect; the dark earth grew darker and damper; the elms lost their reddish brown; the sky became leaden behind the ridge of the Downs, and the shadow of night fell over the field.

Twenty-five years ago I went into a camera obscura, where you see miniature men and women, coloured photographs alive and moving, trees waving, now and then dogs crossing the bright sun picture. I was only there a few moments, and I have never been in one since, and yet so inexplicable a thing is memory, the picture stands before me now clear as if it were painted and tangible. So many millions of pictures have come and gone upon the retina, and yet I can single out this one in an instant, and take it down as you would a book from a shelf. The millions of coloured etchings that have fixed themselves there in the course of those years are all in due order in the portfolio of the mind, and yet they cannot occupy the space of a pin's point. They have neither length, breadth, nor thickness, none of the qualifications of mathematical substance, and yet they must in some way be a species of matter. The fact indicates the possibility of still more subtle existences. Now I wish I could put before you a coloured, living, moving picture, like that of the camera obscura, of some other wheat-fields at a sunnier time. They were painted on the surface of a plain, set round about with a margin of green downs. They were large enough to have the charm of vague, indefinite extension, and yet all could be distinctly seen. Large squares of green corn that was absorbing its yellow from the sunlight, chess squares, irregularly placed, of brown furrows; others of rich blood-red trifolium; others of scarlet sainfoin and blue lucerne, gardens of scarlet poppies here and there. Not all of these, of course, at once, but they followed so quickly in the summer days that they seemed to be one and the same pictures, and had you painted them altogether on the same canvas, together with ripe wheat, they would not have seemed out of place. Never was such brilliant colour; it was chalk there, and on chalk the colours are always clearer, the poppies deeper, the yellow mustard and charlock a keener yellow; the air, too, is pellucid. Waggons going along the tracks; men and women hoeing; ricks of last year still among clumps of trees, where the chimneys and gables of farmhouses are partly visible; red-tiled barns away yonder; a shepherd moving his hurdles; away again the black funnel of an idle engine, and the fly-wheel above hawthorn bushes – all so distinct and close under that you might almost fear to breathe for fear of dimming the mirror. The few white clouds sailing over seemed to belong to the fields on which their shadows were now foreshortened, now lengthened, as if they were really part of the fields, like the crops, and the azure sky so low down as to be the roof of the house and not at all a separate thing. And the sun a lamp that you might almost have pushed along his course faster with your hand; a loving and interesting sun that wanted the wheat to ripen, and stayed there in the slow-drawn arc of the summer day to lend a hand. Sun and sky and clouds close here and not across any planetary space, but working with us in the same field, shoulder to shoulder, with man. Then you might see the white doves yonder flutter up suddenly out of the trees by the farm, little flecks of white clouds themselves, and everywhere all throughout the plain an exquisite silence, a delicious repose, not one clang or harshness of sound to shatter the beauty of it. There you might stand on the high down among the thyme and watch it, hour after hour, and still no interruption; nothing to break it up. It was something like the broad folio of an ancient illuminated manuscript, in gold, gules, blue, green; with foliated scrolls and human figures, somewhat clumsy and thick, but quaintly drawn, and bold in their intense realism.

There was another wheat-field by the side of which I used to walk sometimes in the evenings, as the grains in the ears began to grow firm. The path ran for a mile beside it – a mile of wheat in one piece – all those million million stalks the same height, all with about the same number of grains in each ear, all ripening together. The hue of the surface travelled along as you approached; the tint of yellow shifted farther like the reflection of sunlight on water, but the surface was really much the same colour everywhere. It seemed a triumph of culture over such a space, such regularity, such perfection of myriads of plants springing in their true lines at the same time, each particular ear perfect, and a mile of it. Perfect work with the plough, the drill, the harrow in every detail, and yet such breadth. Let your hand touch the ears lightly as you walk – drawn through them as if over the side of a boat in water – feeling the golden heads. The sparrows fly out every now and then ahead; some of the birds like their corn as it hardens, and some while it is soft and full of milky sap. There are hares within, and many a brood of partridge chicks that cannot yet use their wings. Thick as the seed itself the feathered creatures have been among the wheat since it was sown. Finches more numerous than the berries on the hedges; sparrows like the finches multiplied by finches, linnets, rooks, like leaves on the trees, wood-pigeons whose crops are like bushel baskets for capacity; and now as it ripens the multitude will be multiplied by legions, and as it comes to the harvest there is a fresh crop of sparrows from the nests in the barns, you may see a brown cloud of them a hundred yards long. Besides which there were the rabbits that ate the young green blades, and the mice that will be busy in the sheaves, and the insects from spring-time to granary, a nameless host uncounted. A whole world, as it were, let loose upon the wheat, to eat, consume, and wither it, and yet it conquers the whole world. The great field you see was filled with gold corn four feet deep as a pitcher is filled with water to the brim. Of yore the rich man is said, in the Roman classic, to have measured his money, so here you might have measured it by the rood. The sunbeams sank deeper and deeper into the wheatears, layer upon layer of light, and the colour deepened by these daily strokes. There was no bulletin to tell the folk of its progress, no Nileometer to mark the rising flood of the wheat to its hour of

overflow. Yet there went through the village a sense of expect-
ation, and men said to each other, 'We shall be there soon.' No
one knew the day – the last day of doom of the golden race;
every one knew it was nigh. One evening there was a small
square piece cut at one side, a little notch, and two shocks
stood there in the twilight. Next day the village sent forth its
army with their crooked weapons to cut and slay. It used to be
an era, let me tell you, when a great farmer gave the signal to
his reapers; not a man, woman, or child that did not talk of
that. Well-to-do people stopped their vehicles and walked out
into the new stubble. Ladies came, farmers, men of low degree,
everybody – all to exchange a word or two with the workers.
These were so terribly in earnest at the start they could scarcely
acknowledge the presence even of the squire. They felt themselves so important, and were so full, and so intense and
one-minded in their labour, that the great of the earth might
come and go as sparrows for aught they cared. More men and
more men were put on day by day, and women to bind the
sheaves, till the vast field held the village, yet they seemed but a
handful buried in the tunnels of the golden mine: they were lost
in it like the hares, for as the wheat fell, the shocks rose behind
them, low tents of corn. Your skin or mine could not have
stood the scratching of the straw, which is stiff and sharp, and
the burning of the sun, which blisters like red-hot iron. No one
could stand the harvest-field as a reaper except he had been
born and cradled in a cottage, and passed his childhood
bare-headed in July heats and January snows. I was always
fond of being out of doors, yet I used to wonder how these men
and women could stand it, for the summer day is long, and
they were there hours before I was up. The edge of the
reap-hook had to be driven by force through the stout stalks
like a sword, blow after blow, minute after minute, hour after
hour; the back stooping, and the broad sun throwing his fiery
rays from a full disc on the head and neck. I think some of them
used to put handkerchiefs doubled up in their hats as pads, as
in the East they wind the long roll of the turban about the head,
and perhaps they would have done better if they had adopted

the custom of the South and wound a long scarf about the middle of the body, for they were very liable to be struck down with such internal complaints as come from great heat. Their necks grew black, much like black oak in old houses. Their open chests were always bare, and flat, and stark, and never rising with rounded bust-like muscle as the Greek statues of athletes.

The breast-bone was burned black, and their arms, tough as ash, seemed cased in leather. They grew visibly thinner in the harvest-field, and shrunk together – all flesh disappearing, and nothing but sinew and muscle remaining. Never was such work. The wages were low in those days, and it is not long ago, either – I mean the all-year-round wages; the reaping was piece-work at so much per acre – like solid gold to men and women who had lived on dry bones, as it were, through the winter. So they worked and slaved, and tore at the wheat as if they were seized with a frenzy; the heat, the aches, the illness, the sunstroke, always impending in the air – the stomach hungry again before the meal was over, it was nothing. No song, no laugh, no stay – on from morn till night, possessed with a maddened desire to labour, for the more they could cut the larger the sum they would receive; and what is man's heart and brain to money? So hard, you see, is the pressure of human life that these miserables would have prayed on their knees for permission to tear their arms from the socket, and to scorch and shrivel themselves to charred human brands in the furnace of the sun.

Does it not seem bitter that it should be so? Here was the wheat, the beauty of which I strive in vain to tell you, in the midst of the flowery summer, scourging them with the knot of necessity; that which should give life pulling the life out of them, rendering their existence below that of the cattle, so far as the pleasure of living goes. Without doubt many a low mound in the churchyard – once visible, now level – was the sooner raised over the nameless dead because of that terrible strain in the few weeks of the gold fever. This is human life, real human life – no rest, no calm enjoyment of the scene, no generous gift of food and wine lavishly offered by the gods – the hard fist of necessity for ever battering man to a shapeless and hopeless fall.

The whole village lived in the field; a corn-land village is always the most populous, and every rood of land thereabouts, in a sense, maintains its man. The reaping, and the binding up and stacking of the sheaves, and the carting and building of the ricks, and the gleaning, there was something to do for every one, from the 'olde, olde, very olde man', the Thomas Parr of the hamlet, down to the very youngest child whose little eye could see, and whose little hand could hold a stalk of wheat. The gleaners had a way of binding up the collected wheatstalks together so that a very large quantity was held tightly in a very small compass. The gleaner's sheaf looked like the knot of a girl's hair woven in and bound. It was a tradition of the wheat-field handed down from generation to generation, a thing you could not possibly do unless you had been shown the secret – like the knots the sailors tie, a kind of hand art. The wheatstalks being thick at one end makes the sheaf heavier and more solid there, and so in any manner of fastening it or stacking it, it takes a rounded shape like a nine-pin; the round ricks are built thick in the middle and lessen gradually toward the top and toward the ground. The warm yellow of the straw is very pleasant to look at on a winter's day under a grey sky; so, too, the straw looks nice and warm and comfortable, thrown down thickly in the yards for the roan cattle.

After the village has gone back to its home still the work of the wheat is not over; there is the thatching with straw of last year, which is bleached and contrasts with the yellow of the fresh-gathered crop. Next the threshing; and meantime the ploughs are at work, and very soon there is talk of seed-time.

I used to look with wonder when I was a boy at the endless length of wall and the enormous roof of a great tithe barn. The walls of Spanish convents, with little or no window to break the vast monotony, somewhat resemble it: the convent is a building, but does not look like a home; it is too big, too gen-eral. So this barn, with its few windows, seemed too immense to belong to any one man. The tithe barn has so completely dropped out of modern life that it may be well to briefly men-tion that its use was to hold the tenth sheaf from every wheat-field in the parish. The parson's tithe was the real actual

tenth sheaf bodily taken from every field of corn in the district.
A visible tenth, you see; a very solid thing. Imagine the vast
heap they would have made, imagine the hundreds and hundreds of sacks of wheat they filled when they were threshed. I
have often thought that it would perhaps be a good thing if this
contribution of the real tenth could be brought back again for
another purpose. If such a barn could be filled now, and its produce applied to the help of the poor and aged and injured of the
village, we might get rid of that blot on our civilization – the
workhouse. Mr Besant, in his late capital story, 'The Children
of Gibeon', most truly pointed out that it was custom which
rendered all men indifferent to the sufferings of their fellow-
creatures. In the old Roman days men were crucified so often
that it ceased even to be a show; the soldiers played at dice
under the miserable wretches; the peasant women stepping by
jested and laughed and sang. Almost in our own time dry skeletons creaked on gibbets at every cross-road:

> When for thirty shillings men were hung,
> And the thirst for blood grew stronger,
> Men's lives were valued then at a sheep's –
> Thank God that lasts no longer.

So strong is custom and tradition, and the habit of thought it
weaves about us, that I have heard ancient and grave farmers,
when the fact was mentioned with horror, hum, and ah! and
handle their beards, and mutter that 'they didn't know as 'twas
altogether such a bad thing as they was hung for sheep-stealing'.
There were parsons then, as now, in every rural parish preaching and teaching something they called the Gospel. Why did
they not rise as one man and denounce this ghastly iniquity,
and demand its abolition? They did nothing of the sort; they
enjoyed their pipes and grog very comfortably.

The gallows at the cross-roads is gone, but the workhouse
stands, and custom, cruel custom, that tyrant of the mind, has
inured us (to use an old word) to its existence in our midst.
Apart from any physical suffering, let us only consider the slow
agony of the poor old reaper when he feels his lusty arm wither,

and of the grey bowed wife as they feel themselves drifting like
a ship ashore to that stony waiting-room. For it is a waiting-room
till the grave receives them. Economically, too, the workhouse
is a heavy loss and drag.

Could we, then, see the tithe barn filled again with golden
wheat for this purpose of help to humanity, it might be a great
and wonderful good. With this tenth to feed the starving and
clothe the naked; with the tenth to give the little children a midday meal at the school – that would be natural and true. In the
course of time, as the land laws lessen their grip, and the people
take possession of the earth on which they stand, it is more
than probable that something of this kind will really come about.
It would be only simple justice after so many centuries – it
takes so many hundreds of years to get even that.

'Workhouse, indeed!' I have heard the same ancient well-
to-do greybeards ejaculate, 'workhouse! they ought to be very
thankful they have got such a place to go to!'

All the village has been to the wheat-field with reaping-hooks,
and waggons and horses, the whole strength of man has been
employed upon it; little brown hands and large brown hands,
blue eyes and dark eyes have been there searching about; all
the intelligence of human beings has been brought to bear, and
yet the stubble is not empty. Down there come again the
ever-increasing clouds of sparrows; as a cloud rises here another
cloud descends beyond it, a very mist and vapour as it were of
wings. It makes one wonder to think where all the nests could
have been; there could hardly have been enough eaves and
barns for all these to have been bred in. Every one of the multitude has a keen pair of eyes and a hungry beak, and every
single individual finds something to eat in the stubble. Something that was not provided for them, crumbs that have escaped
from this broad table, and there they are every day for weeks
together, still finding food. If you will consider the incredible
number of little mouths, and the busy rate at which they ply
them hour by hour, you may imagine what an immense number
of grains of wheat must have escaped man's hand, for you must
remember that every time they peck they take a whole grain.
Down, too, come the grey-blue wood-pigeons and the wild

turtle-doves. The singing linnets come in parties, the happy greenfinches, the streaked yellowhammers, as if any one had delicately painted them in separate streaks, and not with a wash of colour, the brown buntings, chaffinches – out they come from the hazel copses, where the nuts are dropping, and the hedge berries turning red, and every one finds something to his liking. There are the seeds of the charlock and the thistle, and a hundred other little seeds, insects, and minute atom-like foods it needs a bird's eye to know. They are never still, they sweep up into the hedges and line the boughs, calling and talking, and away again to another rood of stubble without any order or plan of search, just sowing themselves about like wind-blown seeds. Up and down the day through with a zest never failing. It is beautiful to listen to them and watch them, if any one will stay under an oak by the nut-tree boughs, where the dragon-flies shoot to and fro in the shade as if the direct rays of the sun would burn their delicate wings; they hunt chiefly in the shade. The linnets will suddenly sweep up into the boughs and converse sweetly over your head. The sunshine lingers and grows sweeter as the autumn gives tokens of its coming in the buff bryony leaf, and the acorn filling its cup. They are so happy, the birds, yet there are few to listen to them. I have often looked round and wondered that no one else was about hearkening to them. Altogether, perhaps, they lead safer lives in England than anywhere else. We do not shoot them; the fowlers do mischief, still they make but little impression; there are few birds of prey, and there is not that fearful bloodthirstiness that makes a tropical forest so terrible in fact, under its outward show of glowing colour. There, with cruel hawks and owls, and serpents, and beasts of prey, a bird's life is one long terror. They are ever on the watch here, but they are not so fearfully harassed, and are not certain as it were beforehand to be torn to pieces. The land is well cultivated, and the more the culture the more the food for them. Frost and snow are their greatest enemies, but even these do not often last a great while. It is a land of woods, and above all of hedges, which are much more favourable to birds than forests, so that they are better off in England than in other countries. From the sowing to the reaping, the wheat-field gives a constant dole like the monasteries of old, only here it is no crust, but a free and bountiful largess. Then the stubble must be broken up by the plough, and again there is a fresh helping for them. Brown partridge, and black rook, and yellowhammer, all hues and degrees, come to the wheat-field.

Nature and Books

First published in the *Fortnightly Review*, May 1887
First collected in *Field and Hedgerow*, 1889

What is the colour of the dandelion? There are many dandelions:
that which I mean flowers in May, when the meadow-grass
has started and the hares are busy by daylight. That which
flowers very early in the year has a thickness of hue, and is not
interesting; in autumn the dandelions quite change their colour
and are pale. The right dandelion for this question is the one
that comes about May with a very broad disc, and in such
quantities as often to cover a whole meadow. I used to admire
them very much in the fields by Surbiton (strong clay soil), and
also on the towing-path of the Thames where the sward is very
broad, opposite Long Ditton; indeed, I have often walked up
that towing-path on a beautiful sunny morning, when all was
quiet except the nightingales in the Palace hedge, on purpose to
admire them. I dare say they are all gone now for evermore;
still, it is a pleasure to look back on anything beautiful. What
colour is this dandelion? It is not yellow, nor orange, nor gold;
put a sovereign on it and see the difference. They say the gipsies
call it the Queen's great hairy dog-flower – a number of words
to one stalk; and so, to get a colour to it, you may call it the
yellow-gold-orange plant. In the winter, on the black mud
under a dark, dripping tree, I found a piece of orange peel,
lately dropped – a bright red orange speck in the middle of the
blackness. It looked very beautiful, and instantly recalled to my
mind the great dandelion discs in the sunshine of summer. Yet
certainly they are not red-orange. Perhaps, if ten people answered
this question, they would each give different answers. Again, a
bright day or a cloudy, the presence of a slight haze, or the
juxtaposition of other colours, alters it very much; for the

dandelion is not a glazed colour, like the buttercup, but sensitive. It is like a sponge, and adds to its own hue that which is passing, sucking it up.

The shadows of the trees in the wood, why are they blue? Ought they not to be dark? Is it really blue, or an illusion? And what is their colour when you see the shadow of a tall trunk aslant in the air like a leaning pillar? The fallen brown leaves wet with dew have a different brown from those that are dry, and the upper surface of the green growing leaf is different from the under surface. The yellow butterfly, if you meet one in October, has so toned down his spring yellow that you might fancy him a pale green leaf floating along the road. There is a shining, quivering, gleaming; there is a changing, fluttering, shifting; there is a mixing, weaving – varnished wings, translucent wings, wings with dots and veins, all playing over the purple heath; a very tangle of many-toned lights and hues. Then come the apples: if you look upon them from an upper window, so as to glance along the level plane of the fruit, delicate streaks of scarlet, like those that lie parallel to the eastern horizon before sunrise; golden tints under bronze, and apple-green, and some that the wasps have hollowed, more glowingly beautiful than the rest; sober leaves and black and white swallows: to see it you must be high up, as if the apples were strewn on a sward of foliage. So have I gone in three steps from May dandelion to September apple; an immense space measured by things beautiful, so filled that ten folio volumes could not hold the description of them, and I have left out the meadows, the brooks, and hills. Often in writing about these things I have felt very earnestly my own incompetence to give the least idea of their brilliancy and many-sided colours. My gamut was so very limited in its terms, and would not give a note to one in a thousand of those I saw. At last I said, I will have more words; I will have more terms; I will have a book on colour, and I will find and use the right technical name for each one of these lovely tints. I was told that the very best book was by Chevreul, which had tinted illustrations, chromatic scales, and all that could be desired.

Quite true, all of it; but for me it contained nothing. There was a good deal about assorted wools, but nothing about leaves; nothing by which I could tell you the difference between the light scarlet of one poppy and the deep purple-scarlet of another species. The dandelion remained unexplained; as for the innumerable other flowers, and wings, and sky-colours, they were not even approached. The book, in short, dealt with the artificial and not with nature. Next I went to science – works on optics, such a mass of them. Some I had read in old time, and turned to again; some I read for the first time, some translated from the German, and so on. It appeared that, experimenting with physical colour, tangible paint, they had found out that red, yellow, and blue were the three primary colours; and then, experimenting with light itself, with colours not tangible, they found out that red, green, and violet were the three primary colours; but neither of these would do for the dandelion. Once upon a time I had taken an interest in spectrum analysis, and the theory of the polarization of light was fairly familiar; any number of books, but not what I wanted to know. Next the idea occurred to me of buying all the colours used in painting, and tinting as many pieces of paper a separate hue, and so comparing these with petals, and wings, and grass, and trifolium. This did not answer at all; my unskilful hands made a very poor wash, and the yellow paper set by a yellow petal did not agree, the scientific reason of which I cannot enter into now. Secondly, the names attached to many of these paints are unfamiliar to general readers; it is doubtful if bistre, Leitch's blue, oxide of chromium, and so on, would convey an idea. They might as well be Greek symbols: no use to attempt to describe hues of heath or hill in that way. These, too, are only distinct colours. What was to be done with all the shades and tones? Still there remained the language of the studio; without doubt a master of painting could be found who would quickly supply the technical term of anything I liked to show him; but again no use, because it would be technical. And a still more unsurmountable difficulty occurs: in so far as I have looked at pictures, it seems as if the artists had met with the same obstacle in paints as I have in words – that is to say, a deficiency. Either painting is incompetent to express the extreme beauty of nature, or in some way the canons of art forbid the attempt. Therefore I had to turn back, throw down my books with a bang, and get me to a bit of fallen timber in the open air to meditate.

Would it be possible to build up a fresh system of colour language by means of natural objects? Could we say pine-wood green, larch green, spruce green, wasp yellow, humble-bee amber? And there are fungi that have marked tints, but the Latin names of these agarics are not pleasant. Butterfly blue – but there are several varieties; and this plan is interfered with by two things: first, that almost every single item of nature, however minute, has got a distinctly different colour, so that the dictionary of tints would be immense; and next, so very few would know the object itself that the colour attached to it would have no meaning. The power of language has been gradually enlarging for a great length of time, and I venture to say that the English language at the present time can express more, and is more subtle, flexible, and, at the same time, vigorous, than any of which we possess a record. When people talk to me about studying Sanscrit, or Greek, or Latin, or German, or, still more absurd, French, I feel as if I could fell them with a mallet happily. Study the English, and you will find everything there, I reply. With such a language I fully anticipate, in years to come, a great development in the power of expressing thoughts and feelings which are now thoughts and feelings only. How many have said of the sea, 'It makes me feel something I cannot say'! Hence it is clear there exists in the intellect a layer, if I may so call it, of thought yet dumb – chambers within the mind which require the key of new words to unlock. Whenever that is done a fresh impetus is given to human progress. There are a million books, and yet with all their aid I cannot tell you the colour of the May dandelion. There are three greens at this moment in my mind: that of the leaf of the flower-de-luce, that of the yellow iris leaf, and that of the bayonet-like leaf of the common flag. With admission to a million books, how am I to tell you the difference between these tints? So many, many books, and such a very, very little bit of nature in them! Though we have been so many thousand years upon the earth we do not seem to have done any more as yet than walk along beaten footpaths, and sometimes really it would seem as if there were something in the minds of many men quite artificial, quite distinct from the sun and trees and hills – altogether house people, whose gods must be set in four-cornered buildings. There is nothing in books that touches my dandelion.

It grows, ah yes, it grows! How does it grow? Builds itself up somehow of sugar and starch, and turns mud into bright colour and dead earth into food for bees, and some day perhaps for you, and knows when to shut its petals, and how to construct the brown seeds to float with the wind, and how to please the children, and how to puzzle me. Ingenious dandelion! If you find out that its correct botanical name is *Leontodon taraxacum*, or *Leontodon densleonis*, that will bring it into botany; and there is a place called Dandelion Castle in Kent, and a bell with the inscription –

> John de Dandelion with his great dog
> Brought over this bell on a mill cog –

which is about as relevant as the mere words *Leontodon tarax-acum*. Botany is the knowledge of plants according to the accepted definition; naturally, therefore, when I began to think I would like to know a little more of flowers than could be learned by seeing them in the fields, I went to botany. Nothing could be more simple. You buy a book which first of all tells you how to recognize them, how to classify them; next instructs you in their uses, medical or economical; next tells you about the folk-lore and curious associations; next enters into a lucid explanation of the physiology of the plant and its relation to other creatures; and finally, and most important, supplies you with the ethical feeling, the ideal aspiration to be identified with each particular flower. One moderately thick volume would probably suffice for such a modest round as this.

Lo! now the labour of Hercules when he set about bring-ing up Cerberus from below, and all the work done by Apollo in the years when he ground corn, are but a little matter compared with the attempt to master botany. Great minds have been at it these two thousand years, and yet we are still only nibbling at the edge of the leaf, as the ploughboys bite the young hawthorn in spring. The mere classification – all plant-lore was a vast chaos till there came the man of Sweden, the great Linnæus, till the sexes were recognized, and everything was ruled out and set in place again. A wonderful man! I think it would be true to say it was Linnæus who set the world on its present twist of thinking, and levered our mental glove a little more perpendicular to the ecliptic. He actually gathered the dandelion and took it to bits like a scientific child; he touched nature with his fingers instead of sitting looking out of window – perhaps the first man who had ever done so for seventeen hundred years or so, since superstition blighted the progress of pagan Rome. The work he did! But no one reads Linnæus now; the folios, indeed, might moulder to dust without loss, because his spirit has got into the minds of men, and the text is of little consequence. The best book he wrote to read now is the delightful 'Tour in Lapland', with its quaint pen-and-ink sketches, so realistically vivid, as if the thing sketched had been banged on the paper and so left its impress. I have read it three times, and I still cherish the old yellow pages; it is the best botanical book, written by the greatest of botanists, specially sent on a botanical expedition, and it contains nothing about botany. It tells you about the canoes, and the hard cheese, and the Laplander's warehouse on top of a pole, like a pigeon-house; and the innocent way in which the maiden helped the traveller in his bath, and how the aged men ran so fast that the devil could not catch them; and, best of all, because it gives a smack in the face to modern pseudo-scientific medical cant about hygiene, showing how the Laplanders break every 'law', human and 'divine', ventilation, bath, and diet – all the trash – and therefore enjoy the most excellent health, and live to a great old age. Still I have not succeeded in describing the immense labour there was in learning to distinguish plants on the Linnæan system. Then comes in order of time the natural system, the geographical distribution; then there is the geological relationship, so to say, to Pliocene plants, natural selection and evolution. Of that let us say nothing; let sleeping dogs lie, and evolution is a very weary dog. Most charming, however, will be found the later studies of naturalists on the interdependence of flowers and insects; there is another work the dandelion has got to do – endless, endless botany! Where did the plants come from at first? Did they come creeping up out of the sea at the edge of the estuaries, and gradually run their roots into the ground, and so make green the earth? Did Man come out of the sea, as the Greeks thought? There are so many ideas in plants. Flora, with a full lap, scattering knowledge and flowers together; everything good and sweet seems to come out of flowers, up to the very highest thoughts of the soul, and we carry them daily to the very threshold of the other world. Next you may try the microscope and its literature, and find the crystals in the rhubarb.

I remember taking sly glances when I was a very little boy at an old Culpepper's Herbal, heavily bound in leather and curiously illustrated. It was so deliciously wicked to read about the poisons; and I thought perhaps it was a book like that, only in papyrus rolls, that was used by the sorceress who got ready the poisoned mushrooms in old Rome. Youth's ideas are so imaginative, and bring together things that are so widely separated. Conscience told me I had no business to read about poisons; but there was a fearful fascination in hemlock, and I recollect tasting a little bit – it was very nasty. At this day, nevertheless, if any one wishes to begin a pleasant, interesting, unscientific acquaintance with English plants, he would do very well indeed to get a good copy of Culpepper. Grey hairs had insisted in showing themselves in my beard when, all those weary years afterwards, I thought I would like to buy the still older Englishman, Gerard, who had no Linnæus to guide him, who walked about our English lanes centuries ago. What wonderful scenes he must have viewed when they were all a tangle of wild flowers, and plants that are now scarce were common, and the old ploughs, and the curious customs, and the wild red-deer – it would make a good picture, it really would, Gerard studying English orchids! Such a volume! – hundreds of pages, yellow of course, close type, and marvellously well printed. The minute care they must have taken in those early days of printing to get up such a book – a wonderful volume both in bodily shape and contents. Just then the only copy I could hear of was much damaged. The cunning old bookseller said he could make it up; but I have no fancy for patched books, they are not genuine; I would rather have them deficient; and the price was rather long, and so I went Gerardless. Of folk-lore and medicinal use and history and associations here you have hints. The bottom of the sack is not yet; there are the monographs, years of study expended upon one species of plant growing in one locality, perhaps; some made up into thick books and some into broad quarto pamphlets, with most beautiful plates, that, if you were to see them, would tempt you to cut them out and steal them, all sunk and lost like dead ships under the sand: piles of monographs. There are warehouses in London that are choked to the beams of the roof with them, and every fresh exploration furnishes another shelf-load. The source of the Nile was unknown a very few years ago, and now, I have no doubt, there are dozens of monographs on the flowers that flourish there. Indeed, there is not a thing that grows that may not furnish a monograph. The author spends perhaps twenty years in collecting his material, during which time he must of course come across a great variety of amusing information, and then he spends another ten years writing out a fair copy of his labours. Then he thinks it does not quite do in that form, so he snips a paragraph out of the beginning and puts it at the end; next he shifts some more matter from the middle to the preface; then he thinks it over. It seems to him that it is too big, it wants condensation. The scientific world will say he has made too much of it; it ought to read very slight, and present the facts while concealing the labour. So he sets about removing the superfluous – leaves out all the personal observations, and all the little adventures he has met with in his investigations; and so, having got it down to the dry bones and stones thereof, and omitted all the mortar that stuck them together, he sends for the engraver, and the next three years are occupied in working up the illustrations. About this time some new discovery is made by a foreign observer, which necessitates a complete revision of the subject; and so having shifted the contents of the book about hither and thither till he does not know which is the end and which is the beginning, he pitches the much-mutilated copy into a drawer and turns the key. Farewell, no more of this; his declining days shall be spent in peace. A few months afterwards a work is announced in Leipsic which 'really trenches on my favourite subject, and really after spending a lifetime I can't stand it'. By this time his handwriting has become so shaky he can hardly read it himself, so he sends in despair for a lady who works a type-writer, and with infinite patience she makes a clean manuscript of the muddled mass. To the press at last, and the proofs come rapidly. Such a relief! How joyfully easy a thing is when you set about it! but by-and-by this won't do. Sub-section A ought to be in a foot-note, family B is doubtful; and so the corrections grow and run over the margin in a thin treble hand, till they approach the bulk of the original book – a good profit for the printer; and so after about forty years the monograph is published – the work of a life is accomplished. Fifty copies are sent round to as many public libraries and learned societies, and the rest of the impression lies on the shelves till dust and time and spiders' webs have buried it. Splendid work in it too. Looked back upon from to-day with the key of modern thought, these monographs often contain a whole chest of treasure. And still there are the periodicals, a century of magazines and journals and reviews and notices that have been coming out these hundred years and dropping to the ground like dead leaves unnoticed. And then there are the art works – books about shape and colour and ornament, and a naturalist lately has been trying to see how the leaves of one tree look fitted on the boughs of another. Boundless is the wealth of Flora's lap; the ingenuity of man has been weaving wreaths out of it for ages, and still the bottom of the sack is not yet. Nor have we got much news of the dandelion. For I sit on the thrown timber under the trees and meditate, and I want something more: I want the soul of the flowers.

The bee and the butterfly take their pollen and their honey, and the strange moths so curiously coloured, like the curious colouring of the owls, come to them by night, and they turn towards the sun and live their little day, and their petals fall, and where is the soul when the body decays? I want the inner meaning and the understanding of the wild flowers in the meadow. Why are they? What end? What purpose? The plant knows, and sees, and feels; where is its mind when the petal falls? Absorbed in the universal dynamic force, or what? They make no shadow of pretence, these beautiful flowers, of being beautiful for my sake, of bearing honey for me; in short, there does not seem to be any kind of relationship between us, and yet – as I said just now – language does not express the dumb feelings of the mind any more than the flower can speak. I want to know the soul of the flowers, but the word soul does not in the smallest degree convey the meaning of my wish. It is quite inadequate; I must hope that you will grasp the drift of my meaning. All these life-laboured monographs, these classifications, works of Linnæus, and our own classic Darwin, microscope, physiology, and the flower has not given us its message yet. There are a million books; there are no books: all the books have to be written. What a field! A whole million of books have got to be written. In this sense there are hardly a dozen of them done, and these mere primers. The thoughts of man are like the foraminifera, those minute shells which build up the solid chalk hills and lay the level plain of endless sand; so minute that, save with a powerful lens, you would never imagine the dust on your fingers to be more than dust. The thoughts of man are like these: each to him seems great in his day, but the ages roll, and they shrink till they become triturated dust, and you might, as it were, put a thousand on your thumb-nail. They are not shapeless dust for all that; they are organic, and they build and weld and grow together, till in the passage of time they will make a new earth and a new life. So I think I may say there are no books; the books are yet to be written.

Let us get a little alchemy out of the dandelions. They were not precise, the Arabian sages, with their flowing robes and handwriting; there was a large margin to their manuscripts, much imagination. Therein they failed, judged by the monograph standard, but gave a subtle food for the mind. Some of this I would fain see now inspiring the works and words of our great men of science and thought – a little alchemy. A great change is slowly going forward all over the printing-press world, I mean wherever men print books and papers. The Chinese are perhaps outside that world at present, and the other Asian races; the myriads, too, of the great southern islands and of Africa. The change is steadily, however, proceeding wherever the printing-press is used. Nor Pope, nor Kaiser, nor Czar, nor Sultan, nor fanatic monk, nor muezzin, shouting in vain from his minaret, nor, most fanatic of all, the fanatic shouting in vain in London, can keep it out – all powerless against a bit of printed paper. Bits of printed paper that listen to no command, to which none can say, 'Stand back; thou shalt not enter.' They rise on the summer whirlwinds from the very dust of the road, and float over the highest walls; they fall on the well-kept lawns – monastery, prison, palace – there is no fortress against a bit of printed paper. They penetrate where even Danaë's gold cannot go. Our Darwins, our Lyalls, Herschels, Faradays – all the immense army of those that go down to nature with considering eye – are steadfastly undermining and obliterating the superstitious past, literally burying it under endless loads of accumulated facts; and the printing-presses, like so many Argos, take these facts on their voyage round the world. Over go temples, and minarets, and churches, or rather there they stay, the hollow shells, like the snail shells which thrushes have picked clean; there they stay like Karnac, where there is no more incense, like the stone circles on our own hills, where there are no more human sacrifices. Thus men's minds all over the printing-press world are unlearning the falsehoods that have bound them down so long; they are unlearning, the first step to learn. They are going down to nature and taking up the clods with their own hands, and so coming to have touch of that which is real. As yet we are in the fact stage; by-and-by we shall come to the alchemy, and get the honey for the inner mind and soul. I found, therefore, from the dandelion that there were no books, and it came upon me, believe me, as a great surprise, for I had lived quite certain that I was surrounded with them. It is nothing but unlearning, I find now; five thousand books to unlearn.

Then to unlearn the first ideas of history, of science, of social institutions, to unlearn one's own life and purpose; to unlearn the old mode of thought and way of arriving at things; to take off peel after peel, and so get by degrees slowly towards the truth – thus writing as it were, a sort of floating book in the mind, almost remaking the soul. It seems as if the chief value of books is to give us something to unlearn. Sometimes I feel indignant at the false views that were instilled into me in early days, and then again I see that that very indignation gives me a moral life. I hope in the days to come future thinkers will unlearn us, and find ideas infinitely better. How marvellous it seems that there should be found communities furnished with the printing-press and fully convinced they are more intelligent than ants, and yet deliberately refusing by a solid 'popular' vote to accept free libraries! They look with scorn on the mediaeval times, when volumes were chained in the college library or to the desk at church. Ignorant times those! A good thing it would be if only three books were chained to a desk, open and free in every parish throughout the kingdom now. So might the wish to unlearn be at last started in the inert mind of the mass. Almost the only books left to me to read, and not to unlearn very much, are my first books – the graven classics of Greece and Rome, cut with a stylus so deeply into the tablet they cannot be erased. Little of the monograph or of classification, no bushel baskets full of facts, no minute dissection of nature, no attempt to find the soul under the scalpel. Thoughts which do not exactly deal with nature direct in a mechanical way, as the chemist labels all his gums and spices and earths in small boxes – I wonder if anybody at Athens ever made a collection of the coleoptera? Yet in some way they had got the spirit of the earth and sea, the soul of the sun. This never dies; this I wish not to unlearn; this is ever fresh and beautiful as a summer morning: –

> Such the golden crocus,
> Fair flower of early spring; the gopher white,
> And fragrant thyme, and all the unsown beauty
> Which in moist grounds the verdant meadows bear;
> The ox-eye, the sweet-smelling flower of Jove,

> The chalca, and the much-sung hyacinth,
> And the low-growing violet, to which
> Dark Proserpine a darker hue has given.

They come nearest to our own violets and cowslips – the unsown beauty of our meadows – to the hawthorn leaf and the high pinewood. I can forget all else that I have read, but it is difficult to forget these even when I will. I read them in English. I had the usual Latin and Greek instruction, but I read them in English deliberately. For the inflexion of the vowel I care nothing; I prize the idea. Scholars may regard me with scorn. I reply with equal scorn. I say that a great classic thought is greater to an English mind in English words than in any other form, and therein fits best to this our life and day. I read them in English first, and intend to do so to the end. I do not know what set me on these books, but I began them when about eighteen. The first of all was Diogenes Laertius's *Lives of the Philosophers*. It was a happy choice; my good genius, I suppose, for you see I was already fairly well read in modern science, and these old Greek philosophies set me thinking backwards, unwinding and unlearning, and getting at that eidolon which is not to be found in the mechanical heavens of this age. I still read him. I still find new things, quite new, because they are so very, very old, and quite true; and with his help I seem in a measure to look back upon our thoughts now as if I had projected myself a thousand years forward in space. An imperfect book, say the critics. I do not know about that; his short paragraphs and chapters in their imperfect state convey more freshness to the mind than the thick, laboured volumes in which modern scholarship professes to describe ancient philosophy. I prefer the imperfect original records. Neither can I read the ponderous volumes of modern history, which are nothing but words. I prefer the incomplete and shattered chronicles themselves, where the swords shine and the armour rings, and all is life though but a broken frieze. Next came Plato (it took me a long time to read Plato, and I have had to unlearn much of him) and Xenophon. Socrates' dialectic method taught me how to write, or rather how to put ideas in sequence. Sophocles, too; and last, that wonderful encyclopaedia

of curious things, Athenaeus. So that I found, when the idea of
the hundred best books came out, that between seventy and
eighty of them had been my companions almost from boyhood,
those lacking to complete the number being chiefly ecclesiastical
or Continental. Indeed, some years before the hundred books
were talked of, the idea had occurred to me of making up a
catalogue of books that could be bought for ten pounds. In an
article in the *Pall Mall Gazette* on 'The Pigeons at the British
Museum' I said, 'It seems as if all the books in the world – really
books – can be bought for 10. Man's whole thought is purchasable at that small price – for the value of a watch, of a good
dog.' The idea of making a 10. catalogue was in my mind – I did
make a rough pencil one – and I still think that a 10. library is
worth the notice of the publishing world. My rough list did not
contain a hundred. These old books of nature and nature's mind
ought to be chained up, free for every man to read in every parish. These are the only books I do not wish to unlearn, one item
only excepted, which I shall not here discuss. It is curious, too,
that the Greek philosophers, in the more rigid sense of science,
anticipated most of the drift of modern thought. Two chapters
in Aristotle might almost be printed without change as summa-
ries of our present natural science. For the facts of nature, of
course, neither one hundred books nor a 10. library would be
worth mentioning; say five thousand, and having read those,
then go to Kew, and spend a year studying the specimens of
wood only stored there, such a little slice after all of the whole.
You will then believe what I have advanced, that there are no
books as yet; they have got to be written; and if we pursue the
idea a little further, and consider that these are all about the
crude clods of life – for I often feel what a very crude and clumsy
clod I am – only of the earth, a minute speck among one hundred millions of stars, how shall we write what is *there*? It is
only to be written by the mind or soul, and that is why I strive
so much to find what I have called the alchemy of nature. Let us
not be too entirely mechanical, Baconian, and experimental
only; let us let the soul hope and dream and float on these oceans
of accumulated facts, and feel still greater aspiration than it has
ever known since first a flint was chipped before the glaciers.

Man's mind is the most important fact with which we are yet acquainted. Let us not turn then against it and deny its existence with too many brazen instruments, but remember these are but a means, and that the vast lens of the Californian refractor is but glass – it is the infinite speck upon which the ray of light will fall that is the one great fact of the universe. By the mind, without instruments, the Greeks anticipated almost all our thoughts; by-and-by, having raised ourselves up upon these huge mounds of facts, we shall begin to see still greater things; to do so we must look not at the mound under foot, but at the starry horizon.

Absence of Design in Nature – The Prodigality of Nature and Niggardliness of Man

Unpublished in author's lifetime
First published in *The Old House at Coate*, 1948

In the parlour to which I have retired from the heat there is a chair and a table, and a picture on the wall: the chair was made for an object and a purpose, to sit in; the table for a purpose, to write on; the picture was painted for a purpose, to please the eye. But outside, in the meadow, in the hedge, on the hill, in the water; or, looking still farther, to the sun, the moon, and stars, I see no such chair, or table, or picture.

Pondering deeply and for long upon the plants, the living things (myself, too, as a physical being): upon the elements, on the holy miracle, water; the holy miracle, sunlight; the earth, and the air, I come at last – and not without, for a while, sorrow – to the inevitable conclusion that there is no object, no end, no purpose, no design, and no plan; no anything, that is.

By a strong and continued effort, I compelled myself to see the world mentally: with my mind, as it were, abstracted; hold yourself, as it were, apart from it, and there is no object, and no plan; no law, and no rule.

From childhood we build up for ourselves an encyclopaedia of the world, answering all questions: we turn to Day, and the reply is Light; to Night, and the reply is Darkness. It is difficult to burst through these fetters and to get beyond Day and Night: but, in truth, there is no Day and Night; the sun always shines. It is our minds which supply the purpose, the end, the plan, the law, and the rule. For the practical matters of life, these are sufficient – they are like conventional agreements. But if you wish to really know the truth, there is none. When you first realize this, the whole arch of thought falls in; the structure the brain has reared, or, rather, which so many minds have reared for it, becomes a crumbling ruin, and there seems nothing left. I felt crushed when I first saw that there was no chair, no table, no picture, in nature: I use 'nature' in the widest sense; in the cosmos then. Nothing especially made for man to sit on, to write on, to admire – not even the colour of the buttercups or the beautiful sun-gleam which had me spellbound glowing on the water in my hand in the rocky cell.

The rudest quern ever yet discovered in which the earliest man ground his wheat did not fall from the sky; even that poor instrument, the mere hollowed stone, was not thrown to him prepared for use; he had to make it himself. There neither is, nor has been, nor will be any chair, or table, or picture, or quern in the cosmos. Nor is there any plan even in the butter-cups themselves, looked at for themselves: they are not geomet-rical, or mathematical; nor precisely circular, nor anything regular. A general pattern, as a common colour, may be claimed for them, a pattern, however, liable to modification under cul-tivation; but, fully admitting this, it is no more than saying that water is water: that one crystal is always an octahedron, another a dodecahedron; that one element is oxygen and another hydrogen; that the earth is the earth; and the sun, the sun. It is only stating in the simplest way the fact that a thing *is*: and, after the most rigid research, that is, in the end, all that can be stated.

To say that there is a general buttercup pattern is only saying that it is not a bluebell or violet. Perhaps the general form of the buttercup is not absolutely necessary to its existence; many birds can fly equally well if their tails be removed, or even a great part of their wings. There are some birds that do not fly at all. Some further illustrations presently will arise; indeed, nothing could be examined without affording some. I had forgotten that the parlour, beside the chair and table, had a car-pet. The carpet has a pattern: it is woven; the threads can be discerned, and a little investigation shows beyond doubt that it was designed and made by a man. It is certainly pretty and ingenious. But the grass of my golden meadow has no design, and no purpose: it is beautiful, and more; it is divine.

When at last I had disabused my mind of the enormous imposture of a design, an object, and an end, a purpose or a system, I began to see dimly how much more grandeur, beauty and hope there is in a divine chaos – not chaos in the sense of disorder or confusion but simply the absence of order – than there is in a universe made by pattern. This draught-board universe my mind had laid out: this machine-made world and piece of mechanism; what a petty, despicable, micro-cosmus I had substituted for the reality.

Logically, that which has a design or a purpose has a limit. The very idea of a design or a purpose has since grown repulsive to me, on account of its littleness. I do not venture, for a moment, even to attempt to supply a reason to take the place of the exploded plan. I simply deliberately deny, or, rather, I have now advanced to that stage that to my own mind even the admission of the subject to discussion is impossible. I look at the sunshine and feel that there is no contracted order: there is divine chaos, and, in it, limitless hope and possibilities.

Without number, the buttercups crowd the mead: not one here and there, or sufficient only to tint the sward. There is not just enough for some purpose: there they are without number, in all the extravagance of uselessness and beauty. The apple-bloom – it is falling fast now as the days advance – who can count the myriad blossoms of the orchard? There are leaves upon the hedges which bound that single meadow on three sides (the fourth being enclosed by a brook) enough to occupy the whole summer to count; and before it was half done they would be falling. But that half would be enough for shadow – for use.

Half the rain that falls would be enough. Half the acorns on the oaks in autumn, more than enough. Wheat itself is often thrown into the sty. Famines and droughts occur, but whenever any comes it is in abundance – sow a grain of wheat, and the stalk, one stalk alone, of those that rise from it will yield forty times.

There is no *enough* in nature. It is one vast prodigality. It is a feast. There is no economy: it is all one immense extravagance.

It is all giving, giving, giving: no saving, no penury; a golden shower of good things is for ever descending. I love beyond all things to contemplate this indescribable lavishness – I would it could be introduced into our human life. I know, none better, having gone through the personal experience myself, that it is at the present moment impossible to practise it: that each individual is compelled, in order to exist, to labour, to save, and to economize. I know, of course, as all do who have ever read a book, that attempts to distribute possessions, to live in community of goods, have each failed miserably. If I rightly judge, the human race would require a century of training before even an approximation to such a thing were possible. All this, and much more to the same effect, I fully admit. But still the feeling remains and will not be denied. I dislike the word economy: I detest the word thrift; I hate the thought of saving. Maybe some scheme in the future may be devised whereby such efforts may be turned to a general end. This alone I am certain of: there is no economy, thrift, or saving, in nature; it is one splendid waste. It is that waste which makes it so beautiful, and so irresistible! Now nature was not made by man, and is a better exemplar than he can furnish: each thread in this carpet goes to form the pattern; but go out into my golden mead and gather ten thousand blades of grass, and it will not destroy it.

Perhaps there never were so many houses upon the face of the earth as at the present day: so luxuriously appointed, so comfortable, so handsomely furnished. Yet, with all this wealth and magnificence, these appointments and engineering: with all these many courses at dinner and array of wines, it has ever seemed to me a mean and penurious age. It is formal and in order; there is no heart in it. Food should be broadcast, open, free: wine should be in flagons, not in tiny glasses; in a word, there should be genial waste. Let the crumbs fall: there are birds enough to pick them up.

The greatest proof of the extreme meanness of the age is the long list of names appended to a subscription for a famine or a fashionable charity. Worthy as are these objects, the donors write down their own unutterable meanness. There are men in their warehouses, their offices, on their lands, who have served them honourably for years and have received for their wage just exactly as much as experience has proved can be made to support life. No cheque with a great flourishing signature has ever been presented to them.

I say that the entire labouring population – some skilled trades excepted as not really labouring – is miserably underpaid, not because there is a pressure or scarcity, a trouble, a famine, but from pure selfishness. This selfishness, moreover, is not intentional, but quite unconscious; and individuals are not individually guilty, because they are within their rights. A man has a hundred thousand pounds: he eats and drinks and pleases his little whims – likely enough quite innocent little whims – but he never gives to a friend, or a relation; never assists, does nothing with it. This is commercially right, but it is not the buttercups in the golden mead; it is not the grain of wheat that yielded forty times. It is not according to the exemplar of nature. Therefore I say that although I admit all attempts to adjust possessions have been and for the age at least must prove failures, yet my feeling remains the same. Thrift, economy, accumulation of wealth, are inventions; they are not nature. As there are more than enough buttercups in this single meadow for the pleasure of all the children in the hamlet, so too it is a fact, a very stubborn fact, that there is more than enough food in the world for all its human children. In the year 1880, it was found, on careful calculation made for strictly commercial purposes, that there was a surplus grain production of* bushels. That is to say, if every buttercup in this meadow represented a bushel of wheat, there would be all that over and above what was necessary. This is a very extraordinary fact. That the wheat has to be produced, to be distributed; that there are a thousand social complications to be considered, is, of course, incontrovertible. Still, there was the surplus; bushels of golden grain as numerous as the golden buttercups.

But that does not represent the capacity of the earth for production: it is not possible to gauge that capacity – so practically inexhaustible is it.

---

* There is a blank in the manuscript here.

Thrift and economy and accumulation, therefore, represent a state of things contrary to the exemplar of nature, and in individual life they destroy its beauty. There is no pleasure without waste: the banquet is a formality; the wine tasteless, unless the viands and the liquor are in prodigal quantities. Give me the lavish extravagance of the golden mead!

One of the New Voters

First published in the *Manchester Guardian*,
24 and 31 January 1885
First collected in *The Open Air*, 1885

I

If any one were to get up about half-past five on an August morning and look out of an eastern window in the country, he would see the distant trees almost hidden by a white mist. The tops of the larger groups of elms would appear above it, and by these the line of the hedgerows could be traced. Tier after tier they stretch along, rising by degrees on a gentle slope, the space between filled with haze. Whether there were cornfields or meadows under this white cloud he could not tell – a cloud that might have come down from the sky, leaving it a clear azure. This morning haze means intense heat in the day. It is hot already, very hot, for the sun is shining with all his strength, and if you wish the house to be cool it is time to set the sunblinds.

Roger, the reaper, had slept all night in the cowhouse, lying on the raised platform of narrow planks put up for cleanliness when the cattle were there. He had set the wooden window wide open and left the door ajar when he came stumbling in overnight, long after the late swallows had settled in their nests on the beams, and the bats had wearied of moth catching. One of the swallows twittered a little, as much as to say to his mate, 'My love, it is only a reaper, we need not be afraid', and all was silence and darkness. Roger did not so much as take off his boots, but flung himself on the boards crash, curled himself up hedgehog fashion with some old sacks, and immediately began to breathe heavily. He had no difficulty in sleeping, first because his muscles had been tried to the utmost, and next because his skin was full to the brim, not of jolly 'good ale and old', but of the very smallest and poorest of wish-washy beer. In his own words, it 'blowed him up till he very nigh bust'. Now the great authorities on dyspepsia, so eagerly studied by the wealthy folk whose stomachs are deranged, tell us that a very little flatulence will make the heart beat irregularly and cause the most distressing symptoms.

Roger had swallowed at least a gallon of a liquid chemically designed, one might say, on purpose to utterly upset the internal economy. Harvest beer is probably the vilest drink in the world. The men say it is made by pouring muddy water into empty casks returned sour from use, and then brushing them round and round inside with a besom. This liquid leaves a stickiness on the tongue and a harsh feeling at the back of the mouth which soon turns to thirst, so that having once drunk a pint the drinker must go on drinking. The peculiar dryness caused by this beer is not like any other throat drought – worse than dust, or heat, or thirst from work; there is no satisfying it. With it there go down the germs of fermentation, a sour, yeasty, and, as it were, secondary fermentation; not that kind which is necessary to make beer, but the kind that unmakes and spoils beer. It is beer rotting and decomposing in the stomach. Violent diarrhoea often follows, and then the exhaustion thus caused induces the men to drink more in order to regain the strength necessary to do their work. The great heat of the sun and the heat of hard labour, the strain and perspiration, of course try the body and weaken the digestion. To distend the stomach with half a gallon of this liquor, expressly compounded to ferment, is about the most murderous thing a man could do – murderous because it exposes him to the risk of sunstroke. So vile a drink there is not elsewhere in the world; arrack, and potato-spirit, and all the other killing extracts of the distiller are not equal to it. Upon this abominable mess the golden harvest of English fields is gathered in.

Some people have in consequence endeavoured to induce the harvesters to accept a money payment in place of beer, and to a certain extent successfully. Even then, however, they must drink something. Many manage on weak tea after a fashion, but not so well as the abstainers would have us think. Others have brewed for their men a miserable stuff in buckets, an infusion of oatmeal, and got a few to drink it; but English labourers will never drink oatmeal-water unless they are paid to do it. If they are paid extra beer-money and oatmeal-water is made for them gratis, some will, of course, imbibe it, especially if they see that thereby they may obtain little favours from their employer by yielding to his fad. By drinking the crotchet perhaps they may get a present now and then – food for themselves, cast-off clothes for their families, and so on. For it is a remarkable feature of human natural history, the desire to proselytize. The spectacle of John Bull – jovial John Bull – offering his men a bucket of oatmeal liquor is not a pleasant one. Such a John Bull ought to be ashamed of himself.

The truth is the English farmer's man was and is, and will be, a drinker of beer. Neither tea, nor oatmeal, nor vinegar and water (coolly recommended by indoor folk) will do for him. His natural constitution rebels against such 'peevish' drink. In winter he wants beer against the cold and the frosty rime and the heavy raw mist that hangs about the hollows; in spring and autumn against the rain, and in summer to support him under the pressure of additional work and prolonged hours. Those who really wish well to the labourer cannot do better than see that he really has beer to drink – real beer, genuine brew of malt and hops, a moderate quantity of which will supply force to his thews and sinews, and will not intoxicate or injure. If by giving him a small money payment in lieu of such large quantities you can induce him to be content with a little, so much the better. If an employer followed that plan, and at the same time once or twice a day sent out a moderate supply of genuine beer as a gift to his men, he would do them all the good in the world, and at the same time obtain for himself their goodwill and hearty assistance, that hearty work which is worth so much.

Roger breathed heavily in his sleep in the cowhouse, because the vile stuff he had taken puffed him up and obstructed nature. The tongue in his open mouth became parched and cracked, swollen and dry; he slept indeed, but he did not rest; he groaned heavily at times and rolled aside. Once he awoke choking – he could not swallow, his tongue was so dry and large; he sat up, swore, and again lay down. The rats in the sties had already discovered that a man slept in the cowhouse, a place they rarely visited, as there was nothing there to eat; how they found it out no one knows. They are clever creatures, the despised rats. They came across in the night and looked under his bed, supposing that he might have eaten his bread-and-cheese for supper there, and that fragments might have dropped between the boards. There were none. They mounted the boards and sniffed round him; they would have stolen the food from his very pocket if it had been there. Nor could they find a bundle in a handkerchief, which they would have gnawn through speedily. Not a scrap of food was there to be smelt at, so they left him. Roger had indeed gone supperless, as usual; his supper he had swilled and not eaten. His own fault; he should have exercised self-control. Well, I don't know; let us consider further before we judge.

In houses the difficulty often is to get the servants up in the morning; one cannot wake, and the rest sleep too sound – much the same thing; yet they have clocks and alarums. The reapers are never behind. Roger got off his planks, shook himself, went outside the shed, and tightened his shoelaces in the bright light. His rough hair he just pushed back from his forehead, and that was his toilet. His dry throat sent him to the pump, but he did not swallow much of the water – he washed his mouth out, and that was enough; and so without breakfast he went to his work. Looking down from the stile on the high ground there seemed to be a white cloud resting on the valley, through which the tops of the high trees penetrated; the hedgerows beneath were concealed, and their course could only be traced by the upper branches of the elms. Under this cloud the wheat-fields were blotted out; there seemed neither corn nor grass, work for man nor food for animal; there could be nothing doing there surely. In the stillness of the August morning, without song of bird, the sun, shining brilliantly high above the mist, seemed to be the only living thing, to possess the whole and reign above absolute peace. It is a curious sight to see the early harvest morn – all hushed under the burning sun, a morn that you know is full of life and meaning, yet quiet as if man's foot had never trodden the land. Only the sun is there, rolling on his endless way.

Roger's head was bound with brass, but had it not been he would not have observed anything in the aspect of the earth. Had a brazen band been drawn firmly round his forehead it could not have felt more stupefied. His eyes blinked in the sunlight; every now and then he stopped to save himself from staggering; he was not in a condition to think. It would have mattered not at all if his head had been clear; earth, sky, and sun were nothing to him; he knew the footpath, and saw that the day would be fine and hot, and that was sufficient for him, because his eyes had never been opened.

The reaper had risen early to his labour, but the birds had preceded him hours. Before the sun was up the swallows had left their beams in the cowshed and twittered out into the air. The rooks and wood-pigeons and doves had gone to the corn, the blackbird to the stream, the finch to the hedgerow, the bees to the heath on the hills, the humble-bees to the clover in the plain. Butterflies rose from the flowers by the footpath, and fluttered before him to and fro and round and back again to the place whence they had been driven. Goldfinches tasting the first thistledown rose from the corner where the thistles grew thickly. A hundred sparrows came rushing up into the hedge, suddenly filling the boughs with brown fruit; they chirped and quarrelled in their talk, and rushed away again back to the corn as he stepped nearer. The boughs were stripped of their winged brown berries as quickly as they had grown. Starlings ran before the cows feeding in the aftermath, so close to their mouths as to seem in danger of being licked up by their broad tongues. All creatures, from the tiniest insect upward, were in reality busy under that curtain of white-heat haze. It looked so still, so quiet, from afar; entering it and passing among the fields, all that lived was found busy at its long day's work. Roger did not interest himself in these things, in the wasps that left the gate as he approached – they were making *papier-maché* from the wood of the top bar, – in the bright poppies brushing against his drab unpolished boots, in the hue of the wheat or the white convolvulus; they were nothing to him.

Why should they be? His life was work without skill or thought, the work of the horse, of the crane that lifts stones and timber. His food was rough, his drink rougher, his lodging dry planks. His books were – none; his picture-gallery a coloured print at the alehouse – a dog, dead, by a barrel, 'Trust is dead; Bad Pay killed him.' Of thought he thought nothing; of hope his idea was a shilling a week more wages; of any future for himself of comfort such as even a good cottage can give – of any future whatever – he had no more conception than the horse in the shafts of the waggon. A human animal simply in all this, yet if you reckoned upon him as simply an animal – as has been done these centuries – you would now be mistaken. But why should he note the colour of the butterfly, the bright light of the sun, the hue of the wheat? This loveliness gave him no cheese for breakfast; of beauty in itself, for itself, he had no idea. How should he? To many of us the harvest – the summer – is a time of joy in light and colour; to him it was a time for adding yet another crust of hardness to the thick skin of his hands.

Though the haze looked like a mist it was perfectly dry; the wheat was as dry as noon; not a speck of dew, and the pimpernels wide open for a burning day. The reaping-machine began to rattle as he came up, and work was ready for him. At breakfast-time his fellows lent him a quarter of a loaf, some young onions, and a drink from their tea. He ate little, and the tea slipped from his hot tongue like water from the bars of a grate; his tongue was like the heated iron the housemaid tries before using it on the linen. As the reaping-machine went about the gradually decreasing square of corn, narrowing it by a broad band each time, the wheat fell flat on the short stubble. Roger stopped, and, gathering sufficient together, took a few straws, knotted them to another handful as you might tie two pieces of string, and twisted the band round the sheaf. He worked stooping to gather the wheat, bending to tie it in sheaves; stooping, bending – stooping, bending, – and so across the field. Upon his head and back the fiery sun poured down the ceaseless and increasing heat of the August day. His face grew red, his neck black; the drought of the dry ground rose up

and entered his mouth and nostrils, a warm air seemed to rise
from the earth and fill his chest. His body ached from the ferment of the vile beer, his back ached with stooping, his forehead
was bound tight with a brazen band. They brought some beer
at last; it was like the spring in the desert to him. The vicious
liquor – 'a hair of the dog that bit him' – sank down his throat,
grateful and refreshing to his disordered palate as if he had drunk
the very shadow of green boughs. Good ale would have seemed
nauseous to him at that moment, his taste and stomach destroyed
by so many gallons of this. He was 'pulled together', and worked
easier; the slow hours went on, and it was luncheon. He could have
borrowed more food, but he was content instead with a screw of
tobacco for his pipe and his allowance of beer.

They sat in the corner of the field. There were no trees for
shade; they had been cut down as injurious to corn, but there
were a few maple bushes and thin ash sprays, which seemed
better than the open. The bushes cast no shade at all, the sun
being so nearly overhead, but they formed a kind of enclosure,
an open-air home, for men seldom sit down if they can help it
on the bare and level plain; they go to the bushes, to the corner,
or even to some hollow. It is not really any advantage; it is
habit; or shall we not rather say that it is nature? Brought back
as it were in the open field to the primitive conditions of life,
they resumed the same instincts that controlled man in the ages
past. Ancient man sought the shelter of trees and banks, of
caves and hollows, and so the labourers under somewhat the
same conditions came to the corner where the bushes grew.
There they left their coats and slung up their luncheon-bundles
to the branches; there the children played and took charge of
the infants; there the women had their hearth and hung their
kettle over a fire of sticks.

II

In August the unclouded sun, when there is no wind, shines as
fervently in the harvest-field as in Spain. It is doubtful if the
Spanish people feel the heat so much as our reapers; they have

their siesta; their habits have become attuned to the sun, and it is no special strain upon them. In India our troops are carefully looked after in the hot weather, and everything made as easy for them as possible; without care and special clothing and coverings for the head they could not long endure. The English simoon of heat drops suddenly on the heads of the harvesters and finds them entirely unprepared; they have not so much as a cooling drink ready; they face it, as it were, unarmed. The sun spares not; it is fire from morn till night. Afar in the town the sunblinds are up, there is a tent on the lawn in the shade, people drink claret-cup and use ice; ice has never been seen in the harvest-field. Indoors they say they are melting lying on a sofa in a darkened room, made dusky to keep out the heat. The fire falls straight from the sky on the heads of the harvesters – men, women, and children – and the white-hot light beats up again from the dry straw and the hard ground.

The tender flowers endure; the wide petal of the poppy, which withers between the fingers, lies afloat on the air as the lilies on water, afloat and open to the weight of the heat. The red pimpernel looks straight up at the sky from the early morning till its hour of closing in the afternoon. Pale blue speedwell does not fade; the pale blue stands the warmth equally with the scarlet. Far in the thick wheat the streaked convolvulus winds up the stalks, and is not smothered for want of air though wrapped and circled with corn. Beautiful though they are, they are bloodless, not sensitive; we have given to them our feelings, they do not share our pain or pleasure. Heat has gone into the hollow stalks of the wheat and down the yellow tubes to the roots, drying them in the earth. Heat has dried the leaves upon the hedge, and they touch rough – dusty rough, as books touch that have been lying unused; the plants on the bank are drying up and turning white. Heat has gone down into the cracks of the ground; the bar of the stile is so dry and powdery in the crevices that if a reaper chanced to drop a match on it there would seem risk of fire. The still atmosphere is laden with heat, and does not move in the corner of the field between the bushes.

Roger the reaper smoked out his tobacco; the children played round and watched for scraps of food; the women complained of the heat; the men said nothing. It is seldom that a labourer grumbles much at the weather, except as interfering with his work. Let the heat increase, so it would only keep fine. The fire in the sky meant money. Work went on again; Roger had now to go to another field to pitch – that is, help to load the waggon; as a young man, that was one of the jobs allotted to him. This was the reverse. Instead of stooping he had now to strain himself upright and lift sheaves over his head. His stomach empty of everything but small ale did not like this any more than his back had liked the other; but those who work for bare food must not question their employment. Heavily the day drove on; there was more beer, and again more beer, because it was desired to clear some fields that evening. Monotonously pitching the sheaves, Roger laboured by the waggon till the last had been loaded – till the moon was shining. His brazen forehead was unbound now; in spite of the beer the work and the perspiration had driven off the aching. He was weary but well. Nor had he been dull during the day; he had talked and joked – cumbrously in labourers' fashion – with his fellows. His aches, his empty stomach, his labour, and the heat had not overcome the vitality of his spirits. There was life enough left for a little rough play as the group gathered together and passed out through the gateway. Life enough left in him to go with the rest to the alehouse; and what else, oh moralist, would you have done in his place? This, remember, is not a fancy sketch of rural poetry; this is the reaper's real existence.

He had been in the harvest-field fourteen hours, exposed to the intense heat, not even shielded by a pith helmet; he had worked the day through with thew and sinew; he had had for food a little dry bread and a few onions, for drink a little weak tea and a great deal of small beer. The moon was now shining in the sky, still bright with sunset colours. Fourteen hours of sun and labour and hard fare! Now tell him what to do. To go straight to his plank-bed in the cowhouse; to eat a little more dry bread, borrow some cheese or greasy bacon, munch it alone, and sit musing till sleep came – he who had nothing to muse about. I think it would need a very clever man indeed to invent something for him to do, some way for him to spend his

evening. Read! To recommend a man to read after fourteen
hours burning sun is indeed a mockery; darn his stockings
would be better. There really is nothing whatsoever that the
cleverest and most benevolent person could suggest. Before any
benevolent or well-meaning suggestions could be effective the
preceding circumstances must be changed – the hours and conditions of labour, everything; and can that be done? The world
has been working these thousands of years, and still it is the
same; with our engines, our electric light, our printing-press,
still the coarse labour of the mine, the quarry, the field has to
be carried out by human hands. While that is so, it is useless to
recommend the weary reaper to read. For a man is not a horse:
the horse's day's work is over; taken to his stable he is content,
his mind goes no deeper than the bottom of his manger, and so
long as his nose does not feel the wood, so long as it is met by
corn and hay, he will endure happily. But Roger the reaper is
not a horse.

Just as his body needed food and drink, so did his mind
require recreation, and that chiefly consists of conversation.
The drinking and the smoking are in truth but the attributes of
the labourer's public-house evening. It is conversation that
draws him thither, just as it draws men with money in their
pockets to the club and the houses of their friends. Any one can
drink or smoke alone; it needs several for conversation, for
company. You pass a public-house – the reaper's house – in the
summer evening. You see a number of men grouped about
trestle-tables out of doors, and others sitting at the open window; there is an odour of tobacco, a chink of glasses and mugs.
You can smell the tobacco and see the ale; you cannot see the
indefinite power which holds men there – the magnetism of
company and conversation. *Their* conversation, not *your* conversation; not the last book, the last play; not saloon
conversation; but theirs – talk in which neither you nor any one
of your condition could really join. To us there would seem
nothing at all in that conversation, vapid and subjectless; to
them it means much. We have not been through the same circumstances: our day has been differently spent, and the same
words have therefore a varying value. Certain it is, that it is

conversation that takes men to the public-house. Had Roger
been a horse he would have hastened to borrow some food, and,
having eaten that, would have cast himself at once upon his
rude bed. Not being an animal, though his life and work were
animal, he went with his friends to talk. Let none unjustly con-
demn him as a blackguard for that – no, not even though they
had seen him at ten o'clock unsteadily walking to his shed, and
guiding himself occasionally with his hands to save himself from
stumbling. He blundered against the door, and the noise set the
swallows on the beams twittering. He reached his bedstead,
and sat down and tried to unlace his boots, but could not. He
threw himself upon the sacks and fell asleep. Such was one
twenty-four hours of harvest-time.

The next and the next, for weeks, were almost exactly similar; now a little less beer, now a little more; now tying up, now
pitching, now cutting a small field or corner with a fagging-hook.
Once now and then there was a great supper at the farm. Once
he fell out with another fellow, and they had a fight; Roger,
however, had had so much ale, and his opponent so much
whisky, that their blows were soft and helpless. They both fell –
that is, they stumbled, – they were picked up, there was some
more beer, and it was settled. One afternoon Roger became
suddenly giddy, and was so ill that he did no more work that day,
and very little on the following. It was something like a sunstroke, but fortunately a slight attack; on the third day he resumed
his place. Continued labour in the sun, little food and much
drink, stomach derangement, in short, accounted for his illness.
Though he resumed his place and worked on, he was not so
well afterwards; the work was more of an effort to him, and his
face lost its fulness, and became drawn and pointed. Still he
laboured, and would not miss an hour, for harvest was coming
to an end, and the extra wages would soon cease. For the first
week or so of haymaking or reaping the men usually get drunk,
delighted with the prospect before them, then they settle down
fairly well. Towards the end they struggle hard to recover lost
time and the money spent in ale.

As the last week approached, Roger went up into the village
and ordered the shoemaker to make him a good pair of boots.

He paid partly for them then, and the rest next pay-day. This was a tremendous effort. The labourer usually pays a shilling at a time, but Roger mistrusted himself. Harvest was practically over, and after all the labour and the long hours, the exposure to the sun and the rude lodging, he found he should scarcely have thirty shillings. With the utmost ordinary care he could have saved a good lump of money. He was a single man, and his actual keep cost but little. Many married labourers, who had been forced by hard necessity to economy, contrived to put by enough to buy clothes for their families. The single man, with every advantage, hardly had thirty shillings, and even then it showed extraordinary prudence on his part to go and purchase a pair of boots for the winter. Very few in his place would have been as thoughtful as that; they would have got boots some-how in the end, but not beforehand. This life of animal labour does not grow the spirit of economy. Not only in farming, but in navvy work, in the rougher work of factories and mines, the same fact is evident. The man who labours with thew and sinew at horse labour – crane labour – not for himself, but for others, is not the man who saves. If he worked for his own hand possibly he might, no matter how rough his labour and fare; not while working for another. Roger reached his distant home among the meadows at last, with one golden half-sovereign in his pocket. That and his new pair of boots, not yet finished, represented the golden harvest to him. He lodged with his parents when at home; he was so far fortunate that he had a bed to go to; therefore in the estimation of his class he was not badly off. But if we consider his position as regards his own life we must recognize that he was very badly off indeed, so much precious time and the strength of his youth having been wasted.

Often it is stated that the harvest wages recoup the labourer for the low weekly receipts of the year, and if the money be put down in figures with pen and ink it is so. But in actual fact the pen-and-ink figures do not represent the true case; these extra figures have been paid for, and gold may be bought too dear. Roger had paid heavily for his half-sovereign and his boots; his pinched face did not look as if he had benefited greatly. His

cautious old father, rendered frugal by forty years of labour,
had done fairly well; the young man not at all. The old man,
having a cottage, in a measure worked for his own hand. The
young man, with none but himself to think of, scattered his
money to the winds. Is money earned with such expenditure of
force worth the having? Look at the arm of a woman labouring
in the harvest-field – thin, muscular, sinewy, black almost, it
tells of continual strain. After much of this she becomes pulled
out of shape, the neck loses its roundness and shows the sinews, the chest flattens. In time the women find the strain of it
tell severely. I am not trying to make out a case of special hardship, being aware that both men, women, and children work as
hard and perhaps suffer more in cities; I am simply describing
the realities of rural life behind the scenes. The golden harvest
is the first scene; the golden wheat, glorious under the summer
sun. Bright poppies flower in its depths, and convolvulus climbs
the stalks. Butterflies float slowly over the yellow surface as
they might over a lake of colour. To linger by it, to visit it day
by day, at even to watch the sunset by it, and see it pale under
the changing light, is a delight to the thoughtful mind. There is
so much in the wheat, there are books of meditation in it, it is
dear to the heart. Behind these beautiful aspects comes the reality of human labour – hours upon hours of heat and strain;
there comes the reality of a rude life, and in the end little enough
of gain. The wheat is beautiful, but human life is labour.

After the County Franchise

First published in *Longman's Magazine*, February 1884
First collected in *The Hills and the Vale*, 1909

The money-lender is the man I most fear to see in the villages after the extension of the county franchise – the money-lender both in his private and public capacity, the man who has already taken a grasp of most little towns that have obtained incorporation in some form. Like Shylock he demands what is in his bond: he demands his interest, and that means a pull at every man's purse – every man, rich or poor – who lives within the boundary. Borrowing is almost the ruin of many such little towns; rates rise nearly as high as in cities, and people strive all they can to live anywhere outside the limit. Borrowing is becoming one of the curses of modern life, and a sorrowful day it will be when the first village takes to it. The name changes – now it is a local board, now it is commissioners, sometimes a town council: the practice remains the same. These authorities exist but for one purpose – to borrow money, and as any stick will do to beat a dog with, so any pretence will do to exact the uttermost farthing from the inhabitants. Borrowing boards they are, one and all, and nothing else, from whom no one obtains benefit except the solicitor, the surveyor, the lucky architect, and those who secure a despicable living in the rear of the county court. Nothing could better illustrate the strange supineness of the majority of people than the way in which they pay, pay, pay, and submit to every species of extortion at the hands of these incapable blunderers, without so much as a protest. The system has already penetrated into the smallest of the county towns which groan under the incubus; let us hope, let us labour, that it may not continue its course and enter the villages.

It may reasonably be supposed that when once the extension of the franchise becomes an established fact, some kind of local government will soon follow. At present country districts are either without any local government at all – I mean practically, not theoretically – or else they are ruled without the least shadow of real representation. When men are admitted to vote and come to be enlightened as to the full meaning and force of such rights, it is probable that they will shortly demand the power to arrange their own affairs. They will have something to say as to the administration of the poor-law, over which at present they do not possess the slightest control, and they are not at all unlikely to set up a species of self-government in every separate village. I think, in short, that the parish may become the unit in the future to the disintegration of the artificial divisions drawn to facilitate the poor-law. Such divisions, wherein many parishes of the most diverse description and far apart are thrown together anyhow as the gardener pitches weeds into the basket, have done serious harm in the past. They have injured the sense of personal responsibility, they have created a bureaucracy absolutely without feeling, and they have tended to shift great questions out of sight. The shifting of things out of sight – round the corner – is a vile method of dealing with them. Send your wretched poor miles away into a sort of alien workhouse, and then congratulate yourself that you have tided over the difficulty! But the difficulty has not been got over.

A man who can vote, and who is told – as he certainly will be told – that he bears a part in directing the great affairs of his nation, will ask himself why he should not be capable of managing the little affairs of his own neighbourhood. When he has asked himself this question, it will be the first step towards the downfall of the inhuman poor-law. He will go further and say, 'Why should I not settle these things at home? Why should I not walk up to the village from my house in the country lane, and there and then arrange the business which concerns me? Why should I any longer permit it to be done over my head and without my consent by a body of persons in whom I have no confidence, for they do not represent me – they represent property?'

In his own village the voter will observe the school – his own village then is worthy to possess its own school; possibly he may even remotely have some trifling share in the control of the school if there is a board. If that great interest, the children of the parish, can be administered at home, why not the other and much less important interests? Here may be traced a series of reflections, and a succession of steps by which ultimately the whole system of boards of guardians with their attendant powers, as the rural sanitary authority and so forth, may ultimately be swept away. Government will come again to the village.

Then arises the money-lender, and no time should be lost by those who have the good and genuine liberty of the countryside at heart in labouring to prevent his entry into the village. Whatsoever constitution the village obtains in future, let us strive to strictly limit the borrowing powers of its council. No borrowing powers at all would be best – government without loans would be almost ideal – if that cannot be accomplished, then at least lay down a stringent regulation putting a firm and impassable limit. Were every one of my way of thinking, government without loans would be imperative. It would be done if it had to be done. Rugged discomfort is preferable to borrowing.

I dread, in a word, lest the follies perpetrated in towns should get into the villages and hamlets, and want to say a word betimes of warning. Imagine a new piece of roadway required, then to get the money let a penny be added to the rates, and the amount produced laid by at interest year after year, till the sum be made up. Better wait a few years and walk half a mile round than borrow the five or six hundred pounds, and have to pay that back and all the interest on it. Shift somehow, do not borrow.

In the discussions upon the agricultural franchise it has been generally assumed that the changes it portends will be shown in momentous State affairs and questions of principle. But perhaps it will be rather in local and home concerns that the alterations will be most apparent. The agricultural labourer voters – and the numerous semi-agricultural voters, not labourers – are more than likely to look at their own parish as well as at the policy of the Foreign Office. Gradually the parish – that is, the village – must become the centre to men who feel at last that they are their own masters. Under some form or other they will take the parish into their own hands, and insist upon their business being managed at home. Some shape of village council must come presently into existence.

Shrewd people are certain to appear upon the scene, pointing out to the cottager that if he desires to rule himself in his own village, he must insist upon one most important point. This is the exclusion of property representation. Instead of property having an overwhelming share, as now, in the direction of affairs, the owner of the largest property must not weigh any heavier in the village council than the wayside cottager. If farmer or landowner sit there he must have one vote only, the same as any other member. The council, if it is to be independent, must represent men and not land in the shape of landowners, or money in the shape of tenant-farmers. Shrewd people will have no difficulty in explaining the meaning of this to the village voters, because they can quote so many familiar instances. There is the Education Act in part defeated by the combination of property, landowners and farmers paying to escape a school-board – a plan temporarily advantageous to them, but of doubtful benefit, possibly injurious, to the parish at large. Leaving that question alone, the fact is patent that the cottager has no share in the government of his school, because land and money have combined. It may be governed very well; still it is not *his* government, and will serve to illustrate the meaning. There is the board of guardians, nominally elected, really selected, and almost self-appointed. The board of guardians is land and money simply, and in no way whatever represents the people. A favourite principle continually enunciated at the present day is that the persons chiefly concerned should have the management. But the lower classes who are chiefly concerned with poor relief, as a matter of fact, have not the slightest control over that management. Besides the guardians, there is still an upper row, and here the rulers are not even invested with the semblance of representation, for magistrates are not elected, and they are guardians by virtue of their being magistrates. The machinery is thus complete for the defeat of representation and for the despotic control of those who, being principally concerned, ought by all rule and analogy to have the main share of the management. We have seen working men's representatives sit in the House of Commons; did any one ever see a cottage labourer sit as administrator at the board before which the wretched poor of his own neighbourhood appear for relief?

But it may be asked, Is the village council, then, composed of small proprietors, to sit down and vote away the farmer's or landowner's money without farmer or landowner having so much as a voice in the matter? Certainly not. The idea of village self-government supposes a distinct and separate existence, as it were; the village apart from the farmer or landowner, and the latter apart from the village. At present the money drawn in rates from farmer or landowner is chiefly expended on poor-law purposes. But, as will presently appear, village self-government proposes the entire abolition of the poor-law system, and with it the rates which support it, or at least the heaviest part of them. Therefore, as this money would not be concerned, they could receive no injury, even if they did not sit at the village council at all.

Imagine the village, figuratively speaking, surrounded by a high wall like a girdle, as towns were in ancient times, and so cut off altogether from the large properties surrounding it – on the one hand the village supporting and governing itself, and on the other the large properties equally independent.

The probable result would be a considerable reduction in local burdens on land. A self-supporting and self-governing moral population is the first step towards this relief to land so very desirable in the interest of agriculture.

In practice there must remain certain more or less imperial questions, as lines of through road, police, etc., some of which are already managed by the county authority. As these matters affect the farmer and landowner even more than the cottager, clearly they must expect to contribute to the cost, and can rightly claim a share in the management.

Having advanced so far as a village council, and arrived at the stage of managing their own affairs, having, in fact, emerged from pupilage, next comes a question for the council. We now govern our village ourselves; why should we not possess our village? Why should we not live in our own houses? Why should we not have a little share in the land, as much, at least, as we can pay for? At this moment the village, let us say, consists of a hundred cottages, and perhaps there are another hundred scattered about the parish. Of these three-fourths belong to two or three large landowners, and those who reside in them, however protected by enactment, can never have a sense of complete independence. We should own these cottages, so that the inhabitants might practically pay rent to themselves. We must purchase them, a few at a time; the residents can repurchase from us and so become freeholders. For a purchaser there must be a seller, and here one of the questions of the future appears: Can an owner of this kind of property be permitted to refuse to sell? Must he be compelled to sell?

It is clear that if the village voter thoroughly addresses himself to his home affairs there is room for some remarkable incidents. There is reason now, is there not, to dread the appearance of the money-lender?

About this illustrative parish there lie many hundred acres of good land all belonging to one man, while we, the said village council, do not possess a rood apiece, and our constituents not a square yard. Rightfully we ought to have a share, yet we do not agitate for confiscation. Shall we then say that every owner of land should be obliged to sell a certain fixed percentage – a very small percentage would suffice – upon proffer of a reasonable amount, the proffer being made by those who propose to personally settle on it? Of one thousand acres suppose ten or twenty liable to forcible purchase at a given and moderate price. After all it is not a much more overbearing thing than the taking by railways of land in almost any direction they please, and not nearly so tyrannous, so stupidly tyrannous, as some of the acts of folly committed by local boards in towns. Not long since the newspapers reported a case where a local authority actually ran a main sewer across a gentleman's park, and ventilated it at regular intervals, completely destroying the value of an historic mansion, and utterly ruining a beautiful domain. This was fouling their own nest with a vengeance. They should have cherished that park as one of their chiefest glories, their proudest possession. Parks and woods are daily becoming of almost priceless value to the nation; nothing could be so mad as to destroy these last homes of nature. Just conceive the inordinate folly of marking such a property with sewer ventilators. This is a hundred times more despotic than a proposal that say two per cent of land should be forcibly purchasable for actual settlement. Even five per cent would not make an appreciable difference to an estate, though every fraction of the five per cent were taken up.

For such proposals to have any effect, the transfer of real property must be greatly simplified and cheapened. From time to time, whenever a discussion occurs upon this subject, and there are signs that the glacier-like movements of government will be hastened by public stir, up rises some great lawyer and explains to the world that really nothing could be simpler or cheaper than such transfer. All that can be wished in that direction has been accomplished already; there is not the slightest ground for agitation; every obstruction has been removed, and the machinery is now perfect. He quotes a long list of Acts to demonstrate the progress that has been made, and so winds up a very effective speech. Facts, however, are not in accordance with these gracious words. Here is an instance. A cottage in a village was recently sold for seventy pounds; the costs, legal expenses, parchments, all the antiquated formalities absorbed *thirty-two pounds*, only three pounds less than half the value of the little property. Could anything be more obviously wrong than such a system.

The difficulties in the way of simplification are created difficulties, entirely artificial, owing their existence to legal ingenuity. How often has the question been asked and never answered: Why should there be any more expense in transferring the ownership of an acre of land than of £100 stock?

The village council coming into contact with this matter is likely to agitate continuously for its rectification, since otherwise its movements will be seriously hampered. If they succeed in obtaining the abolition of these semi-feudal survivals, they will have conferred a substantial benefit upon the community.

County franchise would be worth the granting merely to secure this.

Let us take the case for a moment of a labourer at this day and consider his position. What has he before him? He has a hand-to-mouth, nomad existence, ending in the inevitable frozen misery of the workhouse. Men with votes and political power are hardly likely to endure this for many more years, and it is much to be hoped that they will not endure it. A labourer may be never so hard-working, so careful, so sober, and yet let his efforts be what they may, his old age finds him helpless. I am sure there is no class of men among whom may be found so many industrious, plodding, sober folk, economical to the verge of starvation. Their straightforward lives are thrown away. Their sons and daughters, warned by example, go to the cities, and there lose the virtues that rendered their forefathers so admirable even in their wretchedness. It will indeed be a blessing if, as I hope, the outcome of the franchise is the foundation of solid inducements to the countryman to stay in the country. I use the phrase countryman purposely, intending it to include small farmers and small farmers' sons; the latter are likewise driven away from the land year by year as much as the young labourers, and are as serious a loss to it. Did the possibility exist of purchasing a cottage and a plot of ground of moderate size, it is more than probable that the labourer's son would remain in the village, or return to it, and his daughter would come back to the village to be married. We hear how the poor Italian or the poor Swiss leaves his native country for our harder climate, how he works and saves, and by-and-by returns to his village and purchases some corner of earth. This seems a legitimate and worthy object. We do not hear of our own sturdy labourers returning to their village with a pocketful of money and purchasing a plot of ground or a cottage. They do not attempt it, because they know that under present conditions it is nearly impossible. There is no land for them to buy. Why not, when the country is nothing but land? Because the owner of ten thousand acres is by no means obliged to part with the minutest fragment of it. If by chance a stray portion be somewhere for sale, the expenses, the costs, the parchments, the antiquated formalities, the semi-feudal routine delay and possibly prevent transfer altogether. If land were accessible, and the cost of transferring cottage property reduced to reasonable proportions, the labourer would have the soundest of all inducements to practise self-denial in his youth. Cities might attract him temporarily for the advantage of higher wages, but he would put the excess by and ultimately bring it home. Even the married cottager with a family would try his hardest to save a little with such a hope before him.

The existing circumstances deny hope altogether. Neither land nor cottages are to be had, there are no sellers, and the cost of transfer is prohibitive; men are shifted on, they have no security of tenure, they are passed on from farm to farm and can settle nowhere. The competition for a house in some districts is keen to the last degree; it seems as if there were eager crowds waiting for homes. Recently while roaming on the Sussex hills I met an ancient shepherd whose hair was white as snow, though he stood upright enough. I inquired the names of the hills there, and he replied that he did not know; he was a stranger, he had only been moved there lately. How strangely changed are things when a grey-headed shepherd does not know the names of his hills! At a time of life when he ought to have been comfortably settled he had had to shift.

Sentiment is more stubborn than fact. People will face the sternest facts, dire facts, stubborn facts, and stay on in spite of all; but once let sentiment alter and away they troop. So I think that some part of the distaste for farming visible about us is due to change of sentiment – to feeling repelled – as well as to unfruitful years. Men have stood out against weary weather in all ages of agriculture, but lately they have felt hurt and repelled, the sentiment of attachment to home has been rudely torn up, and so now the current sets against farming, though farms are often offered on advantageous terms. In the same way, beside the stubborn facts that drive the labourer from the village and prevent his return to settle, there is a yet more stubborn sentiment repelling him. Made a man of by education – not only of books, but the unconscious education of progressive times – the labourer and his son and daughter have thoughts of independence. To

be humbly subservient to the will of those above them, to be
docilely obedient, not only to the employer, but to all in some
sort of authority, is not attractive to them. Plainly put, the rule
of parson and squire, tenant and guardian, is repellent to them
in these days. They would rather go away. If they do save money
in cities, they do not care to return and settle under the thumb
of these their old masters. Besides more attractive facts, the
sentiment of independence must be called into existence before
the labourer, or, for the matter of that, the small farmer's son,
will willingly settle in the village. That sense of independence
can only arise when the village governs itself by its own council, irrespective of parson, squire, tenant, or guardian. Towards
that end the power to vote is almost certain to drift slowly.

Nothing can be conceived more harshly antagonistic to the
feelings of a naturally industrious race of men than the knowledge that as a mass they are looked upon as prospective
'paupers'. I detest this word so much that it is painful to me to
write it; I put it between inverted commas as a sort of protest,
so that it may appear a hated intruder, and not native to the
text. The local government existing at this day in country districts is practically based upon the assumption that every
labouring man will one day be a 'pauper', will one day come to
the workhouse. By the workhouse and its board the cottage is
governed; the workhouse is the centre, the bureau, the *hôtel de
ville*. The venue of local government must be changed before
the labourer can feel independent, and it will be changed doubtless as he becomes conscious of the new power he has acquired.
Shall the bitterness of the workhouse at last pass away? Let us
hope so, let us be thankful indeed if the franchise leads to the
downfall of those cruel walls. Yet what is the cruelty of cold
walls to the cruelty of 'system'? A workhouse in the country is
usually situated as nearly as possible in the centre of the Union,
it may be miles from the outlying parishes. Thither the worn-out
cottager is borne away from the fields, his cronies, his little
helps to old age such as the corner where the sun shines, the
friend who allows little amenities, to dwindle and die. The
workhouse bureau extends its unfeeling hands into every detail
of cottage life. No wonder the labourer does not deny himself

to save money in order to settle where these things are done. A happy day it will be when the workhouse door is shut and the building sold for materials. A gentleman not long since wrote to me a vindication of his workhouse – I cannot at the moment place my hand on the figures he sent me, but I grant that they were conclusive from his point of view; they were not extravagant, the administration appeared correct. But this is not my point of view at all. Figures are not humanity. The workhouse and the poor-law system are inhuman, debasing, and injurious to the whole country, and the better they are administered, the worse it really is, since it affords a specious pretext for their continuance. What would be the use of a captain assuring his passengers that the ship was well found, plenty of coal in the bunkers, the engines oiled and working smoothly, when they did not want to go to the port for which he was steering? An exact dose of poison may be administered, but what comfort is it to the victim to assure him that it was accurately measured to a minim? What is the value of informing me that the 'paupers' are properly looked after when I do not want any 'paupers'?

But how manage without the poor-law system? There are several ways. There is the insurance method: space will not permit of discussion in this paper, but one fact which speaks volumes may be alluded to. Two large societies exist in this country called the 'Oddfellows' and the 'Foresters'; they number their members by the million; they assist their members not only at home, but all over the world (which is what no poor-law has ever done); they govern themselves by their own laws, and they prosper exceedingly – an honour to the nation. They have solved the difficulty for themselves.

When the village governs itself and takes all matters into its own hands, in time the sentiment of independence may grow up and men begin to work and strive and save, that they may settle at home. It would be a very noble thing indeed if the true English feeling for home life should become the dominant passion of the country once again. By home life I mean that which gathers about a house, however small, standing in its own grounds. Something comes into existence about such a house, an influence, a pervading feeling, like some warm colour

softening the whole, tinting the lichen on the wall, even the
very smoke-marks on the chimney. It is home, and the men and
women born there will never lose the tone it has given them.
Such homes are the strength of a land. The emigrant who leaves
us for the backwoods hopes to carve out a home for himself
there, and we consider that an ambition to be admired. I hope
the day will come when some at least of our people may be able
to set up homes for themselves in their own country. To-day,
if they would live, they must crowd into the city, often to dwell
in the midst of hideous squalor, or they must cross the ocean.
They would rather endure the squalor, rather say farewell for
ever and sail for America, than stay in the village where everyone is master, and none of their class can be independent. The
village must be its own master before it becomes popular.
County government may be reformed with advantage, but that
is not enough, because it must necessarily be too far off. People
in the country are scattered, and each little centre is naturally
only concerned with itself. A government having its centre at
the county town is too far away, and is likely to bear too much
resemblance to the boards of guardians and present authorities, to be representative of land and money rather than of men.
Progress can only be made in each little centre separately by means
of village councils, genuinely representative of the village folk,
unswayed by mansion, vicarage, or farm. Then by degrees we
may hope to see the re-awakening of English home-life in con-
tradistinction to that unhappy restlessness which drives so many
to the cities.

Men will then wake up and work with energy because they
will have hope. The slow, plodding manner of the labourer –
the dull ways even of the many industrious cottagers – these
will disappear, giving place to push and enterprise. Why does a
lawyer work as no navvy works? Why does a cabinet minister
labour the year through as hard as a miner? Because they have
a mental object. So will the labourer work when he has a mental object – to possess a home for himself.

Whenever such homes become numerous and the new life of
the country begins to flow, pressure will soon be brought to
bear for the removal of the mediaeval law which prevents the

use of steam on common roads. Modern as the law is, it is mediaeval in its tendency as much as a law would be for the restriction of steam on the ocean. Suppose a statute compelling all ships to sail, or, if they steamed, not to exceed four miles an hour! One of the greatest drawbacks to agriculture is the cost and difficulty of transit; wheat, flour, and other foods come from America at far less expense in proportion than it takes to send a waggon-load to London. This cost of transit in the United Kingdom will ultimately, one would think, become the question of the day, concerning as it does every individual. Agriculture on a large scale finds it a heavy drawback; to agriculture on a small scale it is often prohibitory. A man may cultivate his two-acre plot and produce vegetables and fruit, but if he cannot get his produce to London (or some great city), the demand for it is small, and the value low in proportion. As settlers increase, as the village becomes its own master, and men pass part at least of their time labouring on their own land, the difficulty will be felt to be a very serious one. Transit they must have, and steam alone can supply it. Engines and cars can be built to run on common roads almost as easily as on rails, and as for danger it is merely the interested outcry of those who deal in horses. There is no danger. Fine smooth roads exist all over the country; they have been kept up from coaching days as if in a prophetic spirit for their future use by steam. Upon these roads engines and cars can travel at a good fair pace, collecting produce, and either delivering it to the through lines of rail, or passing it on from road-train to road-train till it reaches the city. This is a very important matter indeed, for in the future easier and quicker transit will become imperative for agriculture. The impost of extraordinary tithe – the whole system of tithe – again, is doomed when once the country begins to live its new life. Freedom of cultivation is ten times more needful to the small than to the large proprietor.

These changes closely examined lose their threatening aspect, so much so that the marvel is they did not commence fifty years ago instead of waiting till now, and even now to be only potential. What is there in the present condition of agriculture to make farmer or landowner anxious that the existing system of

things should continue? Surely nothing; surely every consideration points in favour of moderate change. Those who quote
the example of France, and would argue that dissatisfaction
must, as there, increase with efforts to allay it, must know full
well in their hearts that there is no comparison whatever with
France. The two peoples are so entirely different. So little contents our race that the danger is rather the other way, that they
will be too easily satisfied. Such changes as I have indicated,
when examined closely, are really so mild that in full operation
they would scarcely make any difference in the relation of the
classes. Such village councils would be very anxious for the
existence of the farmer, and for his interests to be respected, for
the sufficient reason that they know the value of wages. Perhaps they might even, under certain conditions, become almost
too willing partisans of the farmer for their best interests to be
served. I can imagine such conditions easily enough, and the
possibility of the three sections, labourer, farmer, and owner,
becoming more closely welded together than ever. There is far
more stolidity to be regretted than revolution to be feared. The
danger is lest the new voters should stolidify – crystallize – in
tacit league with existing conditions; not lest we should go hop,
skip, and jump over Niagara.

A probable result of these changes is an increase in the value
of land: if thousands of people should ever really begin to desire
it, and to work and save for the object of buying it, analogy
would suppose a rise in value. Instead of a loss there would be
a gain to the landowner, and I think to the farmer, who would
have a larger supply of labour, and possibly a strong posse of
supporters at the poll in their men. Instead of division coales-
cence is more probable. The greater his freedom, the greater his
attachment to home, the more settled the labourer, the firmer
will become the position of all three classes. The landowner has
nothing whatever to fear for his park, his mansion, his privacy,
his shooting, or anything else. What is taken will be paid for,
and no more will be taken than needful. Parks and woods are
becoming of priceless value; we should have to preserve a few
landlords if only to have parks and woods. Perfect rights of
possession are not at all incompatible with enjoyment by the

people. There are domains to be found where people wander at their will, and enjoy themselves as much as they please, and yet the owner retains every right. It is true that there are also numerous parks rigidly closed to the public, demonstrating the folly of the proprietors – square miles of folly. The use of a little compulsion to open them would not be at all deplorable. But it must stop there and not encroach farther. Having obtained the use, be careful not to destroy.

The one great aim I have in all my thoughts is the acquisition of public and the preservation of private liberty. Freedom is the most valuable of all things, and is to be sought with all our powers of mind and hand. Freedom does not mean injustice, but neither will it put up with injustice. A singular misapprehension seems to be widely spread in our time, it is that there are two great criminals, the poor man or 'pauper' and the landlord. At opposite extremes of the scale they are regarded as equally guilty. Every right – the right to vote, the right to live in his native village, the right to be buried decently – is taken from the unhappy poor man or 'pauper'. He is a criminal. To own land is to be guilty of unpardonable sin, nothing is so bad; as criminals are ordered to be searched and everything taken from them, so everything is to be taken from the landowner. The injustice to both is equally evident. Any one by chance of circumstances, uncontrollable, may be reduced to extreme poverty; how cruel to punish the unfortunate with the loss of civil rights! Any one by good fortune and labour may acquire wealth, and would naturally wish to purchase land: is he then guilty? In equity both the poor and the rich should enjoy the same civil rights.

Let the new voter then bear in mind above all things the value of individual liberty, and not be too anxious to destroy the liberty of others, an action that invariably recoils. Let him, having obtained his freedom, beware how he surrenders it again either to local influence in the shape of land or money, or to the outside orator who may urge him on for his own ends. Efforts will be made no doubt to use the new voter for the purposes of cliques and fanatics. He can always test the value of their object by the question of wages and food – 'How will

it affect my wages and food?' – and probably that is the test
he will apply. A little knot of resolute and straightforward
men should be formed in every village to see that the natural
outcome of the franchise is obtained. They can begin as vigilance committees, and will ultimately reach to legal status as
councils.

Shooting Poachers

First published in the *Pall Mall Gazette*,
13 December 1884
First collected in *Chronicles of the Hedges*, 1948

The sport of shooting poachers, which comes in towards Christmas, is now in full swing, some capital sport has already been obtained, and there appears to be a plentiful supply of human game on hand. Bands of men go into the woods armed with guns, and bands of men carrying revolvers go to meet them. The savage encounters that ensue read like those with banditti in the days of Königsmark the Robber. Indeed, while our expedition toils up the Nile (to rescue Gordon) and correspondents have little to describe beyond hard rowing, another war is proceeding at home, accompanied with serious bloodshed. If a 'special' were on the spot he would have to relate something like this. The keepers on a large preserve, by means of scouts and vedettes, ascertain the probable intentions of a gang of poachers, and settle themselves in ambush as the night approaches. They are well armed with breech-loading guns and revolvers, six-shooters, in American 'frontier' style, as if for a battle with Indians. The poachers, not having wealthy people to buy good weapons for them, generally have old muzzle-loading guns, and have not yet arrived at the civilization of the revolver. Heavy shadows settle in the hollow by the firs; it is night, and by-and-by a scout creeps up with the intelligence that the enemy is busy at the side of the plantation. Fetching a detour the 'frontier' men suddenly rush out from a gateway. There is a scuffle – curses – quick flashes of red flame light up the scene. On one side a curl of white smoke ascends from the barrel of a levelled gun. On the other a curl of smoke darts from a revolver extended by an arm in velveteen. Two more men are rolling over each other on the ground, bound up inextricably in a great net into which they have fallen and drawn round them. Another lies twisted in a heap, doubled up, hard hit; a pheasant projects from his coat-pocket. Bang! bang! There are groans, curses, a lantern is turned on, and the fight is over. Next morning, if you visited the spot early, you might see scene two. On the wet grass, stained cartridge-cases; marks of heavy iron-shod boots dug deeply into the soil in the struggle; a broken pipe; a hare wire; blood on the grass and on the crushed bunch of rushes, blood which remains though a fine rain is falling, and drip, dripping from the still trees. Some pheasant feathers lie scattered by the ditch. Away in a shed a stiff and human carcass is extended under a sheet. Other human game, wounded but not mortally, is bagged in the cells at the nearest town. Cold and wet the grey winter's morning casts its chill over the view; this is the time to think of the fatherless children and the widow. Is not this a noble sport for Christmas-tide? A grand subject here for the next Academy Exhibition, two panels – (one) 'The Battle': (two) 'Next Morning'.

'The right to kill!' A fresh addition to the rights of man, invented when Madame Clovis Hugues shot M. Morin. In Paris you may avenge your honour – at least, a lady may; these are privileged cases. In England – moral England, which expressed such horror – everybody has a right to kill – a poacher. A keeper is a licensed killer; he shoots cats, weasels, crows, poachers, and other vermin equally. It is his royal pleasure – the keeper s'amuse. The boast of our civilization is the high value we set upon human life. Never, never before in the whole history of man was life so sacred as it is now. The tribunals hold that even starvation does not justify homicide. What, then, can justify this shooting of poachers? Of course a poacher is engaged in an unlawful act, but is that act sufficiently unlawful to render it right to kill him? He is not a burglar, he does not enter a house and put the lives of the inmates in danger. He is not a garrotter – he does not attack people with violence in the street. A wood is not a house – nor even a garden. The argument that he goes by night is merely a legal quibble – poaching by night is the same in this respect as poaching by day; neither by day nor night is there any assault. The poacher, in short, is simply a thief who steals rabbits and pheasants instead of watches from a shop window. It is not nearly so much an assault upon the person as stealing without violence, from the pocket. A man has his pocket picked at Charing-Cross Station; Policeman B. witnesses the robbery, runs up and seizes the thief; suppose Policeman B. drew a revolver from his breast and shot the thief instead? Would that be justifiable? It even remains a moot point what does and what does not justify one in shooting a burglar. Only a poacher may be shot with impunity.

But a poacher goes armed, true, but with the purpose of shooting pheasants. The keeper does not shoot pheasants at night, nor at any time, with revolvers; such weapons are intended to be used upon man. Those who have had any experience of the combative instincts of rude men know very well that there are many keepers – and others – who go to these brutal encounters with delight. Cases have been seen even of young farmers joining the keeper's gang to enjoy the battle. It is altogether nonsense to suppose that they go out armed with revolvers with the purely virtuous intention of protecting property. They like the row; they like to 'do' for somebody. Good keepers are perfectly well acquainted with various ways and means of tracking and identifying poachers, and if the present be not sufficient some one should invent a portable electric lantern to be suddenly turned on, and so, by making the covers as light as day, afford a view. Poachers would dread a bright light – which means identification – far more than gunpowder. The truth is that these bloodthirsty affairs are a disgrace to our boasted humanity. We have just had an outburst of indignation against keepers shooting cats; but shooting a poacher is nothing – it does not happen in Bulgaria, and is no atrocity. The truth also is that these bloodthirsty businesses are part and parcel of a marked change of tone in the population, they belong to the same class of sentiment that promotes prize-fighting, now so much on the increase. It is downright brutality, and nothing else. It is most injurious to the interest of sport, against which it must ultimately create a prejudice. Shooting doves from a trap became a fashionable atrocity a short while since; rank and fashion arrayed themselves on the side of the poor doves. But the poacher is an outlaw, outside the pale of humanity, far below a pigeon. If a man be privy to a murder, though he be not actually present, he is in law an accomplice; if a man sanction his keeper 'going for' poachers with revolvers, what is his position? His conscience at all events cannot be at ease, if slaughter ensues. Poaching is no new thing, but years ago before we became so humane it was the custom to 'go for' poachers armed with good stout cudgels, and with those good stout cudgels many a gang of poachers was captured. Then every consideration was in favour of the keepers; now, by using revolvers, they place themselves obviously in as bad a moral position as the poachers. Nor is suspicion wanting that when these local shooting cases come before local magnates the keepers are usually discharged. The whole thing has a bad odour – a very bad odour. Much blame lies in the law which visits night-poaching with penalties of ridiculous severity, not much better than the old plan of hanging for sheep-stealing. On the one hand, the poacher thinks he may as well be hung (so to say) for a sheep as a lamb; on the other hand, the keeper, knowing that the law is so heavily on his behalf, thinks himself fighting on the 'side of the angels', so that nothing he can do is wrong. It is scarcely possible now to pick up a newspaper without finding 'Serious Poaching Affray', 'Keepers Shot', 'Poachers Wounded', and so on *ad nauseum*. All this is most injurious to sport; as a champion of sport, a true believer in sport, I trust a stop will be put to it, or in time we shall get back to the days (and ways) of spring guns, steel man traps, bloodhounds, and similar amenities. Or shall we go forward and develop, as this is the age of evolution? We shall perhaps find that there are people better off than keepers and poachers who would like a 'brush' of this sort – the people who pay the money for prize fights. Here is a cutting from the sporting paper of the period: – 'The Hon. Jim Masher has a large party of guests staying at Pepperem Hall in anticipation of the Christmas Poacher Shooting. They are all armed with Winchester repeating rifles, and

are looking forward anxiously to the full moon in order to take
better aim. There is a very strong gang of poachers, and splendid sport is expected; they want decimating sadly. The poachers
are said to have a big punt gun, carrying three pounds of shot,
and place much reliance on this field-piece. The *battue* will
probably come off in the Lower Plantations, and will be a noisy
affair. P.S. The J.P.s have been squared.'

Primrose Gold in Our Village

First published in the *Pall Mall Gazette*, 8 June 1887
First collected in *Field and Farm*, 1957

Every one said how beautiful the tall arching boughs of the elms looked meeting over the road at the entrance to the village. As in the East the bazaars and all the life seem to be under domes and covers, so the entry into English country life is very often under elms like these. It is a common scene, and every one says it is beautiful. The houses just beyond are still for the most part thatched, yet there is a certain difference in the general style of the place, if you can imagine it as an engraving before your eye. Outside the blacksmith's shop there are a number of strange machines painted a staring red; things with horrible knives, a machine that would be welcomed by a Chinese executioner for cutting off feet first and hands next, and so on; things with long clawy spikes that seem to prick your eyes if you look at them; and another thing is coming that makes a tremendous groan and clank. I always shrink into a gateway if I can when a traction-engine comes by, with a sort of vague prayer to Fate that it may not burst as it passes and blow me up with all my dreams. Somehow there seems such a vast mass of dust about, the grocer's shop there (which will supply you with French wine) must be sanded with it. There is an unpleasant feeling that this dust is not good, pure road dust; if a little pinch gets up the nose it has a noisome smell. It is like desiccated sewage. A direful odour rises from a grating, and the secret is out: the place has been drained. Till then it was a healthy spot; since then there has been nothing but epidemics. This is a common experience; it is called 'sanitation'. If you Londoners go into the country for a change be careful that you do not go to a village that has been drained. Especially take notice if there are many villas about, for they are dangerous and indicate deadly improvements. Beware of villas.

Still, there are rooks and sunshine and twenty gables to draw, and do what they will they cannot quite obliterate the old place. There is a window under a low-tiled roof with yellow stonecrop above it. Yellow wallflowers, marigolds, musk, evening primrose, crown lilies, dwarf genista, eschscholtzia – everything yellow. Behind the window panes the window flowers are so thick they seem to flatten themselves against the glass: some scarlet geraniums, of course, but chiefly yellow calceolarias. Close to the window there is a sort of abutment also tiled – perhaps it is an oven – and this, too, bears yellow stonecrop. There is a gable above, and a high narrow chimney; a very pleasant 'bit' to sketch or paint. A golden-chain tree stands in front – long pendants of yellow. All the corner seems stained with golden colour. Any stranger passing along the footpath would be sure to stop and look at it and say, 'Ah! that really is a bit of old-fashioned country life. Really genuine. Very pretty indeed.' One would suppose the people who lived there would be in the foremost ranks of everything good.

The village was made upright, but they have found out many inventions; they have invented an *élite*, and found out that they possessed a stratum of 'society' – in short, they have got a Primrose Habitation, which came in with the drains. The rolls are not open to inspection, but it is believed the clergyman and the curate belong to the *élite* – that is, to the Habitation. The old doctor certainly does – a genuine old Tory. The new doctor did not at first, but he found he had better do so afterwards, and he finds it better also to be very regular at the 'celebrations' at the church. The old doctor has spread about an idea among the old maids that the new man, who is very clever, is a dreadful materialist. In the Middle Ages if a man was very clever in chemistry he was supposed to be a necromancer and keep a familiar spirit in the neck of an alembic. To-day, if a man is very clever, there is always a suspicion that he is a wicked materialist, and deals with 'spores', and 'germs', and 'microbes'. There are no spores in the gospel. The professional tradesman, that is to say, the chemist, who is at least a hundred degrees higher in the scale than the old grocer, is thought to be on the list. There are four or five people retired, possibly unprofessional tradesmen once, living in the old farmhouses that have been villafied, who are imagined to supply a good deal of the sinews of war. Of course all the upper class of Tory farmers are affiliated in some way, and there are one or two county families, the M.P. of the district, and four or five of his more or less titled friends, honorary subscribers, and several semi-county families, neither farmers, gentlemen, nor lords. The bulk of the work, however, is got through by a sort of quasi-secretary, who does all the calls and three-line whips, and arranges the meetings and carries out everything, and who is casually alluded to by the big folk as a 'very good fellow, you know; don't know what we should do without him', but they don't ask him to dinner. This is very nearly all that is known by the vulgar of the village caucus, for such it is – for ways that are 'dark and tricks that are vain', commend me to the heathen Tory. There is a still darker branch of this mysterious craft – it is the ladies, great Dames, to whom be honour and glory. What they do I do not know, but there are whispers that there are social divisions, and that one Dame is greater than another Dame, inasmuch that if a great Dame, one of the big folk, proposes a resolution, the resolution is carried, but if a lesser Dame makes a resolution it falls to the ground. Hence it appears that there are heartburnings among the angels. Still, they belong to the order of the *élite*, and the discipline is perfect.

Now a local village is a very local place. There is no very great variety of streets, no Charing-Cross, no floating population that drifts up the Strand in endless stream, that drops in at a shop and buys a cigarette for a penny or an ormolu clock for seven guineas. The same customer is never seen again there, but to-morrow a fresh one takes his place. In the local village the customers are always the same. They are a fixed quantity; a glass is full of water and you cannot put any more in, there are so many beads on a string, and count them as many times as you like they are still the same number. Pictorially thus: the old grocer, who is not a 'professional tradesman', who exposes dirty Radical prints in his window for sale, who said several

hard words to the clergyman a few years ago for refusing to
bury his Nonconformist baby, who is a regular old sanded
brute – is not boycotted. Certainly not. No private notice sent
round, or placards stuck up remarking that if you deal there
you will get lead pepper. Still it is not necessary to buy there if
the 'professional' tradesman's brother sets up another shop. It
is not that you shall not go to the old grocer, but it is suggested
how much better it would be to go to the other one and so
encourage him. The caucus does not say you shall not deal
here; the caucus says you *shall* deal *there*. It is boycotting
reversed. By-and-by the doctors found out that the prevalence
of disease was due to there not being sufficient air-holes to the
drains; so in making these improvements one was casually
opened by the old grocer's shop. Always a beastly Radical
effluvia just there. Don't stop there – spores, germs, pah! The
old gentleman has written letters about it, but somehow the
official wheels don't move. *Ex-officio* people are plentiful on
country boards, and they are mostly heathen Tories.

A man who lives in the cottage with the beautiful flowery
window was once the dog in the village with a bad name. He is
a little owner, a little occupier, he has a little dairy and a little
poultry farm, and a heavy mortgage. He was a shocking Radical and upset everything; he was so rough he did not care for
threats of action for libel or slander; he did not care if he did go
to gaol – a man fearfully and wonderfully made in contempt of
authority. Mostly he cursed a good deal, especially about a
green and succulent meadow with a pond of never-failing water
next to his own arid and waterless fields. This meadow and
pond was part of the glebe land, and the clergyman would not
let it to such a drunken reprobate. By-and-by, when the Habitation was formed and Primrose gold began to work its way,
some one whispered a whisper, and the pond and the meadow
were placed at the disposal of this dreadful fellow. He is now
shaven and wears a clean smock-frock and goes to church a'
Sundays. Next the villa folk came down to buy his beautiful
butter and make much of his wife, a very respectable woman
with a fancy for flowers – a very nice pot came down now and
then from the greenhouses. Next it was found out that one of

the dry and arid fields was very level and would make an excellent tennis ground for the Primrose Club. Accordingly a square acre or so was rented at a liberal price, and now you may see the stately Knights and Dames disporting where once did grow the weeds of treason rank.

Once now and then a real lord or a real lady who happens to be visiting one of the county families is marched round to the cottages and takes off his hat and says a few words about the crops, or perhaps my lady strokes the cat. This is not boycotting, it is Primrosing. The golden party work by finding out the soft places, and by making things very pleasant for those who will come under its wings. The voice of the reprobate is still, and the heart of the enemy is broken. The cobbler was another horror; he was consumptive too – evidently a judgment on the wretched atheist. The curate could do nothing with him, till by-and-by he had a great inspiration. 'He wants encouragement,' said the curate. The caucus thought so too. After this, about forty pairs of boots came floating in, gentlemen's and ladies' boots, neat repairs wanted, 2s. 6d., 3s. 6d. each. By-and-by the curate said 'You have got a dreadful cough', and the upshot was they sent him to the seaside for a month, and when he came back his cough was gone and also many of his ancient prejudices. He had no further objection to any number of half-crowns – another vote secure.

Primrosing goes a great deal higher than cobblers and dairymen. If you are pliant and flexible and don't mind being petted you have nice things put in your way, and you are passed not only in the local village, but right up to London if you want to do business there. If you are not pliant, you are not harrowed, but you are not watered, and it is best to get out of the local village. Then there are decorations, and the *élite* of the Dames wear Special Service brooches. What these mysterious special services are, no one knows. Certain, however, it is that a powerful caucus is being established everywhere throughout the country, and the same style of thing is carried on where there is not a formal Habitation.

Hours of Spring

First published in *Longman's Magazine*, May 1886
First collected in *Field and Hedgerow*, 1889

It is sweet on awaking in the early morn to listen to the small bird singing on the tree. No sound of voice or flute is like the bird's song; there is something in it distinct and separate from all other notes. The throat of woman gives forth a more perfect music, and the organ is the glory of man's soul. The bird upon the tree utters the meaning of the wind – a voice of the grass and wild flower, words of the green leaf; they speak through that slender tone. Sweetness of dew and rifts of sunshine, the dark hawthorn touched with breadths of open bud, the odour of the air, the colour of the daffodil – all that is delicious and beloved of spring-time are expressed in his song. Genius is nature, and his lay, like the sap in the bough from which he sings, rises without thought. Nor is it necessary that it should be a song; a few short notes in the sharp spring morning are sufficient to stir the heart. But yesterday the least of them all came to a bough by my window, and in his call I heard the sweet-briar wind rushing over the young grass. Refulgent fall the golden rays of the sun; a minute only, the clouds cover him and the hedge is dark. The bloom of the gorse is shut like a book; but it is there – a few hours of warmth and the covers will fall open. The meadow is bare, but in a little while the heart-shaped celandine leaves will come in their accustomed place. On the pollard willows the long wands are yellow-ruddy in the passing gleam of sunshine, the first colour of spring appears in their bark. The delicious wind rushes among them and they bow and rise; it touches the top of the dark pine that looks in the sun the same now as in summer; it lifts and swings the arching trail of bramble; it dries and crumbles the earth in its fingers; the hedge-sparrow's feathers are fluttered as he sings on the bush.

I wonder to myself how they can all get on without me – how they manage, bird and flower, without me to keep the calendar for them. For I noted it so carefully and lovingly, day by day, the seed-leaves on the mound in the sheltered places that come so early, the pushing up of the young grass, the succulent dandelion, the coltsfoot on the heavy, thick clods, the trodden chickweed despised at the foot of the gatepost, so common and small, and yet so dear to me. Every blade of grass was mine, as though I had planted it separately. They were all my pets, as the roses the lover of his garden tends so faithfully. All the grasses of the meadow were my pets, I loved them all; and perhaps that was why I never had a 'pet', never cultivated a flower, never kept a caged bird, or any creature. Why keep pets when every wild free hawk that passed overhead in the air was mine? I joyed in his swift, careless flight, in the throw of his pinions, in his rush over the elms and miles of woodland; it was happiness to see his unchecked life. What more beautiful than the sweep and curve of his going through the azure sky? These were my pets, and all the grass. Under the wind it seemed to dry and become grey, and the starlings running to and fro on the surface that did not sink now stood high above it and were larger. The dust that drifted along blessed it and it grew. Day by day a change; always a note to make. The moss drying on the tree trunks, dog's-mercury stirring under the ash-poles, bird's-claw buds of beech lengthening; books upon books to be filled with these things. I cannot think how they manage without me.

To-day through the window-pane I see a lark high up against the grey cloud, and hear his song. I cannot walk about and arrange with the buds and gorse-bloom; how does he know it is the time for him to sing? Without my book and pencil and observing eye, how does he understand that the hour has come? To sing high in the air, to chase his mate over the low stone wall of the ploughed field, to battle with his high-crested rival, to balance himself on his trembling wings outspread a few yards above the earth, and utter that sweet little loving kiss, as it were, of song – oh, happy, happy days! So beautiful to watch

as if he were my own, and I felt it all! It is years since I went out
amongst them in the old fields, and saw them in the green corn,
they must be dead, dear little things, by now. Without me to tell
him, how does this lark to-day that I hear through the window
know it is his hour?

The green hawthorn buds prophesy on the hedge; the reed
pushes up in the moist earth like a spear thrust through a shield;
the eggs of the starling are laid in the knot-hole of the pollard
elm – common eggs, but within each a speck that is not to be
found in the cut diamond of two hundred carats – the dot of
protoplasm, the atom of life. There was one row of pollards
where they always began laying first. With a big stick in his
beak the rook is blown aside like a loose feather in the wind;
he knows his building-time from the fathers of his house –
hereditary knowledge handed down in settled course: but the
stray things of the hedge, how do they know? The great blackbird has planted his nest by the ash-stole, open to every one's
view, without a bough to conceal it and not a leaf on the ash –
nothing but the moss on the lower end of the branches. He does
not seek cunningly for concealment. I think of the drift of time,
and I see the apple bloom coming and the blue veronica in the
grass. A thousand thousand buds and leaves and flowers and
blades of grass, things to note day by day, increasing so rapidly
that no pencil can put them down and no book hold them, not
even to number them – and how to write the thoughts they give?
All these without me – how can they manage without me?

For they were so much to me, I had come to feel that I was
as much in return to them. The old, old error: I love the earth,
therefore the earth loves me – I am her child – I am Man, the
favoured of all creatures. I am the centre, and all for me was
made.

In time past, strong of foot, I walked gaily up the noble hill
that leads to Beachy Head from Eastbourne, joying greatly in
the sun and the wind. Every step crumbled up numbers of minute grey shells, empty and dry, that crunched under foot like
hoar-frost or fragile beads. They were very pretty; it was a
shame to crush them – such vases as no king's pottery could
make. They lay by millions in the depths of the sward, and I

thought as I broke them unwillingly that each of these had once
been a house of life. A living creature dwelt in each and felt the
joy of existence, and was to itself all in all – as if the great sun
over the hill shone for it, and the width of the earth under was
for it, and the grass and plants put on purpose for it. They were
dead, the whole race of them, and these their skeletons were as
dust under my feet. Nature sets no value upon life neither of
minute hill-snail nor of human being.

I thought myself so much to the earliest leaf and the first
meadow orchis – so important that I should note the first
zee-zee of the titlark – that I should pronounce it summer,
because now the oaks were green; I must not miss a day nor an
hour in the fields lest something should escape me. How beautiful the droop of the great brome-grass by the wood! But
to-day I have to listen to the lark's song – not out of doors with
him, but through the window-pane, and the bullfinch carries
the rootlet fibre to his nest without me. They manage without
me very well; they know their times and seasons – not only the
civilized rooks, with their libraries of knowledge in their old
nests of reference, but the stray things of the hedge and the
chiffchaff from over sea in the ash wood. They go on without
me. Orchis flower and cowslip – I cannot number them all – I
hear, as it were, the patter of their feet – flower and bud and the
beautiful clouds that go over, with the sweet rush of rain and
burst of sun glory among the leafy trees. They go on, and I am
no more than the least of the empty shells that strewed the
sward of the hill. Nature sets no value upon life, neither of
mine nor of the larks that sang years ago. The earth is all in all
to me, but I am nothing to the earth: it is bitter to know this
before you are dead. These delicious violets are sweet for themselves; they were not shaped and coloured and gifted with that
exquisite proportion and adjustment of odour and hue for me.
High up against the grey cloud I hear the lark through the window singing, and each note falls into my heart like a knife.

Now this to me speaks as the roll of thunder that cannot be
denied – you must hear it; and how can you shut your ears to
what this lark sings, this violet tells, this little grey shell writes
in the curl of its spire? The bitter truth that human life is no

more to the universe than that of the unnoticed hill-snail in the grass should make us think more and more highly of ourselves as human – as men – living things that think. We must look to ourselves to help ourselves. We must think ourselves into an earthly immortality. By day and by night, by years and by centuries, still striving, studying, searching to find that which shall enable us to live a fuller life upon the earth – to have a wider grasp upon its violets and loveliness, a deeper draught of the sweet-briar wind. Because my heart beats feebly to-day, my trickling pulse scarcely notating the passing of the time, so much the more do I hope that those to come in future years may see wider and enjoy fuller than I have done; and so much the more gladly would I do all that I could to enlarge the life that shall be then. There is no hope on the old lines – they are dead, like the empty shells; from the sweet delicious violets think out fresh petals of thought and colours, as it were, of soul.

Never was such a worshipper of earth. The commonest pebble, dusty and marked with the stain of the ground, seems to me so wonderful; my mind works round it till it becomes the sun and centre of a system of thought and feeling. Sometimes moving aside the tufts of grass with careless fingers while resting on the sward, I found these little pebble stones loose in the crumbly earth among the rootlets. Then, brought out from the shadow, the sunlight shone and glistened on the particles of sand that adhered to it. Particles adhered to my skin – thousands of years between finger and thumb, these atoms of quartz, and sunlight shining all that time, and flowers blooming and life glowing in all, myriads of living things, from the cold still limpet on the rock to the burning, throbbing heart of man. Sometimes I found them among the sand of the heath, the sea of golden brown surging up yellow billows six feet high about me, where the dry lizard hid, or basked, of kin, too, to old time. Or the rush of the sea wave brought them to me, wet and gleaming, up from the depths of what unknown Past? where they nestled in the root crevices of trees forgotten before Egypt. The living mind opposite the dead pebble – did you ever consider the strange and wonderful problem there? Only the thickness of the skin of the hand between them. The chief use of matter is to demonstrate to us the existence of the soul. The pebble-stone tells me I am a soul because I am not that that touches the nerves of my hand. We are distinctly two, utterly separate, and shall never come together. The little pebble and the great sun overhead – millions of miles away: yet is the great sun no more distinct and apart than this which I can touch. Dull-surfaced matter, like a polished mirror, reflects back thought to thought's self within.

I listened to the sweet-briar wind this morning; but for weeks and weeks the stark black oaks stood straight out of the snow as masts of ships with furled sails frozen and ice-bound in the haven of the deep valley. Each was visible to the foot, set in the white slope, made individual in the wood by the brilliance of the background. Never was such a long winter. For fully two months they stood in the snow in black armour of iron bark unshaken, the front rank of the forest army that would not yield to the northern invader. Snow in broad flakes, snow in semi-flakes, snow raining down in frozen specks, whirling and twisting in fury, ice raining in small shot of frost, howling, sleeting, groaning; the ground like iron, the sky black and faintly yellow – brutal colours of despotism – heaven striking with clenched fist. When at last the general surface cleared, still there remained the trenches and traverses of the enemy, his ramparts drifted high, and his roads marked with snow. The black firs on the ridge stood out against the frozen clouds, still and hard; the slopes of leafless larches seemed withered and brown; the distant plain far down gloomy with the same dull yellowish blackness. At a height of seven hundred feet the air was sharp as a scythe – a rude barbarian giant wind knocking at the walls of the house with a vast club, so that we crept sideways even to the windows to look out upon the world. There was everything to repel – the cold, the frost, the hardness, the snow, dark sky and ground, leaflessness; the very furze chilled and all benumbed. Yet the forest was still beautiful. There was no day that we did not, all of us, glance out at it and admire it, and say something about it. Harder and harder grew the frost, yet still the forest-clad hills possessed a something that drew the mind open to their largeness and grandeur. Earth is always beautiful – always. Without colour, or leaf, or sunshine, or song of bird and flutter of butterfly's wing; without anything sensuous, without advantage or gilding of summer – the power is ever there. Or shall we not say that the desire of the mind is ever there, and *will* satisfy itself, in a measure at least, even with the barren wild? The heart from the moment of its first beat instinctively longs for the beautiful; the means we possess to gratify it are limited – we are always trying to find the statue in the rude block. Out of the vast block of the earth the mind endeavours to carve itself loveliness, nobility, and grandeur. We strive for the right and the true: it is circumstance that thrusts wrong upon us.

One morning a labouring man came to the door with a spade, and asked if he could dig the garden, or try to, at the risk of breaking the tool in the ground. He was starving; he had had no work for two months; it was just six months, he said, since the first frost started the winter. Nature and the earth and the gods did not trouble about *him*, you see; he might grub the rock-frost ground with his hands if he chose – the yellowish black sky did not care. Nothing for man! The only good he found was in his fellow-men; they fed him after a fashion – still they fed him. There was no good in anything else. Another aged man came once a week regularly; white as the snow through which he walked. In summer he worked; since the winter began he had had no employment, but supported himself by going round to the farms in rotation. They all gave him a trifle – bread and cheese, a penny, a slice of meat – something; and so he lived, and slept the whole of that time in outhouses wherever he could. He had no home of any kind. Why did he not go into the workhouse? 'I be afeared if I goes in there they'll put me with the rough uns, and very likely I should get some of my clothes stole.' Rather than go into the workhouse he would totter round in the face of the blasts that might cover his weak old limbs with drift. There was a sense of dignity and manhood left still; his clothes were worn, but clean and decent; he was no companion of rogues; the snow and frost, the straw of the outhouses, was better than that. He was struggling against age, against nature, against circumstance; the entire weight of society, law, and order pressed upon him to force him to lose his self-respect and liberty. He would rather risk his life in the snowdrift. Nature, earth, and the gods did not help him; sun and stars, where were they? He knocked at the doors of the farms and found good in man only – not in Law or Order, but in individual man alone.

The bitter north wind drives even the wild fieldfare to the berries in the garden hedge; so it drives stray human creatures to the door. A third came – an old gipsy woman – still stout and hearty, with green fresh brooms to sell. We bought some brooms – one of them was left on the kitchen floor, and the tame rabbit nibbled it; it proved to be heather. The true broom is as green and succulent in appearance in January as June. She would see the 'missis'. 'Bless you, my good lady, it be weather, bean't it? I hopes you'll never know what it be to want, my good lady. Ah, well, you looks good-tempered if you don't want to buy nothing. Do you see if you can't find me an old body, now, for my girl – now do'ee try; she's confined in a tent on the common – nothing but one of our tents, my good lady – that's true – and she's doing jest about well' (with briskness and an air of triumph), 'that she is! She's got twins, you see, my lady, but she's all right, and as well as can be. She wants to get up; and she says to me, "Mother, do'ee try and get me a body; 'tis hard to lie here abed and be well enough to get up, and be obliged to stay here because I've got nothing but a bedgown." For you see, my good lady, we managed pretty well with the first baby, but the second bothered us, and we cut up all the bits of things we could find, and there she ain't got nothing to put on. Do'ee see if'ee can't find her an old body.' The common is an open piece of furze and heath at the verge of the forest; and here, in a tent just large enough to creep in, the gipsy woman had borne twins in the midst of the snow and frost. They could not make a fire of the heath and gorse even if they cut it, the snow and whirling winds would not permit. The old gipsy said if they had little food they could not do without fire, and they were compelled to get coke and coal somehow – apologizing for such a luxury. There was no whining – not a bit of it; they were evidently quite contented and happy, and the old woman proud of her daughter's hardihood. By-and-by the husband came round with straw beehives to sell, and cane to mend chairs – a strong, respectable-looking man. Of all the north wind drove to the door, the outcasts were the best off – much better off than the cottager who was willing to break his spade to earn a shilling; much better off than the white-haired labourer, whose strength was spent, and who had not even a friend to watch with him in the dark hours of the winter evening – not even a fire to rest by. The gipsy nearest to the earth was the best off in every way; yet not even for primitive man and woman did the winds cease. Broad flakes of snow drifted up against the low tent, beneath which the babes were nestling to the breast. Not even for the babes did the snow cease or the keen wind rest; the very fire could scarcely struggle against it. Snow-rain and ice-rain; frost-formed snow-granules, driven along like shot, stinging and rattling against the tent-cloth, hissing in the fire; roar and groan of the great wind among the oaks of the forest. No kindness to man, from birth-hour to ending; neither earth, sky, nor gods care for him, innocent at the mother's breast. Nothing good to man but man. Let man, then, leave his gods and lift up his ideal beyond them.

Something grey and spotted and puffy, not unlike a toad, moved about under the gorse of the garden hedge one morning, half-hidden by the stalks of old grasses. By-and-by it hopped out – the last thrush, so distended with puffed feathers against the frost as to be almost shapeless. He searched about hopelessly round the stones and in the nooks, all hard and frostbound; there was the shell of a snail, dry and whitened and empty, as was apparent enough even at a distance. His keen eye must have told him that it was empty; yet such was his hunger and despair that he took it and dashed it to pieces against a stone. Like a human being, his imagination was stronger than his experience; he tried to persuade himself that there might be something there; hoping against hope. Mind, you see, working in the bird's brain, and overlooking facts. A mere mechanism

would have left the empty and useless shell untouched – would
have accepted facts at once, however bitter, just as the balance
on the heaviest side declines immediately, obeying the fact of an
extra grain of weight. The bird's brain was not mechanical, and
therefore he was not wholly mastered by experience. It was a
purely human action – just what we do ourselves. Next he
came across to the door to see if a stray berry still remained on
a creeper. He saw me at the window, and he came to the
window – right to it – and stopped and looked full at me some
minutes, within touch almost, saying as plainly as could be
said, 'I am starving – help me.' I never before knew a thrush
make so unmistakable an appeal for assistance, or deliberately
approach so near (unless previously encouraged). We tried to
feed him, but we fear little of the food reached him. The wonder of the incident was that a thrush should still be left – there
had not been one in the garden for two months. Berries all
gone, ground hard and foodless, streams frozen, snow lying for
weeks, frost stealing away the vital heat – ingenuity could not
devise a more terrible scene of torture to the birds. Neither for
the thrushes nor for the new-born infants in the tent did the
onslaught of the winter slacken. No pity in earth or heaven.
This one thrush did, indeed, by some exceptional fortune, survive; but where were the family of thrushes that had sung so
sweetly in the rainy autumn? Where were the blackbirds?

Looking down from the stilts of seven hundred feet into the
deep coombe of black oaks standing in the white snow, day by
day, built round about with the rugged mound of the hills,
doubly locked with the key of frost – it seemed to me to take on
itself the actuality of the ancient faith of the Magi. How the
seeds of all living things – the germs – of bird and animal, man
and insect, tree and herb, of the whole earth – were gathered
together into a foursquare rampart, and there laid to sleep in
safety, shielded by a spell-bound fortification against the coming flood, not of water, but of frost and snow! With snow and
frost and winter the earth was overcome, and the world perished, stricken dumb and dead, swept clean and utterly
destroyed – a winter of the gods, the silence of snow and uni-

versal death. All that had been passed away, and the earth was depopulated. Death triumphed. But under the snow, behind the charmed rampart, slept the living germs. Down in the deep coombe, where the dark oaks stood out individually in the whiteness of the snow, fortified round about with immovable hills, there was the actual presentment of Zoroaster's sacred story. Locked in sleep lay bud and germ – the butterflies of next summer were there somewhere, under the snow. The earth was swept of its inhabitants, but the seeds of life were not dead. Near by were the tents of the gipsies – an Eastern race, whose forefathers perhaps had seen that very Magian worship of the Light; and in those tents birth had already taken place. Under the Night of winter – under the power of dark Ahriman, the evil spirit of Destruction – lay bud and germ in bondage, waiting for the coming of Ormuzd, the Sun of Light and Summer. Beneath the snow, and in the frozen crevices of the trees, in the chinks of the earth, sealed up by the signet of frost, were of the life that would replenish the air in time to come, the seeds. The buzzing crowds of summer were still under the snow.

This forest land is marked by the myriads of insects that roam about it in the days of sunshine. Of all the million million heathbells – multiply them again by a million million more – that purple the acres of rolling hills, mile upon mile, there is not one that is not daily visited by these flying creatures. Countless and incalculable hosts of the yellow-barred hover-flies come to them; the heath and common, the moor and forest, the hedge-row and copse, are full of insects. They rise under foot, they rise from the spray brushed by your arm as you pass, they settle down in front of you – a rain of insects, a coloured shower. Legion is a little word for the butterflies; the dry pastures among the woods are brown with meadow-brown; blues and coppers float in endless succession; all the nations of Xerxes' army were but a handful to these. In their millions they have perished; but somewhere, coiled up, as it were, and sealed under the snow, there must have been the mothers and germs of the equally vast crowds that will fill the atmosphere this year. The great humble-bee that shall be mother of hundreds, the yellow wasp that shall be mother of thousands, were hidden there somewhere. The food of the migrant birds that are coming from over sea was there dormant under the snow. Many nations have a tradition of a former world destroyed by a deluge of water, from the East to the West, from Greece to Mexico, where the tail of a comet was said to have caused the flood; but in the strange characters of the Zend is the legend of an ark (as it were) prepared against the snow. It may be that it is the dim memory of a glacial epoch. In this deep coombe, amid the dark oaks and snow, was the fable of Zoroaster. For the coming of Ormuzd, the Light and Life Bringer, the leaf slept folded, the butterfly was hidden, the germ concealed, while the sun swept upwards towards Aries.

There is nothing so wearying as a long frost – the endless monotony, which makes one think that the very fault we usually find with our climate – its changeableness – is in reality its best quality. Rain, mist, gales – anything; give us anything but weary, weary frost. But having once fixed its mind, the weather will not listen to the usual signs of alteration.

The larks sang at last high up against the grey cloud over the frostbound earth. They could not wait longer; love was strong in their little hearts – stronger than the winter. After a while the hedge-sparrows, too, began to sing on the top of the gorse-hedge about the garden. By-and-by a chaffinch boldly raised his voice, ending with the old story, 'Sweet, will you, will you kiss – me – dear?' Then there came a hoar-frost, and the earth, which had been black became white, as its evaporated vapours began to gather and drops of rain to fall. Even then the obstinate weather refused to quite yield, wrapping its cloak, as it were, around it in bitter enmity. But in a day or two white clouds lit up with sunshine appeared drifting over from the southward, and that was the end. The old pensioner came to the door for his bread and cheese: 'The wind's in the south,' he said, 'and I hopes she'll stay there.' Five dull yellow spots on the hedge – gorse bloom – that had remained unchanged for so many weeks, took a fresh colour and became golden. By the constant passing of the waggons and carts along the road that had been so silent it was evident that the busy time of spring was here.

There would be rough weather, doubtless, now and again, but it would not again be winter.

Dark patches of cloud – spots of ink on the sky, the 'messengers' – go drifting by; and after them will follow the water-carriers, harnessed to the south and west winds, drilling the long rows of rain like seed into the earth. After a time there will be a rainbow. Through the bars of my prison I can see the catkins thick and sallow-grey on the willows across the field, visible even at that distance; so great the change in a few days, the hand of spring grows firm and takes a strong grasp of the hedges. My prison bars are but a sixteenth of an inch thick; I could snap them with a fillip – only the window-pane, to me as impenetrable as the twenty-foot wall of the Tower of London. A cart has just gone past bearing a strange load among the carts of spring; they are talking of poling the hops. In it there sat an old man, with the fixed stare, the animal-like eye, of extreme age; he is over ninety. About him there were some few chairs and articles of furniture, and he was propped against a bed. He was being moved – literally carted – to another house, not home, and he said he could not go without his bed; he had slept on it for seventy-three years. Last Sunday his son – himself old – was carted to the churchyard, as is the country custom, in an open van; to-day the father, still living, goes to what will be to him a strange land. His home is broken up – he will potter no more with maize for the chicken; the gorse hedges will become solid walls of golden bloom, but there will never again be a spring for him. It is very hard, is it not, at ninety? It is not the tyranny of any one that has done it; it is the tyranny of circumstance, the lot of man. The song of the Greeks is full of sorrow; man was to them the creature of grief, yet theirs was the land of violets and pellucid air. This has been a land of frost and snow, and here, too, it is the same. A stranger, I see, is already digging the old man's garden.

How happy the trees must be to hear the song of birds again in their branches! After the silence and the leaflessness, to have the birds back once more and to feel them busy at the nest-building; how glad to give them the moss and fibres and the crutch of the boughs to build in! Pleasant it is now to watch

the sunlit clouds sailing onwards; it is like sitting by the sea.
There is voyaging to and fro of birds; the strong wood-pigeon
goes over – a long course in the air, from hill to distant copse;
a blackbird starts from an ash, and, now inclining this way and
now that, traverses the meadows to the thick corner hedge;
finches go by, and the air is full of larks that sing without ceas-
ing. The touch of the wind, the moisture of the dew, the
sun-stained raindrop, have in them the magic force of life – a
marvellous something that was not there before. Under it the
narrow blade of grass comes up freshly green between the old
white fibres the rook pulled; the sycamore bud swells and
opens, and takes the eye instantly in the still dark wood; the
starlings go to the hollow pollards; the lambs leap in the mead.
You never know what a day may bring forth – what new thing
will come next. Yesterday I saw the ploughman and his team,
and the earth gleam smoothed behind the share; to-day a butterfly has gone past; the farm-folk are bringing home the fagots
from the hedgerows; to-morrow there will be a merry, merry
note in the ash copse, the chiffchaffs' ringing call to arms, to
arms, ye leaves! By-and-by a bennet, a bloom of the grass; in
time to come the furrow, as it were, shall open, and the great
buttercup of the waters will show a broad palm of gold. You
never know what will come to the net of the eye next – a bud,
a flower, a nest, a curled fern, or whether it will be in the woodland or by the meadow path, at the water's side or on the dead
dry heap of fagots. There is no settled succession, no fixed and
formal order – always the unexpected; and you cannot say, 'I
will go and find this or that.' The sowing of life in the spring-
time is not in the set straight line of the drill, nor shall you find
wild flowers by a foot measure. There are great woods without
a lily of the valley; the nightingale does not sing everywhere.
Nature has no arrangement, no plan, nothing judicious even;
the walnut trees bring forth their tender buds, and the frost
burns them – they have no mosaic of time to fit in, like a Roman
tesselated pavement; nature is like a child, who will sing and
shout though you may be never so deeply pondering in the
study, and does not wait for the hour that suits your mind. You
do not know what you may find each day; perhaps you may

only pick up a fallen feather, but it is beautiful, every filament. Always beautiful! everything beautiful! And are these things new – the ploughman and his team, the lark's song, the green leaf! Can they be new? Surely they have been of old time! They are, indeed, new – the only things that are so; the rest is old and grey, and a weariness.

My Old Village

First published in *Longman's Magazine*, October 1887
First collected in *Field and Hedgerow*, 1889

'John Brown is dead,' said an aged friend and visitor in answer to my inquiry for the strong labourer.

'Is he really dead?' I asked, for it seemed impossible.

'He is. He came home from his work in the evening as usual, and seemed to catch his foot in the threshold and fell forward on the floor. When they picked him up he was dead.'

I remember the doorway; a raised piece of wood ran across it, as is commonly the case in country cottages, such as one might easily catch one's foot against if one did not notice it; but he knew that bit of wood well. The floor was of brick, hard to fall on and die. He must have come down over the crown of the hill, with his long slouching stride, as if his legs had been half pulled away from his body by his heavy boots in the furrows when a ploughboy. He must have turned up the steps in the bank to his cottage, and so, touching the threshold, ended. He is gone through the great doorway, and one pencil-mark is rubbed out. There used to be a large hearth in that room, a larger room than in most cottages; and when the fire was lit, and the light shone on the yellowish red brick beneath and the large rafters overhead, it was homely and pleasant. In summer the door was always wide open. Close by on the high bank there was a spot where the first wild violets came. You might look along miles of hedgerow, but there were never any until they had shown by John Brown's.

If a man's work that he has done all the days of his life could be collected and piled up around him in visible shape, what a vast mound there would be beside some! If each act or stroke

was represented, say by a brick, John Brown would have stood
the day before his ending by the side of a monument as high as
a pyramid. Then if in front of him could be placed the sum and
product of his labour, the profit to himself, he could have held
it in his clenched hand like a nut, and no one would have seen
it. Our modern people think they train their sons to strength by
football and rowing and jumping, and what are called athletic
exercises; all of which it is the fashion now to preach as very
noble, and likely to lead to the goodness of the race. Certainly
feats are accomplished and records are beaten, but there is no
real strength gained, no hardihood built up. Without hardihood it is of little avail to be able to jump an inch farther than
somebody else. Hardihood is the true test, hardihood is the
ideal, and not these caperings or ten minutes' spurts.

Now, the way they made the boy John Brown hardy was to
let him roll about on the ground with naked legs and bare head
from morn till night, from June till December, from January till
June. The rain fell on his head, and he played in wet grass to his
knees. Dry bread and a little lard was his chief food. He went
to work while he was still a child. At half-past three in the
morning he was on his way to the farm stables, there to help
feed the cart-horses, which used to be done with great care very
early in the morning. The carter's whip used to sting his legs,
and sometimes he felt the butt. At fifteen he was no taller than
the sons of well-to-do people at eleven; he scarcely seemed to
grow at all till he was eighteen or twenty, and even then very
slowly, but at last became a tall big man. That slouching walk,
with knees always bent, diminished his height to appearance;
he really was the full size, and every inch of his frame had been
slowly welded together by this ceaseless work, continual life in
the open air, and coarse hard food. This is what makes a man
hardy. This is what makes a man able to stand almost anything,
and gives a power of endurance that can never be obtained by
any amount of gymnastic training.

I used to watch him mowing with amazement. Sometimes he
would begin at half-past two in the morning, and continue till
night. About eleven o'clock, which used to be the mowers'

noon, he took a rest on a couch of half-dried grass in the shade
of the hedge. For the rest, it was mow, mow, mow for the long
summer day.

John Brown was dead: died in an instant at his cottage door.
I could hardly credit it, so vivid was the memory of his strength.
The gap of time since I had seen him last had made no impression on me; to me he was still in my mind the John Brown of
the hayfield; there was nothing between then and his death.

He used to catch us boys the bats in the stable, and tell us
fearful tales of the ghosts he had seen; and bring the bread from
the town in an old-fashioned wallet, half in front and half
behind, long before the bakers' carts began to come round in
country places. One evening he came into the dairy carrying a
yoke of milk, staggering, with tipsy gravity; he was quite sure
he did not want any assistance, he could pour the milk into the
pans. He tried, and fell at full length and bathed himself from
head to foot. Of later days they say he worked in the town a
good deal, and did not look so well or so happy as on the farm.
In this cottage opposite the violet bank they had small-pox
once, the only case I recollect in the hamlet – the old men used
to say everybody had it when they were young; this was the
only case in my time, and they recovered quickly without any
loss, nor did the disease spread. A roomy well-built cottage like
that, on dry ground, isolated, is the only hospital worthy of the
name. People have a chance to get well in such places; they have
very great difficulty in the huge buildings that are put up expressly
for them. I have a Convalescent Home in my mind at the
moment, a vast building. In these great blocks what they call
ventilation is a steady draught, and there is no 'home' about it.
It is all walls and regulations and draughts, and altogether miserable. I would infinitely rather see any friend of mine in John
Brown's cottage. That terrible disease, however, seemed to quite
spoil the violet bank opposite, and I never picked one there
afterwards. There is something in disease so destructive, as it were,
to flowers.

The hundreds of times I saw the tall chimney of that cottage
rise out of the hill-side as I came home at all hours of the day
and night! the first chimney after a long journey, always com-

fortable to see, especially so in earlier days, when we had a kind of halting belief in John Brown's ghosts, several of which were dotted along that road according to him. The ghosts die as we grow older, they die and their places are taken by real ghosts. I wish I had sent John Brown a pound or two when I was in good health; but one is selfish then, and puts off things till it is too late – a lame excuse verily. I can scarcely believe now that he is really dead, gone as you might casually pluck a hawthorn leaf from the hedge.

The next cottage was a very marked one, for houses grow to their owners. The low thatched roof had rounded itself and stopped down to fit itself to Job's shoulders; the walls had got short and thick to suit him, and they had a yellowish colour, like his complexion, as if chewing tobacco had stained his cheeks right through. Tobacco juice had likewise penetrated and tinted the wall. It was cut off as it seemed by a party-wall into one room, instead of which there were more rooms beyond which no one would have suspected. Job had a way of shaking hands with you with his right hand, while his left hand was casually doing something else in a detached sort of way. 'Yes, sir,' and 'No, sir,' and nodding to everything you said all so complaisant, but at the end of the bargain you generally found yourself a few shillings in some roundabout manner on the wrong side. Job had a lot of shut-up rooms in his house and in his character, which never seemed to be opened to daylight. The eaves hung over and beetled like his brows, and he had a forelock, a regular antique forelock, which he used to touch with the greatest humility. There was a long bough of an elm hanging over one gable just like the forelock. His face was a blank, like the broad end wall of the cottage, which had no window – at least you might think so until you looked up and discovered one little narrow slit, one narrow pane, and woke with a start to the idea that Job was always up there watching and listening. That was how he looked out of his one eye so intensely cunning, the other being a wall eye – that is, the world supposed so, as he kept it half shut, always between the lights; but whether it was really blind or not I cannot say. Job caught rats and rabbits and moles, and bought fagots or potatoes, fruit or rabbit-skins, or rusty iron: wonderful how he seemed to have command of money. It was done probably by buying and selling almost simultaneously, so that the cash passed really from one customer to another, and was never his at all. Also he worked as labourer, chiefly piece-work; also Mrs Job had a shop window about two feet square: snuff and tobacco, bread and cheese, immense big round jumbles and sugar, kept on the floor above, and reached down by hand, when wanted, through the opening for the ladder stairs. The front door – Job's right hand – was always open in summer, and the flagstones of the floor chalked round their edges; a clean table, clean chairs, decent crockery, an old clock about an hour slow, a large hearth with a minute fire to boil the kettle without heating the room. Tea was usually at half-past three, and it is a fact that many well-to-do persons, as they came along the road hot and dusty, used to drop in and rest and take a cup – very little milk and much gossip. Two paths met just there, and people used to step in out of a storm of rain, a sort of thatched house club. Job was somehow on fair terms with nearly everybody, and that is a wonderful thing in a village, where everybody knows everybody's business, and petty interests continually cross. The strangest fellow and the strangest way of life, and yet I do not believe a black mark was ever put against him; the shiftiness was all for nothing. It arose, no doubt, out of the constant and eager straining to gain a little advantage and make an extra penny. Had Job been a Jew he would have been rich. He was the exact counterpart of the London Jew dealer, set down in the midst of the country. Job should have been rich. Such immense dark brown jumbles, such cheek-distenders – never any French sweetmeats or chocolate or bonbons to equal these. I really think I could eat one now. The pennies and fourpenny bits – there were fourpenny bits in those days – that went behind that two-foot window, goodness! there was no end. Job used to chink them in a pint pot sometimes before the company, to give them an idea of his great hoards. He always tried to impress people with his wealth, and would talk of a fifty-pound con-tract as if it was nothing to him. Jumbles are eternal, if nothing else is. I thought then there was not such another shop as Job's in the universe. I have found since that there is a Job shop in every village, and in every street in every town – that is to say, a window for jumbles and rubbish; and if you don't know it, you may be quite sure your children do, and spend many a sly penny there. Be as rich as you may, and give them gilded sweet-meats at home, still they will slip round to the Job shop.

It was a pretty cottage, well backed with trees and bushes, with a south-east mixture of sunlight and shade, and little touches that cannot be suggested by writing. Job had not got the Semitic instinct of keeping. The art of acquisition he possessed to some extent, that was his right hand; but somehow the half-crowns slipped away through his unstable left hand, and fortune was a greasy pole to him. His left hand was too cunning for him, it wanted to manage things too cleverly. If it had only had the Semitic grip, digging the nails into the flesh to hold tight each separate coin, he would have been village rich. The great secret is the keeping. Finding is by no means keeping. Job did not flourish in his old days; the people changed round about. Job is gone, and I think every one of that cottage is either dead or moved. Empty.

The next cottage was the water-bailiff's, who looked after the great pond or 'broad'. There were one or two old boats, and he used to leave the oars leaning against a wall at the side of the house. These oars looked like fragments of a wreck, broken and irregular. The right-hand scull was heavy, as if made of ironwood, the blade broad and spoon-shaped, so as to have a most powerful grip of the water. The left-hand scull was light and slender, with a narrow blade like a marrow scoop; so when you had the punt, you had to pull very hard with your left hand and gently with the right to get the forces equal. The punt had a list of its own, and no matter how you rowed, it would still make leeway. Those who did not know its character were perpetually trying to get this crooked wake straight, and consequently went round and round exactly like the whirligig beetle. Those who knew used to let the leeway proceed a good way and then alter it, so as to act in the other direction like an elongated zigzag. These sculls the old fellow would bring you as if they were great treasures, and watch you off in the punt as

if he was parting with his dearest. At that date it was no little
matter to coax him round to unchain his vessel. You had to
take an interest in the garden, in the baits, and the weather, and
be very humble; then perhaps he would tell you he did not
want it for the trimmers, or the withy, or the flags, and you
might have it for an hour as far as he could see; 'did not think
my lord's steward would come over that morning; of course, if
he did you must come in', and so on; and if the stars were pro-
pitious, by-and-by the punt was got afloat. These sculls were
tilted up against the wall, and as you innocently went to take
one, Wauw! – a dirty little ill-tempered mongrel poodle rolled
himself like a ball to your heels and snapped his teeth – Wauw!
At the bark, out rushed the old lady, his housekeeper, shouting
in the shrillest key to the dog to lie still, and to you that the
bailiff would be there in a minute. At the sound of her shrewish
'yang-yang' down came the old man from the bank, and so one
dog fetched out the lot. The three were exactly alike somehow.
Beside these diamond sculls he had a big gun, with which he
used to shoot the kingfishers that came for the little fish; the
number he slaughtered was very great; he persecuted them as
Domitian did the flies: he declared that a kingfisher would
carry off a fish heavier than itself. Also he shot rooks, once now
and then strange wild fowl with this monstrous iron pipe, and
something happened with this gun one evening which was wit-
nessed, and after that the old fellow was very benevolent, and
the punt was free to one or two who knew all about it. There is
an old story about the stick that would not beat the dog, and
the dog would not bite the pig, and so on; and so I am quite
sure that ill-natured cur could never have lived with that
'yang-yang' shrew, nor could any one else but he have turned
the gear of the hatch, nor have endured the dog and the woman,
and the constant miasma from the stagnant waters. No one else
could have shot anything with that cumbrous weapon, and no
one else could row that punt straight. He used to row it quite
straight, to the amazement of a wondering world, and somehow supplied the motive force – the stick – which kept all these
things going. He is gone, and, I think, the housekeeper too, and

the house has had several occupants since, who have stamped down the old ghosts and thrust them out of doors.

After this the cottages and houses came in little groups, some up crooked lanes, hidden away by elms as if out of sight in a cupboard, and some dotted along the brooks, scattered so that, unless you had connected them all with a very long rope, no stranger could have told which belonged to the village and which did not. They drifted into various tithings, and yet it was all the same place. They were all thatched. It was a thatched village. This is strictly accurate and strictly inaccurate, for I think there were one or two tiled and one 'slated', and perhaps a modern one slated. Nothing is ever quite rigid or complete that is of man; all rules have a chip in them. The way they builded the older thatched farmhouses was to put up a very high wall in front and a very low one behind, and then the roof in a general way sloped down from the high wall to the low wall, an acre broad of thatch. These old thatched houses seemed to be very healthy so long as the old folk lived in them in the old-fashioned way. Thatch is believed to give an equable temperature. The air blew all round them, and it might be said all through them; for the front door was always open three parts of the year, and at the back the dairies were in a continual blow. Upstairs the houses were only one room thick, so that each wall was an outside wall, or rather it was a wall one side and thatched the other, so that the wind went through if a window was open. Modern houses are often built two rooms thick, so that the air does not circulate from one side to the other. No one seemed to be ill, unless he brought it home with him from some place where he had been visiting. The diseases they used to have were long-lived, such as rheumatism, which may keep a man comfortably in aches and pains forty years. My dear old friend, however, taking them one by one, went through the lot and told me of the ghosts. The forefathers I knew are all gone – the stout man, the lame man, the paralysed man, the gruff old stick: not one left. There is not one left of the old farmers, not a single one. The fathers, too, of our own generation have been dropping away. The strong young man who used to fill us with such astonishment at the feats he would achieve without a thought, no gymnastic training, to whom a sack of wheat was a toy. The strong young man went one day into the harvest-field, as he had done so many times before. Suddenly he felt a little dizzy. By-and-by he went home and became very ill with sunstroke; he recovered, but he was never strong again; he gradually declined for twelve months, and next harvest-time he was under the daisies. Just one little touch of the sun, and the strength of man faded as a leaf. The hardy dark young man, built of iron, broad, thick, and short, who looked as if frost, snow, and heat were all the same to him, had something go wrong in his lung: one twelve-month, and there was an end. This was a very unhappy affair. The pickaxe and the spade have made almost a full round to every door; I do not want to think any more about this. Family changes and the pressure of these hard times have driven out most of the rest; some seem to have quite gone out of sight; some have crossed the sea; some have abandoned the land as a livelihood. Of the few, the very few that still remain, still fewer abide in their original homes. Time has shuffled them about from house to house like a pack of cards. Of them all, I verily believe there is but one soul living in the same old house. If the French had landed in the mediaeval way to harry with fire and sword, they could not have swept the place more clean.

Almost the first thing I did with pen and ink as a boy was to draw a map of the hamlet with the roads and lanes and paths, and I think some of the ponds, and with each of the houses marked and the occupier's name. Of course it was very roughly done, and not to any scale, yet it was perfectly accurate and full of detail. I wish I could find it, but the confusion of time has scattered and mixed these early papers. A map by Ptolemy would bear as much resemblance to the same country in a modern atlas as mine to the present state of that locality. It is all gone – rubbed out. The names against the whole of those houses have been altered, one only excepted, and changes have taken place there. Nothing remains. This is not in a century, half a century, or even in a quarter of a century, but in a few ticks of the clock.

I think I have heard that the oaks are down. They may be standing or down, it matters nothing to me; the leaves I last saw upon them are gone for evermore, nor shall I ever see them come there again ruddy in spring. I would not see them again even if I could; they could never look again as they used to do. There are too many memories there. The happiest days become the saddest afterwards; let us never go back, lest we too die. There are no such oaks anywhere else, none so tall and straight, and with such massive heads, on which the sun used to shine as if on the globe of the earth, one side in shadow, the other in bright light. How often I have looked at oaks since, and yet have never been able to get the same effect from them! Like an old author printed in another type, the words are the same, but the sentiment is different. The brooks have ceased to run. There is no music now at the old hatch where we used to sit in danger of our lives, happy as kings, on the narrow bar over the deep water. The barred pike that used to come up in such numbers are no more among the flags. The perch used to drift down the stream, and then bring up again. The sun shone there for a very long time, and the water rippled and sang, and it always seemed to me that I could feel the rippling and the singing and the sparkling back through the centuries. The brook is dead, for when man goes nature ends. I dare say there is water there still but it is not the brook; the brook is gone like John Brown's soul. There used to be clouds over the fields, white clouds in blue summer skies. I have lived a good deal on clouds; they have been meat to me often; they bring something to the spirit which even the trees do not. I see clouds now sometimes when the iron grip of hell permits for a minute or two; they are very different clouds, and speak differently. I long for some of the old clouds that had no memories. There were nights in those times over those fields, not darkness, but Night, full of glowing suns and glowing richness of life that sprang up to meet them. The nights are there still; they are everywhere, nothing local in the night; but it is not the Night to me seen through the window.

There used to be footpaths. Following one of them, the first field always had a good crop of grass; over the next stile there

was a great oak standing alone in the centre of the field, generally a great cart-horse under it, and a few rushes scattered
about the furrows; the fourth was always full of the finest clover; in the fifth you could scent the beans on the hill, and there
was a hedge like a wood and a nest of the long-tailed tit; the
sixth had a runnel and blue forget-me-nots; the seventh had a
brooklet and scattered trees along it; from the eighth you
looked back on the slope and saw the thatched houses you had
left behind under passing shadows, and rounded white clouds
going straight for the distant hills, each cloud visibly bulging
and bowed down like a bag. I cannot think how the distant
thatched houses came to stand out with such clear definition
and etched outline and bluish shadows; and beyond these was
the uncertain vale that had no individuality, but the trees put
their arms together and became one. All these were meadows,
every step was among grass, beautiful grass, and the cuckoos
sang as if they had found paradise. A hundred years ago a little
old man with silver buckles on his shoes used to walk along
this footpath once a week in summer, taking his children over
to drink milk at the farm; but though he set them every time to
note the number of fields, so busy were they with the nests and
the flowers, they could never be sure at the end of the journey
whether there were eight or nine. To make quite sure at last, he
took with them a pocket full of apples, one of which was eaten
in each field, and so they came to know for certain that the
number of meadows was either eight or nine, I forget which;
and so you see this great experiment did not fix the faith of
mankind. Like other great truths, it has grown dim, but it
seems strange to think how this little incident could have been
borne in mind for a century. There was another footpath that
led through the peewit field, where the green plovers for evermore circle round in spring; then past the nightingale field, by
the largest maple trees that grew in that country; this too was
all grass. Another led along the water to bluebell land; another
into the coombs of the hills; all meadows, which was the beauty
of it; for though you could find wheat in plenty if you liked,
you always walked in grass. All round the compass you could
still step on sward. This is rare. Of one other path I have a

faded memory, like a silk marker in an old book; in truth, I don't want to remember it except the end of it where it came down to the railway. So full was the mind of romance in those days, that I used to get there specially in time to see the express go up, the magnificent engine of the broad gauge that swept along with such ease and power to London. I wish I could feel like that now. The feeling is not quite gone even now, and I have often since seen these great broad-gauge creatures moving alive to and fro like Ezekiel's wheel dream beside the platforms of Babylon with much of the same old delight. Still I never went back with them to the faded footpath. They are all faded now, these footpaths.

The walnut trees are dead at home. They gave such a thick shade when the fruit was juicy ripe, and the hoods cracked as they fell; they peeled as easy as taking off a glove; the sweetest and nuttiest of fruit. It was delicious to sit there with a great volume of Sir Walter Scott, half in sunshine, half in shade, dreaming of 'Kenilworth' and Wayland Smith's cave; only the difficulty was to balance the luxuries, when to peel the walnuts and when to read the book, and how to adjust oneself to perfection so as to get the exact amount of sunshine and shadow. Too much luxury. There was a story, too, told by one Abu-Kaka ibn Ja'is, of the caravan that set forth in 1483 to cross the desert, and being overwhelmed by a sandstorm, lost their way. They wandered for some time till hunger and thirst began to consume them, and then suddenly lit on an oasis unknown to the oldest merchant of Bagdad. There they found refreshing waters and palms and a caravanserai; and, what was most pleasant, the people at the bazaar and the prince hastened to fill them with hospitality; sheep were killed, and kids were roasted, and all was joy. They were not permitted to depart till they had feasted, when they set out again on their journey, and each at leaving was presented with strings of pearls and bags of rubies, so that at last they came home with all the magnificence of kings. They found, however, that instead of having been absent only a month or two they had been gone twenty years, so swiftly had time sped. As they grew old, and their beards grey, and their frames withered, and the pearls were gone, and the

rubies spent, they said, 'We will go back to the city of the oasis.'
They set out, each on his camel, one lame, the other paralytic,
and the third blind, but still the way was plain, for had they not
trodden it before? and they had with them the astrolabe of the
astronomer that fixes the track by the stars. Time wore on, and
presently the camels' feet brought them nearer and nearer the
wished-for spot. One saw the water, and another the palms,
but when they came near, it was the mirage, and deep sand
covered the place. Then they separated, and each hastened
home; but the blind had no leader, and the lame fell from his
camel, and the paralytic had no more dates, and their whited
bones have disappeared.* Many another tale, too, I read under
the trees that are gone like human beings. Sometimes I went
forth to the nooks in the deep meadows by the hazel mounds,
and sometimes I parted the ash-tree wands. In my waistcoat
pocket I had a little red book, made square; I never read it out
of doors, but I always carried it in my pocket till it was frayed
and the binding broken; the smallest of red books, but very
much therein – the poems and sonnets of Mr William Shake-
speare. Some books are alive. The book I have still, it cannot
die; the ash copses are cut, and the hazel mounds destroyed.

Was every one, then, so pleasant to me in those days? were
the people all so beneficent and kindly that I must needs look
back; all welcoming with open hand and open door? No, the
reverse; there was not a single one friendly to me. Still that has
nothing to do with it; I never thought about them, and I am
quite certain they never thought about me. They are all gone,
and there is an end. Incompatibility would describe our con-
nections best. Nothing to do with them at all; it was me. I
planted myself everywhere – in all the fields and under the

---

* The Arabian commentator thinks this story a myth: the oasis in the desert is
the time of youth, which passes so quickly, and is not recognized till it is gone;
the pearls and rubies, the joys of love, which make the fortunate lover as a
king. In old age every man is afflicted with disease or infirmity, every one is
paralytic, lame, or blind. They set out to find a second youth – the dream of
immortality – with the astrolabe, which is the creed or Koran all take as their
guide. And death separated the company. This is only his pragmatic way; the
circumstance is doubtless historic.

trees. The curious part of it is that though they are all dead, and 'worms have eaten them, but not for love', we continually meet them in other shapes. We say, 'Holloa, here is old So-and-so coming; that is exactly his jaw, that's his Flemish face'; or, 'By Jove, yonder is So-and-so; that's his very walk': one almost expects them to speak as one meets them in the street. There seem to be certain set types which continually crop up again whithersoever you go, and even certain tricks of speech and curves of the head – a set of family portraits walking about the world. It was not the people, neither for good, for evil, nor indifference.

I planted myself everywhere under the trees in the fields and footpaths, by day and by night, and that is why I have never put myself into the charge of the many wheeled creatures that move on the rails and gone back thither, lest I might find the trees look small, and the elms mere switches, and the fields shrunken, and the brooks dry, and no voice anywhere. Nothing but my own ghost to meet me by every hedge. I fear lest I should find myself more dead than all the rest. And verily I wish, could it be without injury to others, that the sand of the desert would rise and roll over and obliterate the place for ever and ever.

I need not wish, for I have been conversing again with learned folk about this place, and they begin to draw my view to certain considerations. These very learned men point out to me a number of objections, for the question they sceptically put is this: are you quite certain that such a village ever existed? In the first place, they say, you have only got one other witness beside yourself, and she is aged, and has defective sight; and really we don't know what to say to accepting such evidence unsupported. Secondly, John Brown cannot be found to bear testimony. Thirdly, there are no ghosts there; that can be demonstrated. It renders a case unsubstantial to introduce these flimsy spirits. Fourthly, the map is lost, and it might be asked was there ever such a map? Fifthly, the people are all gone. Sixthly, no one ever saw any particular sparkle on the brook there, and the clouds appear to be of the same commonplace order that go about everywhere. Seventhly, no one can find these footpaths, which probably led nowhere; and as for the little old man with silver buckles on his shoes, it is a story only fit for some one in his dotage. You can't expect grave and considerate men to take your story as it stands; they must consult the Ordnance Survey and Domesday Book; and the fact is, you have not got the shadow of a foundation on which to carry your case into court. I may resent this, but I cannot deny that the argument is very black against me, and I begin to think that my senses have deceived me. It is as they say. No one else seems to have seen the sparkle on the brook, or heard the music at the hatch, or to have felt back through the centuries; and when I try to describe these things to them they look at me with stolid incredulity. No one seems to understand how I got food from the clouds, nor what there was in the night, nor why it is not so good to look at it out of window. They turn their faces away from me, so that perhaps after all I was mistaken, and there never was any such place or any such meadows, and I was never there. And perhaps in course of time I shall find out also, when I pass away physically, that as a matter of fact there never was any earth.

Bibliography

1. Books and pamphlets published during Jefferies' lifetime

Reporting, Editing, and Authorship, London: John Snow, 1873 (pamphlet).

Jack Brass, Emperor of England, London: T. Pettitt, 1873 (pamphlet).

A Memoir of the Goddards of North Wilts, Compiled from Ancient Records, Registers and Family Papers, London: Simmons and Botten, 1873.

The Scarlet Shawl: A Novel, London: Tinsley, 1874.

Restless Human Hearts, 3 vols., London: Tinsley, 1875.

Suez-cide!! Or How Miss Britannia Bought a Dirty Puddle and Lost Her Sugar-plums, London: John Snow, 1876 (pamphlet).

World's End: A Story in Three Books, 3 vols., London: Tinsley, 1877.

The Gamekeeper at Home; or, Sketches of Natural History and Rural Life, London: Smith Elder, 1878.

Wild Life in a Southern County, London: Smith Elder, 1879.

The Amateur Poacher, London: Smith Elder, 1879.

Hodge and His Masters, 2 vols., London: Smith Elder, 1880.

Greene Ferne Farm, London: Smith Elder, 1880.

Round About a Great Estate, London: Smith Elder, 1880.

Wood Magic: A Fable, 2 vols., London: Cassell, 1881.

Bevis: The Story of a Boy, 3 vols., London: Sampson Low, 1882.

Nature Near London, London: Chatto & Windus, 1883.

Society Novelettes, by various authors, 2 vols., London: Vizetelly, 1883 (Jefferies contributed two short stories, 'Kiss and Try' in volume I, 'Out of the Season' in volume II. Volume I was reprinted in 1886 as *No Rose Without a Thorn, and Other Tales*, volume II as *The Dove's Nest, and Other Tales*).

The Story of My Heart: My Autobiography, London: Longmans, 1883.

Red Deer, London: Longmans, 1884.

The Life of the Fields, London: Chatto & Windus, 1884.

The Dewy Morn, 2 vols., London: Bentley, 1884.

After London; or, Wild England, London: Cassell, 1885.

The Open Air, London: Chatto & Windus, 1885.

Introduction to White, Gilbert, *The Natural History of Selborne* (1789), London: Walter Scott, 1887.

Amaryllis at the Fair, London: Sampson Low, 1887.

2. Collections, etc., published posthumously

Field and Hedgerow: Being the Last Essays of Richard Jefferies, Collected by His Widow, London: Longmans, 1889.

The Toilers of the Field, London: Longmans, 1892.

The Early Fiction of Richard Jefferies, edited by Grace Toplis, London: Simpkin, Marshall, 1896.

Jefferies' Land: A History of Swindon and Its Environs, edited by Grace Toplis, London: Simpkin, Marshall, 1896.

T. T. T., Wells: A. Young, 1896 (short story).

The Hills and the Vale, with an introduction by Edward Thomas, London: Duckworth, 1909.

The Old House at Coate, and Other Hitherto Unprinted Essays, edited by Samuel J. Looker, London: Lutterworth Press, 1948.

The Nature Diaries and Note-Books of Richard Jefferies, edited by Samuel J. Looker, London: Grey Walls Press, 1948.

Chronicles of the Hedges, and Other Essays, edited by Samuel J. Looker, London: Phoenix House, 1948.

Field and Farm: Essays Now First Collected, with some from MSS, edited by Samuel J. Looker, London: Phoenix House, 1957.

Landscape and Labour, edited by John Pearson, Bradford-on-Avon: Moonraker Press, 1979.

A complete list of Jefferies' essays and journalism appears in the Bibliography of *Landscape and Labour* (see above).

PENGUIN CLASSICS

CONFESSIONS OF AN ENGLISH OPIUM EATER
THOMAS DE QUINCEY

'Thou hast the keys of Paradise, oh just, subtle, and mighty opium!'

Confessions is a remarkable account of the pleasures and pains of worshipping at the 'Church of Opium'. Thomas De Quincey consumed large daily quantities of laudanum (at the time a legal painkiller), and this autobiography of addiction hauntingly describes his surreal visions and hallucinatory nocturnal wanderings though London, along with the nightmares, despair and paranoia to which he became prey. The result is a work in which the effects of drugs and the nature of dreams, memory and imagination are seamlessly interwoven. *Confessions* forged a link between artistic self-expression and addiction, paving the way for later generations of literary drug-users from Baudelaire to Burroughs, and anticipating psychoanalysis with its insights into the subconscious.

This edition is based on the original serial version of 1821, and reproduces the two 'sequels', 'Suspiria De Profundis' (1845) and 'The English Mail-Coach' (1849). It also includes a critical introduction discussing the romantic figure of the addict and the tradition of confessional literature, and an appendix on opium in the nineteenth century.

Edited with an introduction by Barry Milligan

PENGUIN CLASSICS

THE ROAD TO OXIANA
ROBERT BYRON

'Neither an Afghan saddle nor the pangs of starvation could spoil the beauty of our ride among the glistening silver hills'

In 1933 Robert Byron began a journey to Persia and Afghanistan, via Jerusalem, Damascus and Baghdad, in search of the origins of Islamic architecture. *The Road to Oxiana* is the record of his ten-month voyage and the characters, landscapes and buildings he encountered: from diary entries, historical vignettes, comic conversations and magnificent evocations of architecture. At once poetic, scholarly and acidly humorous, Byron's travel journal is a passionate ode to the pursuit of experience and a portrait of an extraordinary traveller.

In his new introduction, Colin Thubron discusses Byron's life and travels, and the impact *The Road to Oxiana* had on travel writing.

'One of the best, most learned and most entertaining of all books of literary travel' *Independent*

'What *Ulysses* is to the novel between the wars and what *The Waste Land* is to poetry, *The Road to Oxiana* is to the travel book' Paul Fussell

With an introduction by Colin Thubron

THE STORY OF PENGUIN CLASSICS

Before 1946 ... 'Classics' are mainly the domain of academics and students; readable editions for everyone else are almost unheard of. This all changes when a little-known classicist, E. V. Rieu, presents Penguin founder Allen Lane with the translation of Homer's *Odyssey* that he has been working on in his spare time.

1946 Penguin Classics debuts with *The Odyssey*, which promptly sells three million copies. Suddenly, classics are no longer for the privileged few.

1950s Rieu, now series editor, turns to professional writers for the best modern, readable translations, including Dorothy L. Sayers's *Inferno* and Robert Graves's unexpurgated *Twelve Caesars*.

1960s The Classics are given the distinctive black covers that have remained a constant throughout the life of the series. Rieu retires in 1964, hailing the Penguin Classics list as 'the greatest educative force of the twentieth century.'

1970s A new generation of translators swells the Penguin Classics ranks, introducing readers of English to classics of world literature from more than twenty languages. The list grows to encompass more history, philosophy, science, religion and politics.

1980s The Penguin American Library launches with titles such as *Uncle Tom's Cabin*, and joins forces with Penguin Classics to provide the most comprehensive library of world literature available from any paperback publisher.

1990s The launch of Penguin Audiobooks brings the classics to a listening audience for the first time, and in 1999 the worldwide launch of the Penguin Classics website extends their reach to the global online community.

The 21st Century Penguin Classics are completely redesigned for the first time in nearly twenty years. This world-famous series now consists of more than 1300 titles, making the widest range of the best books ever written available to millions – and constantly redefining what makes a 'classic'.

The Odyssey continues ...

The best books ever written

PENGUIN ⟨𝕬⟩ CLASSICS

SINCE 1946